Logistical Excellence

It's Not Business as Usual

Donald J. Bowersox
Patricia J. Daugherty
Cornelia L. Dröge
Richard N. Germain
Dale S. Rogers

DIGITAL
PRESS

Printed in the United States of America
9 8 7 6 5 4 3
Order number EY-H953E-DP

The publisher offers discounts on bulk orders of this book. For information, please write:
Special Sales Department
Digital Press
One Burlington Woods Drive
Burlington, MA 01803

Design: Joyce C. Weston
Production: Herbert Nolan
Composition: DEKR Corporation
Printing: The Maple-Vail Book Manufacturing Group

Trademarks and trademarked products mentioned in this book include: American Telephone and Telegraph Corporation, AT&T; the Digital logo, which is a registered trademark of the Digital Equipment Company; IBM PC, IBM PC XT, IBM AT, which are registered trademarks of International Business Machines Corporation; Levi Strauss LeviLink; Lithonia Lighting Light*Link; Owens-Corning Fiberglas PinkLink; Xerox Corporation.

The views expressed in this book are those of the authors, not of the publisher. Digital Equipment Corporation is not responsible for any errors that may appear in this book.

Library of Congress Cataloging-in-Publication Data

Logistical excellence : it's not business as usual / Donald J.
  Bowersox . . . [et. al.].
      p.   cm.
    Includes index.
    ISBN 1-55558-087-4 (hardcover) :
    1. Business logistics.   I. Bowersox, Donald J.
  HD38.5.L6   1992
  658.5—dc20   91-40228
                                              CIP

Contents

Logistics: 1990s Style:
Charlie realizes that logistical
excellence transcends
trucking schedules and
warehouse location!

Assessment: Charlie takes
a critical look at his firm's
performance, and the system
assessment pinpoints areas
of improvement in the
conduct of value-added
activities.

Moving the Mountain:
Charlie tackles the obstacles
to change: If everyone agrees
that something has to be
done, why can it not get
done?

6. The Keys to Success   112

The Keys to Success:
Charlie accepts that the
burden of proof is his, and he
backs up his case with
detailed research findings.

7. Developing Strategic Alliances   138

**Developing Strategic
Alliances:** Charlie's vision
incorporates channel
alliances with suppliers,
customers, and third-party
service providers.

8. The Day After Success   163

The Day After Success:
Just as Charlie is winning the
game, providence changes
the playing field. But Charlie
does not have to start at
square one all over again.

Preface

This book about logistical excellence is the second of two books written by faculty and doctoral students at Michigan State University. The first, *Leading Edge Logistics: Competitive Positioning for the 1990s*, was a research report that presented statistical evidence about the best practices of logistics management in North America. This book is not a sequel. Although this volume is based on research, it is clearly not a research report. Instead, the authors offer their interpretation of research findings in an effort to help improve the practice of logistics management. *Logistical Excellence* conveys a message based upon continued updating, analysis, and interpretation of the earlier research. For example, to enrich the original data set, case studies have been included to illustrate the formation and operation of strategic alliances. The responses of firms that participated in the original research were subjected to extensive analysis regarding major trading relationships. The result is a model to guide managers as they seek to improve their firms' overall logistical competency.

Logistical Excellence is directed toward managers who face the challenge of improving logistical performance within their organizations. The basic topic is change management. When a firm comes face to face with the challenge of improving logistical competency, what must the responsible managers do to grasp leadership of the change process? Improving logistical performance within the context of a dynamic environment, but with a static organization resistant to change is not simple!

To facilitate interest and ease of reading, an action-oriented case dialogue runs throughout the text. The case is the story of a manager, Charlie Change, who tackles the task of improving the logistical competency of his firm. The dialogue initially tracks Charlie's efforts to become fully knowledgeable about the potential benefits that can result from logistical excellence. Attention is directed to the process by which he takes ownership of the commitment to change. The case dialogue then follows Charlie as he develops and implements an improvement program. From chapter to chapter, the dialogue tracks the highs and the lows of Charlie's initiative to create significant improvement in his firm's logistical competency. Each chapter begins with an appropriate case dialogue, and thus a reader can gain a good overview of the managerial significance of the book's message by initially reading only the case dialogue for each chapter, skipping the chapter contents. It is hoped that Charlie's story will stimulate the reader to examine the supporting evidence within the chapters.

The authors are extremely grateful to numerous individuals and organizations for their support. The expanded research was funded by basic grants from Digital Equipment Corporation (DEC). Managers who benefit from the research owe DEC a debt of gratitude for their continued support of the logistics profession by sponsorship of public research.

To provide updated understanding of how information technology is being adopted and exploited, several in-depth case studies were completed. The authors wish to acknowledge the contribution of Joseph C. Andraski, Vice President of Distribution, Nabisco Foods Company; Charles Darnell, Executive Vice President, Lithonia Lighting; Jeffrey A. Kernan, Vice President, Information and Management Services, Lithonia Lighting; Tom Dutton, Director of Systems and Programming, Kuppenheimer Men's Clothiers; Bernard J. Hale, Vice President of Human Resources and Logistics, McGaw, Inc. and previously Vice President of Distribution Services, Bergen Brunswig Corporation; Bill Lane, Corporate EDI Coordinator, J. C. Penney Company; and Tom Moriarity, Senior Distribution Engineer, J. C. Penney Company.

The development proposal and initial manuscript were reviewed by a number of practitioners for content and method of presentation. The time and effort expended by the following individuals were invaluable for the development of the manuscript: Raymond Bard, Bard Productions; Marvin Collins, Digital Equipment Corporation; Wade H. Culberson, Digital Equipment Corporation; Bernard J. Hale, McGaw, Inc.; Charles P. Johansen, Zellerbach Corporation; Maurice P. Lundrigan, Owens-Corning Fiberglas; Jack Mileski, Digital Equipment Corporation; Burt Reynolds, Digital Equipment Corporation;

D. J. Scott, The Kellogg Company; Richard J. Sherman, Digital Equipment Corporation; Herb Shumway, Digital Equipment Corporation; and Hank Weiland, Digital Equipment Corporation.

Finally, the support of Michigan State University was essential to completing this book. Dean Richard Lewis and Chairperson Robert Nason continue to provide an environment that permits research to be completed and reported in a timely manner. Both Carrie Closs and Tricia Walters performed assignments critical to completion of the manuscript. David Frayer and Carol Neckel served as research assistants. In particular, David played a key role in coordinating development of the manuscript.

With so much able assistance, it is difficult to offer any excuse for whatever shortcomings this book may have. To the extent that faults exist, they are the sole responsibility of the research team.

December 1991

D. J. B.
P. J. D.
C. L. D.
R. N. G.
D. S. R.

The Setting

HISTORIANS will record the last ninety days of 1989 and the entire year of 1990 as one of the most significant periods of change in recent history. In what seemed like a matter of hours, forty years of cold war stagnation became the victim of a mass human outcry for economic and political freedom. Eastern Europe underwent radical change as socialist nations such as East Germany, Poland, Czechoslovakia, and Hungary turned to the promises of a free market system in an effort to reverse decades of economic decay.

Within the first few months of 1990, even the Soviet Union began to talk about the difficult process of abandoning the constructs and ideals of socialism for a market economy. Under the shaky leadership of President Gorbachev, the Soviet Union tentatively began the tedious "perestroika" initiative. Power struggles and policy reversals ensued. The following comments of Russian Vitaly Korotich, editor-in-chief of *Ogonyok* magazine, delivered before the Committee for Economic Development of Australia, captured the desperation of the Soviet crisis.

Nobody in the Soviet Union really knows what a market economy means. But we want one. We need one to overcome the crippling shortages and inefficiencies. People stock up what food they can in their fridges. I remember in China once the authorities solved this problem by stopping the supply of fridges.

We have more combine harvesters than the United States, six times as many tractors and twice as many farmers, but we have nothing in our shops. We still can't feed ourselves. Every year we lose half our vegetables and much of our meat before they reach [the] market.[1]

In 1990 Soviet agriculture had a bumper crop; however, lack of labor, poorly maintained equipment, strikes, hoarding, black markets, and inadequate processing capacity caused the Soviet agribusiness system to fail to meet basic food requirements.[2] Indeed, by mid-1990 bread was rationed in the Soviet Union. Although only a segment of the United States population will remember World War II food rationing and shortages, even at the height of the war a staple as fundamental as bread was in abundant supply. Therefore it is clearly difficult for consumers throughout the free market world to relate to the utter despair of the socialist-bloc nations. What the world was about to witness was a superpower attempting to move at a breathtaking pace to undergo basic and elementary economic change. By December 1990, the United States had entered into special trade agreements with the Soviet Union, which included $1 billion in loan guarantees for Russia to buy United States food. Included was a pledge to provide distribution and marketing assistance to help Russia move the food produced on its farms to food processing plants and then to markets. Although it became clear that the attractions of the free market system had outpowered the missiles and nuclear weapons of the cold war, it was still not clear what direction the Soviet Union would finally take. The failed August 1991 coup and abolishment of the Communist Party serve to underline the instability of this situation.

Fundamental to the inability of a planned market system to satisfy consumer wants and needs is the failure of such arrangements over time to develop and support an adequate distribution infrastructure. To effectively and efficiently move products to market, adequate transportation and storage facilities must be in place. In free market societies such as Western Germany, Great Britain, Japan, and the United States, the presence of a distribution infrastructure is almost invisible—it is taken for granted. Although government plays a role in the establishment, maintenance, and safety of the basic transportation system, its operation is left to free enterprise.

Substantial differences among firms are clearly apparent as to how individual firms manage the logistical aspects of their business. These differences and their implications for competition are the focus of this book. At this point, it suffices to say that some firms are logistically superior to others. Taken as a whole, however, firms in a free market economy perform day in and out at a level that provides their constituents with the highest standard of living ever enjoyed by the human race. In the United States alone, over $600 billion will be expended during 1991 to logistically support this standard of living.[3] The logistics of private enterprise is big business.

It is an uncontested fact that a significant difference exists between the free market and socialist systems in terms of relative logistical competency. As noted above, however, the logistics of a free market system functions without much public notice. Of course, consumers become irritated when they have to wait at a railroad crossing for a double-stack container train to pass by or angry when they become bogged down in metropolitan traffic gridlock because of numerous semi-trucks. Seldom, if ever, do consumers attempt to reconcile these discomforts with their continuous demand for convenience. Consumers in a free market economy expect retail shelves to be full of an ever-increasing assortment of new and convenient products.

Then everything was changed by the Gulf crisis! In a few hours of an otherwise quiet day in August 1990, Saddam Hussein occupied Kuwait and sparked a retaliatory buildup of massive military strength authorized by the United Nations. By the end of 1990, the United Nations Security Council had passed a resolution permitting the use of force if necessary to liberate Kuwait, and on January 17, 1991, the allied forces initiated what was to be a six-day war with Iraq. The Gulf war and subsequent events served to awaken the general population of the free world to the critical nature of logistics in at least five highly visible ways. Logistics became a more active and meaningful word in the world's everyday vocabulary.

First, the news media made the world aware of the fundamental importance of logistics to the implementation of the economic trade sanctions against Iraq backed by the United Nations. A shipping embargo was implemented to restrict goods from flowing into Iraq, which was highly dependent upon world trade to obtain vital food and medical supplies. Although such embargoes require substantial time to become fully effective, Iraq began to feel the pressure within months.

The second way in which the world became aware of the importance of logistics was the large fluctuation in world fuel costs, which was a direct result of the Gulf crisis. As crude oil prices temporarily doubled overnight, the sparks of inflation spread throughout a world on the brink of economic recession. Despite an adequate supply of crude oil, gasoline pump prices spiraled up so rapidly that congressional hearings resulted. Fuel surcharges implemented by trucking firms became an instant challenge to business profits. Airlines were forced into aggressive fare increases to cover escalating costs.

Third was the slow pace of the initial military buildup, which made the world aware of the logistical complexity required to move a large military force from the countries allied against Iraq to Saudi Arabia. After a flurry of flying advance forces, it became clear that the logistics of the buildup would require several months before the military was strategically positioned to launch a war. In fact, the military command was criticized for moving small headquarters units to the Saudi desert during Desert Shield, the occupation that preceded the actual war, in advance of core troops and equipment. Although such a tactic may have had strategic value, it served to underline the fact that despite relatively high levels of logistical expertise, the military needed time to support an initiative as sudden and comprehensive as Desert Storm.

The fourth way in which logistics became visibly important emerged during the later months of 1990 and the first months of 1991 when the military activated record peacetime numbers of national guard and reserve units to support Desert Shield and later Desert Storm. The reason for this massive call to duty was not as much based on the overall need for combat troops as it was motivated by a need for specific talents. Next to medical detachments, those units most frequently called to active duty were transportation and supply specialists. As neighbors and family members departed from community after community, it became clear that logistical resources were in critically short supply.

The fifth and final visible demonstration of the importance of logistics occurred in the aftermath of the war when reports from Iraq detailed the difficulties of life without such basic infrastructure as bridges. At the same time, the Kurdish refugee problem brought to the American living room the logistical nightmare of feeding up to a million people. While food, tents, blankets, and other supplies sat in Turkish cities, the Kurds starved and froze in an inaccessible mountain terrain.

All of the above events as well as many other events established the background for *Logistical Excellence*. This book conveys a message based on research, and is directed to managers who seek to improve logistical competency; it seeks to isolate what's important in leveraging performance and how to go about getting it done.

LOOKING BACK ACROSS THE 1980s

During the decade of the 1980s, the availability of information reshaped traditional business practices. In looking over the events of the 1980s, it appears that world–class organizations seized opportunities generated by four basic forces: (1) political or legal changes; (2) the technology explosion; (3) business and economic structural changes; and (4) globalization. The multiple impacts of these forces are briefly reviewed.

During the 1980s, the prevailing regulatory philosophy of North America changed dramatically. In both Canada and the United States, deregulation of major sectors of the economy occurred, not the least of which was in transportation. Transportation deregulation served as a stimulant for logistical creativity. Such creativity was further motivated by significant changes in the antitrust enforcement practices of the Justice Department. Strategic alliances, which would have been closely scrutinized or prohibited in earlier years, became common by the late 1980s. The National Cooperative Research and Development Act of 1984 and subsequent modifications of the act established and institutionalized a philosophy encouraging cooperative arrangements. Subsequent implementation of provisions of this act has introduced new ways and means to leverage logistics.

The impact of technology on the practice of logistics during the 1980s was striking. The increasing power and declining cost of computers stimulated an information revolution. Logistics managers confronted a staggering array of choices. What constitutes state-of-the-art information technology is expanding at an increasing rate. Electronic Data Interchange (EDI), satellites, and cellular telephones changed the way in which business communicates. One leading-edge retail firm operates a sophisticated satellite system to accumulate sales and inventory information on a real-time basis while at the same time serving as a closed-circuit television network to inform sales associates and managers about merchandising strategies. Firms using such technology tend to perform key business processes faster than their competitors. Bar coding and scanning technologies are capable of making downstream or market sales information available so rapidly that the need for selected traditional forecasting is eliminated. Firms operating in real time know every minute of every hour exactly where they stand. Furthermore, some firms know how to exploit such information capabilities. Knowledge-based systems are rapidly being implemented. Some firms are developing "fuzzy logic" neural networks to mimic and improve the imprecision of the typical human decision-making process.

During the past decade, the structure of traditional industries and even the overall economy have drastically changed. The rash of mergers and acquisitions has served to constantly restructure the demand for logistics services. Many firms faced with the burden of servicing leveraged buy-out debt have looked to their logistical operations for greater efficiencies and cash flow generation. Almost every industry is more concentrated today than it was going into the 1980s. Concentration is a fact at the retail, wholesale, and manufacturing levels of trade. It is also true in service industries such as transportation and warehousing. Concentration is also a reality in the information, health care, hospitality, and entertainment industries. Beyond such formal concentration is the increasing consolidation of resources resulting from strategic alliances and outsourcing. The shape of the business playing field changed dramatically during the 1980s.

Finally, during the 1980s business began to embrace the challenges of globalization. Globalization means global businesses, global organizations, and global competition. With each passing year, an increasing percentage of manufactured goods purchased in the United States is produced elsewhere. The core and leadership of some basic industries such as steel, tires, shoes, consumer electronics, toys, and jewelry have shifted off-shore from the United States. At the same time, new overseas markets are being opened up to United States products. Many firms are trying to sort out exactly what global competition will mean during the 1990s. Few, if any, progressive firms live with the illusion that they can escape direct foreign competition. Significant foreign investment has taken place in, among others, the United States banking, food, transportation, battery, and retail industries. Without doubt, the global village has become a reality, and logistics has a critical role in global organizational strategy.

Some firms may be temporarily able to improve logistical performance without in-depth comprehension of these changed forces. However, it appears unlikely that many firms will be able to achieve and sustain excellence without seizing the inherent opportunities created by such change. Understanding the challenges and opportunities is the first step in avoiding potentially fatal myopia.

MANAGING IN THE 1990s

If the activities of 1990 are any indication, the balance of the decade should provide its share of management challenges. For the logistics managers, the 1990s will represent a period of significant change in traditional paradigms. Although there certainly will be many surprises, logistics management during the 1990s is likely to focus on speed, quality, and structure. Naturally, the roots of such change can be traced to the 1980s.

Speed

Increased focus on speed is a natural outgrowth of the technological advances of the 1980s. The availability of information in real time means that everything is positioned to happen faster. An assessment of performance across the board suggests that some firms are more ideally positioned to capitalize upon speed than others. The focus on speed is beginning to impact directly on three areas of logistical operations: (1) process; (2) information; and (3) decision making. It appears that organizations of the 1990s have different capabilities when it comes to accommodating these dimensions of speed.

Process speed means doing things faster. If the traditional time required to bring a new product to market is five years, it should be cut to much less time and continuously reduced. If the typical order service cycle is ten days, it should be reduced to five days or less and then continuously reduced. If the time required to change over a production process is eight hours, it should be cut to four hours and ways to reduce it to minutes should be explored. Such reduction in time required to perform any process should be achieved while maintaining or increasing efficiency and quality. Unlike past attempts to perform faster, modern concepts of process speed cannot be realized by costly expenditures to achieve the desired performance. Efficiency will not be sacrificed for speed. The goal is to achieve speed with equal or greater productivity. For example, the 1980s gave birth to a form of process speed based on enhanced responsiveness. Such techniques as just-in-time (JIT) and quick response (QR) are examples of responsiveness strategies. Although offering significant improvement, such techniques represent the tip of the iceberg when it comes to potential process speed benefits. The full exploitation of simultaneous or parallel work, quick reconfiguration, postponement, and compression all represent significant alternatives that firms of tomorrow will deploy to modify processes to compete in time more effectively. In a general sense, today's leading-edge firms are rethinking traditional processes to identify ways to leverage speed.[4]

The speed of *information* is a given with today's technology. As noted earlier, firms can now conduct worldwide operations on a real-time basis. Not all firms excel nor are they equal when it comes to developing and maintaining high-quality accurate information. But, across the board, things are getting better. One of the challenges of the 1990s will be learning how to share information in an interorganizational setting. Speed of information takes on a different context when it is shared among organizations. Issues related to database access and degree of connectivity are moving to the top of the agenda. Thus, the real issues of information speed are organizational not technical, and they span the trading channel as contrasted to being within a single firm's operations.

Decision-making speed appears to be the most critical dimension of doing things faster. Progress in speeding up making decisions is lagging development in process and information speed. Decision-making speed relates to empowerment. Faster decision making goes hand in hand with effective delegation of authority. In situations where processes are changing rapidly and information is shared, slow cumbersome decisions can paralyze an organization. If a firm remains committed to the traditional command and control structures typical of functional organizations, it is unlikely that the decision-making processes will keep pace with requirements of competing in time.[5]

Quality

It is becoming abundantly clear that customers expect high-quality products and services. Quality performance will increasingly become a prerequisite for doing business during the decade ahead. Who can be against quality? It's like motherhood and apple pie. For some firms, however, it's an elusive concept. Quality in some processes, such as providing services, is difficult to define and hard to measure. Other firms do not have the patience to sustain a quality initiative. In the 1980s a public quality competition was launched and firms began to compete for national recognition. Motorola, Xerox, Westinghouse, Milliken, Cadillac, Global Metallurgical, Federal Express, IBM, Wallace, Solectron, Zytec, and Marlow Industries were among the initial winners of the Malcolm Baldridge National Quality Award. Florida Power and Light was named a winner of the highly regarded Deming Award. These public acknowledgments reinforced the commitment that "Made in America" will not symbolize inferior goods or poor service. Quality to the logistics manager boils down to three basic commitments: (1) zero defects; (2) continuous improvement; and (3) sustained performance.

Zero defects is a goal of 100-percent performance. Although it is not always possible to achieve in practice, the idea of giving customers what is promised when a sale is made is not a radical notion. In essence, zero defects places emphasis on doing the right thing, on time, every time. To view performance from a perspective of achieving less than perfection is a promise to disappoint some customers. A promise to provide a 95-percent fill rate is equally a promise to provide a 5-percent failure rate. Performance based on averages was acceptable in the days of inaccurate and delayed information. A commitment to average performance was justified in part by an inability to forecast accurately. The notion of planned deficiencies is obsolete in a real-time environment. Firms committed to quality measure their performance in terms of a quest for perfection.

A commitment to *continuous improvement* is a mind set that always searches for new and better ways to perform the logistics process. It is the continuous fixing, calibrating, and upgrading of a process that is currently working well. The idea is to always be seeking continuous small improvements rather than counting on the "home run" or breakthrough. In highly developed logistical situations, such improvements are often only possible by implementing strategic alliances. In the quest of continuous improvement, firms must be willing to test new concepts regardless of how deep they cut into traditional mind sets about how best to perform a specific function.

The idea of *sustained performance* is simple. All new levels of achievement must be maintained over time and this cannot be achieved if core problems remain while only symptoms are addressed. Short bursts of productivity followed by a relapse to old levels of performance are not acceptable. The basic technique, used to assure a sustained level of achievement, is *pay for performance*. Once again the basic notion is simple. Suppliers and other contributors to a process are granted increased rewards only in terms of sustained performance. For example, carriers are not granted rate increases. They are given shares of the productivity benefits that result from improved and sustained performance.[6]

Structure

The 1980s were dominated by significant changes in industry and economic structure. Individual organization management structures began to change to accommodate the technology that emerged during the 1980s. The responses of organizational structure to technology will accelerate in the 1990s. At the heart of organization structural change are three fundamental concepts: (1) networking; (2) outsourcing; and (3) ethics.

The trend toward increased organization *networking* is well documented. Just how organizations of the future will shape up is less clear. Charles Savage sees the management challenges of the 1990s as centering on four basic issues:

(1) How do we move beyond the extreme *fragmentation* of industrial-era companies?
(2) How do we maintain *accountability* in flat, dynamic network organizations?
(3) How do we support the *focusing* and *coordination* of multiple cross-functional task teams?
(4) How do we build into the very structure of the organization the capacity for *continual learning*?[7]

Effective networking raises many operational issues that require creative redesign of basic work. Some experts feel that it will be necessary for traditional organizations to disintegrate before they can evolve to fully take advantage of the power of information.[8] Organizational structures of yesterday are in for some really significant upheavals. At the heart of this change will be a team focus to facilitate or network skill groups throughout the organization to perform selected tasks and processes. Networking will configure around the required tasks in the job to be done and work teams will be formed and dissolved as necessary. The best techniques to empower, create incentive, motivate, compensate, and guide human resource development in a network performance environment are not clear. Network management is a basic challenge to a traditional hierarchical command and control organization structure.

The idea of *outsourcing* activities to specialists has the net effect of expanding the scope of effective management. The concept of outsourcing itself is old and finds its roots in economic specialization.[9] A modern outsourcing format is the strategic alliance. The notion of all outsourcing is to allow specialists to assist in performing selected functions while focusing internal resources on the core competencies of a firm. To the degree that a firm can specialize it has an opportunity to be *both* a low-cost and a high-quality performer. Once again, an old idea is finding renewed application because of the increased ability to manage functional outsourcing made possible by information technology such as Electronic Data Interchange. New attitudes about the importance of customers and suppliers are fostering long-term strategic alliances. A value-added service strategy may even encompass the supplier's suppliers and the customer's customers! As firms pare down their organizations and move toward leaner, flatter structures, they are likely to enter into more alliances and will confront the need to expand their managerial horizons.

Finally, the question of business *ethics* is moving to center stage. The rebirth of attention to the fundamental right and wrong of a business relationship is a reaction to such indiscretions as the insider trading scandals of the late 1980s and the savings and loan (thrift) bailouts and insurance failures of the early 1990s. Traditional procurement practices are coming under close scrutiny. Because of the wide range of materials and services purchased by a typical logistics organization, the potential for ethical violations is significant. Fair play in strategic alliances also requires that performance and compensation be more closely related than ever before.

WHAT DOES IT ALL MEAN?

From a logistics management perspective, doing business in the world of the 1990s will be different and challenging. It appears likely that the practices of management that worked during the past may not be effective in the future. Although some firms are currently changing in an effort to be better positioned to meet the challenges of the future, the vast majority remain in a mind-set of "business as usual." Their primary concerns are quarterly sales and earnings. Each year is devoted to achieving gains in shareholders' wealth with no real attention to improving their long-run competitive posture. They are failing to address the real question of the 1990s—are they ready to compete in a global economy?

When many of these firms are finally forced to come face to face with the challenges of change, it is likely that they will not be ready to manage the process. Most will be cast into a reactive mode rather than in a proactive, creative mode. As such, they will fail to grasp leadership and will not take the initiative to exploit change.

Logistical Excellence is about change management. The focus is on how to go about changing an organization's commitment and culture to support revitalization of its logistical process. The logistical process of a firm cuts across every internal organizational unit and reaches out to encompass customers and suppliers. The work of logistics takes place across a broad geographical playing field twenty-four hours a day, seven days of every week. Since it is not confined to a building or a plant, logistics is a difficult process to manage. It is an even more difficult process to change. Logistical excellence is a moving target.

No clear-cut, sure-fire formula exists to guide the change management processes. Lessons can be learned from a careful examination of what successful firms did to revamp their basic approach to logistics. Such examination reveals some common attributes among successful firms that seem to transcend industry, size, or position in the distribution channel. Similarly, there are some lessons to learn about how such leaders go about managing the process of change.

The chapters that follow address the questions of how to achieve leading-edge logistical competency. To be leading edge means to adopt the best practices of management and to always be "pushing the envelope." It means taking industry leadership in exploiting logistical competency as a way to gain competitive advantage. It means being creative, even visionary!

To present the challenges of change and to map managerial guidelines, each chapter is preceded by a dialogue that flows from chapter to chapter. The dialogue presents the trials and tribulations of a manager—Charlie Change*—who works through the process of improving the logistical competency of his firm. The dialogue tracks Charlie's efforts to become fully knowledgeable about the need for and the potential benefits from improved logistical performance. Subsequent episodes of the dialogue illustrate how Charlie takes ownership of the commitment to change and tracks how he develops and implements an improvement program. From chapter to chapter, the dialogue maps Charlie's initiative and frustration as he strives to create significant improvement in his firm's logistical competency. The chapter content following each "Charlie Change" episode develops the lessons to be learned in greater detail. To set the stage for the book's content, the reader may want to read all of these episodes first.

WHY CHANGE? THE TRIALS AND TRIBULATIONS OF CHARLIE CHANGE!

Charlie Change has always been the type to get things done, or at least that was his reputation throughout the company. It was this reputation that re-

---

* The name Charlie Change was chosen over Charlene Change by a flip of a coin.

sulted in his being selected to go to Europe three years ago to consolidate the company's marketing efforts on the Continent. Soon after top management decided that with "EC 92" coming it was time to get into gear in the European market, Charlie found himself living in France. Charlie successfully completed the European assignment and recently returned to the general office.

During his first week back, Charlie was called into Randy Good's office. Randy was the CEO. Charlie anticipated being debriefed on the European operations and expected to discuss a more specific assignment than "staff assistant to the CEO." To his surprise, after a few complimentary comments concerning how comprehensive and well written Charlie's reports were, Randy didn't seem to want to talk about the past. Instead, he began to discuss an entirely new topic—or at least, it appeared entirely different to Charlie! The topic was logistics. Charlie didn't consider himself much of an expert. In fact, during the subsequent conversation, Charlie was not even sure he understood exactly what Randy was talking about. He was happy when Randy told him that the board of directors wanted him to make an appraisal of what should be done to get the company moving in the logistics area.

That night, Charlie made a list of what he perceived logistics to be all about. Basically, Charlie felt logistics focused on "moving and storing products":

transportation: trucks? planes? Somehow material had to be moved into the plants, it had to be moved around inside the plants, and it had to be moved out of the plants. Somehow the final products had to reach the customers.
warehouses: to store supplies? to store finished goods?
inventory: the company sure had a lot of raw materials and finished goods!!
documentation: everything moved or stored had to be documented.

Charlie looked at his list and began to laugh—the list appeared to be ridiculously simple and incomplete. Worse still, the list appeared to have no or at best limited connection to the things that Randy had been talking about. Charlie reviewed his notes listing some of the key phrases that Randy had used over and over:

integrated logistics
significant and continuous improvements in efficiency and quality
enhanced customer service and satisfaction
JIT and Quick Response capability
EDI linkages with trading partners
sustainable competitive advantage

focused logistics strategy
interrelated systems
reduced costs
flexibility and responsiveness to changing customer requirements
logistical mission/supply chain management
asset management

What did any of these have to do with warehouses? What did they have to do with trucks? Charlie could make some connections between his list and the meeting notes, but they seemed trivial. For example, Charlie thought, we could probably get products to customers a lot faster by using a specialized transportation source. But—we would have to pay a premium. Customers would probably be happy with the fast delivery, but could we pass on the additional cost? Everything that Charlie thought of seemed to contain inherent contradictions with something else on the list.

Charlie decided to proceed systematically. The first thing I need is information, he thought to himself, information about the overall picture concerning what is going on in logistics. He also felt he needed to understand the details. Charlie remembered the confidence Randy had expressed in him: "You're the man for the job—you develop the big picture, you find out what has to be done, and you get it done."

Notes

1. *The Age* (June 26, 1990): 8.
2. *The New York Times* (August 20, 1990): A4.
3. Robert V. Delaney, "State of Logistics Annual Report: Trends in Logistics and Our World Competitiveness," presented at the National Press Club, Washington, D.C., June 15, 1990.
4. Peter G. W. Keen, *Competing in Time*, 2d ed. (New York: Ballinger Publishing Company, 1988).
5. George Stalk, Jr., and Thomas M. Hout, *Competing Against Time* (New York: The Free Press, 1990).
6. James Aaron Cooke, "Xerox's Drive for Logistics Quality," *Traffic Management* (October 1990): 50–58.
7. Charles M. Savage, *5th Generation Management*, (Bedford, Mass.: Digital Press, 1990).
8. Christopher Meyer and David Power, "Enterprise Disintegration: The Storm Before the Calm," *Commentary* (Lexington, Mass.: Temple, Barker and Sloane, Inc., 1989).
9. George E. Stigler, "The Division of Labor is Limited by the Extent of the Market," *Journal of Political Economy* (June 1951): 185–193.

Change Is Everywhere

WITHIN a short time, Charlie realized his company was facing a crisis. There was no drastic drop in profitability. No, thought Charlie, this crisis is far more dangerous. The symptoms are subtle and the core problems are difficult to pinpoint.

Charlie had come to this preliminary conclusion after talking to numerous people throughout the company. Everyone seemed to acknowledge that their department had problems. They were all quick to point out that they weren't alone—other departments also had problems. Sales complained that competition had intensified significantly during the past few years and as a result it was getting far more difficult to get new customers and hold on to the core of the current business. Manufacturing complained that salespeople were making promises to customers that were impossible to keep. Manufacturing and logistics were particularly upset at demands for high levels of service performance on small orders. Sales countered that new customers tested potential suppliers this way. If the supplier didn't perform on the small order task, a big order would never materialize. And so it went—almost everyone Charlie talked to agreed that things were getting tougher.

Charlie remembered one conversation in particular. It would become key to his future actions. Bob was one of the company's top sales managers. Charlie had lunch with Bob at a particularly frustrating time. Like a song that replays uncontrollably in one's mind, so had one of Bob's stories stuck in Charlie's mind . . .

"You know, Charlie, I've been around a long time, and I know everyone in the business." Bob proceeded to name key purchasers, key salespeople in competing firms, who had which account, who bought how much from whom, who was after which account, and so on. Bob knew who could deliver what within which time span. Indeed, Bob's grasp of competitive benchmarking was remarkable.

Thinking back, Charlie remembered being impressed, but not surprised—after all, isn't a sales manager supposed to be on top of things? What *did* surprise Charlie was the name of the competitor Bob was most concerned about . . .

> "Charlie, the numbers tell you that Universal is our main rival. Every guy in the office will tell you that Universal is our main rival. But I'm telling you that they're not. I'm telling you that Special is. They only started two years ago, and in terms of volume they don't compare to Universal—yet. We're much bigger than them—for now. Let me tell you about Special. They'll customize the product down to the last micron . . . we try to convince the customer that our standard unit will somehow fit their needs. Special could ship products faster from the moon than we can ship from 150 miles. Special commits to a specific delivery time when the order is received . . . we're lucky to deliver it in the right year."

Charlie remembered laughing at this obvious exaggeration. However, as the story drifted over and over again through Charlies's mind, Bob's words somehow became less and less amusing. Bob had continued . . .

> "You know Sam, to whom I've been selling for eight years? Last month he placed an order with Special and requested a 3:00 P.M. Tuesday delivery. Sam told me they had bets going at his place over whether Special would make it. Well, their truck was there and waiting to be unloaded at 3:00 P.M. The order was perfect—nothing missing, nothing broken, nothing defective. Sam says he'll have to give them a whole lot more orders in the future. Sure, Sam still orders much more from us—for now."

Charlie thought of what it would take to accomplish 100-percent fill rate on time with zero defects . . . surely no company could perform that well all the time. In fact, several people Charlie had talked to had stated that such service was impossible; some had practically laughed at the suggestion; some thought that Japanese firms might try to do it. Everyone had plenty of reasons why it couldn't be done, although there was substantial disagreement over what the exact reasons were. Charlie remembered the rest of Bob's tale . . .

> "It was two weeks ago that Sam tells me another 'little story.' Seems like one of Sam's machines was busted and they couldn't figure out what was wrong with it. So they called Special to delay delivery of some raw material for a couple of days. Special responds by sending a guy over to help them

get it running. Then this guy phones Special and reschedules delivery. Sam says to me: they saved us a fortune. Well, I got the real message. Do you know what it is, Charlie? We're slightly cheaper than Special, so Sam's still giving us the big orders. But this one event wiped out weeks of those savings. The last straw came yesterday. Sam tells me that Special's representative came in with this new design that could save them hundreds of thousands of dollars and that Sam's engineers are looking into it. Then he tells me—and this is a real bombshell—that his company is planning to drastically reduce the number of suppliers they have traditionally dealt with. Buzz words like "reorganization," "rationalization," and so on are flying, but again, the real message is simple. They want the right product—not 80 percent of the right product and not the product 80 percent right. They want it at the right time, at the right place. And they want it *all* the time, not some of the time, and not most of the time. Finally, they want someone who helps them *make* money—they want a partner. Special's got a good chance. They're flexible, they're fast, they've got salespeople and plant and *everything* hooked up computer-wise, they make decisions fast. Around here, it can take days just to find out the status of an order, and every decision is subject to the 10/10 rule: 10 weeks and 10 signatures before anything major is decided!"

Charlie could still envision Bob's intense expression as these last words were spoken. The story stuck because it seemed to incorporate key elements from some major trends impacting American business—trends that Charlie had identified over the past few weeks through observation, study, and reflection. These trends characterized the macro-environment in which firms had to operate. Charlie reviewed the basic trends one at a time, in no particular order . . .

Trend 1:   The focus is on customer satisfaction
Delighting the customer leads to loyalty.

Trend 2:   Globalization and international competition
The world is shrinking.

Trend 3:   Market concentration in the United States
The middle is squeezed.

Trend 4:   The computer revolution's effects are everywhere
The mechanization of management?

Trend 5:   Many organizations are flatter than before:
Tasks and functions are also being reorganized
Doing things right.

Trend 6: Supplier-customer strategic alliances are being formed: Are corporations becoming hollow?
Recognizing common interests.

Trend 7: The knowledge era and the value of innovativeness
Knowledge and newness pay off.

Trend 8: Strategy in the competitive environment: Implementation has strategic value
Doing the right things right.

Charlie knew that whatever specific change scenario developed in his firm, success could not be assured if major forces in the environment were ignored.

It is important for decision makers to be aware of major macroenvironmental trends. This is true even if a particular trend does not appear to have an immediate effect in a particular industry, company, or functional area. Knowledge has both defensive and offensive strategic value—while lack of knowledge can be disabling. Ignorance is seldom bliss in today's environment; rather, ignorance can be suicide. A proper perspective to guide development of a leading-edge logistical initiative starts with becoming fully aware of key trends that will cast the future. These eight major trends will dominate the early years of the 1990s. They are so pervasive that it would be a rare manager who would not be affected by most of them.

☞ TREND 1: The Focus Is on Customer Satisfaction
Delighting the customer leads to loyalty.

It seems obvious, even trivial, to state that firms make money from customers and that competitors compete for customers. It seems obvious that satisfied customers are more likely to purchase from a firm than are dissatisfied customers and delighted customers are even more likely to repeat their purchasing. It seems obvious that customers will probably be satisfied when their expectations are met, and that they will probably be delighted when their expectations are exceeded. It is almost always cheaper to retain a customer than to obtain a customer, and therefore it seems obvious that customer loyalty is a sensible business goal. It is simple: customers want a quality product and the level of customer service that the company promised!

Yet it is not so simple.[1] First, who is the customer? Different segments of customers want different things and have different expectations. In at least some respects, all major customers are unique. It is productive, however, to focus on their commonalities and to make a list of the minimum that *all* customers *really* want:

- Customers want to receive exactly what they ordered: no more, no less, no substitutions, no defects, no breakage, no spoilage.
- Customers want delivery of their perfectly filled order within the precisely agreed-upon time (sometimes ASAP!).
- Customers want to pay as little as possible.

Each individual customer would probably easily add other things to this basic list. Of course, realistic customers have come to *expect* that even these three desires may not be filled. What customers *expect* to happen is usually quite different from what they would like to happen. When no supplier achieves a 100-percent fill rate, customers do not expect a 100-percent fill rate—but they still *want* a 100-percent fill rate. When no supplier delivers exactly on time, all of the time, customers do not expect on-time delivery—but they still *want* 100-percent on-time delivery. Finally, when a supplier is competitively superior with respect to the first two items on the list, many customers are willing to pay more—but they still *want* to pay as little as possible.

The evaluation of a supplier by a customer depends to some extent on what other suppliers are offering. For example, not all customers demand just-in-time delivery at a particular time. Many customers appear to be satisfied with schedules that promise "the beginning of the week" or "Monday delivery." But how long will they be satisfied with such loose performance when it becomes apparent that "Monday at or about 3:00 P.M." is an attainable delivery goal? How much is "Monday at 3:00 P.M." versus "the beginning of the week" worth to a customer in terms of reduced safety stocks? How much is it worth to a customer to receive exactly what was ordered, without the interminable phone calls and faxes and without the hassles? How much is it worth to a customer to be able to rely absolutely on a supplier to deliver a desired order at the exact time?

Frequently, one supplier begins to offer superior service and other suppliers are forced to follow suit. If competitive service levels are not offered by a particular firm, price cuts often become necessary to entice customers in the resulting competitive environment. On the other hand, providing similar service levels can cost a significant amount of money. Whether a supplier is an innovator, a follower, or a laggard, the impact on sales and profit is profound. Both costs *and* opportunity costs must be considered.

In summary, there are three sets of important questions: they center on *customers, competitors,* and *costs.*

> *First,* who are the current and potential customers? What quality of product and level of services do they expect at present and what would they really like to have? What tradeoffs in price, quality, or service will customers perceive as desirable?

> *Second,* what are the competitors doing for these customers and what do they intend to do in the future? Which products at what level of quality and which services can be provided that yield a differential advantage over these competitors? Is this differential advantage sustainable? Do all value-added services over time become the minimum customers expect? What quality and service must be provided in order to avoid a serious differential *dis*advantage?

> *Third,* how much will it cost to provide the desired levels of service and quality? Will customers be willing to pay for them? Do costs increase exponentially as various levels of service approach 100 percent or zero defects in the product is approached? What is the opportunity cost of *not* offering various services or of *not* offering top quality?

Indeed, these questions are not particularly revolutionary. What makes their consideration newly important—indeed critical—is the rapidly changing environment in which all firms operate. This changing competitive environment is affecting customers at every level in the channel.

"It seems so simple. Businesses exist to serve customers and should bend over backward to satisfy their needs. But too many companies still don't get it and in the 1990s, more customers are likely to take the opportunity to reward those who do."[2] So ended a recent *Business Week* cover story. In essence, customers hate wasting their time and money, and they love companies that listen to what they want and then deliver it. For example, the top peeves of consumers are waiting in line when additional service windows are closed, staying at home for a no-show delivery or salespeople, and being waited on by poorly informed salespeople.[3] From the customer's point of view these peeves are all directly related to their interface with the company. For the customer, the company *is* the individual(s) with whom the *customer* interacts. The contact person is frequently a lower-level employee, not a top manager. Furthermore, customers do not care why something is late or why an order is defective or incomplete—customers are interested in results, not excuses.

Quality and time seem to comprise the essence of competitive service. Time has been called the "cutting edge," especially when it is combined with quality offerings and responsiveness to customers.[4] Time-based competition is reshaping both United States and international competition. Furthermore, some of the basic paradigms of the past, such as the traditional cost–service curve, are being challenged. Do costs increase with reduced lead times, increased flexibility, larger assortments, and increased quality? Does demand increase only marginally when customers are given what they really want?

A "customer service" or "customer focus" on the part of management is insufficient, although such a commitment is certainly necessary in order to institute real changes. Real change demands the reorganization of the entire company to focus on customer desires. It demands reengineering, leadership, vision! Thus, to the three basic questions concerning *customers, competitors,* and *costs,* a fourth can be added: *commitment.*

> How can the commitment necessary to refocus and reorganize the entire company be obtained? Excellence in service is estimated to be worth anywhere from a 10-percent to a 50-percent price differential[5]—is this a sufficiently strong argument? Others may argue that the differential is not sustainable or that the differential exists only at the top end of the market. How can others be convinced that real quality and real service can actually be delivered at a reasonable cost or even at lower cost? How can others be convinced of the value of doing things right the first time, every time? Will the "if we don't do it, someone else will" argument be convincing? How can others be forced to take the longer-term perspective?

☞ TREND 2: Globalization and International Competition
The world is shrinking.

The focus on international business seems to center on two fundamental issues: (1) that certain nation states or geographic areas may have distinct competitive advantages;[6] and (2) that a worldwide trend is toward economic unification. It appears that three distinct trading blocs are emerging: Europe, North America, and the Pacific Rim, dominated by a reunited Germany, the United States, and Japan, respectively. Table

2-1 compares these three countries and reveals that, although most of the world's attention in recent years has been focused on Japan, West Germany actually exports 2.5 times more per capita, runs a larger positive trade balance, and has a much broader export base than Japan.[7] Furthermore, the average German worker works about 450 hours (12 weeks) less per year than the average Japanese worker. The Japanese, however, lead the world in capital investment. In 1989, they outspent the United States $549 to $513 billion, which is the first time any country has outspent the United States since World War II—and Japan has an economy half the size of that of the United States.[8]

Of the largest 100 companies in the world, 43 are Japanese, 38 are American, and the rest are European.[9] This does not mean that wealth can be measured by the number of mega-corporations registered or headquartered within a nation. West Germany, for example, has always relied on its "Mittelstand" (midsized companies often controlled by families), which account for 80 percent of GNP and are the key to its export success. Thus, it is not surprising that of the world's top 1,000 corporations, only 30 are German, while 353 are American and 345 are Japanese. Only about 500 German companies, one quarter as many as in Britain, are traded in stock exchanges.[10]

The situation in Europe is a well-known example of the potential of integration. Market integration of the European Community (EC) is scheduled to be virtually completed by 1992. Less well known is the European Free Trade Association (EFTA), consisting of Switzerland, Sweden, Norway, Iceland, and Austria. The Warsaw Pact has *disinte-grated* recently, however, and the parallel trading bloc Comecon failed as Moscow insisted on hard currency transactions. Many of its members are now seeking ties with the EC and the West. Although suffering

---

TABLE 2-1: *Comparative Economic Indicators*

	United States	*Japan*	*Germany*
GNP (billions of US$)	$ 5,233	$ 2,820	$ 1,373
GNP (US$ per capita)	$21,018	$22,879	$14,910
Exports (billions of US$)	$624	$413	$428
Gross Investment (%GNP)	15%	32%	20%
Hourly Compensation (wages & benefits)	$14.51	$12.42	$17.72

from outmoded manufacturing facilities and decaying logistics infrastructures, these countries constitute significant markets and have large inexpensive labor pools. The scope of the problems involved in East–West economic reintegration is overwhelming. These problems range from macro to micro levels. As an example of a small detail, consider that there were fewer private telephones in eastern Germany in 1989 than there were in 1938. The outcome in Eastern Europe is difficult to predict after forty-five years of economic interdependence focused eastward.

Nationalism seems to be reemerging east of the old Iron Curtain, particularly in the Soviet Union. The major exception is of course "East" Germany, which was already among the top twenty industrialized countries. As a result of unification, East Germany gave up its albeit artificially imposed nationhood and will gain automatic EC "membership." Economic unification with West Germany is well under way, with 95 percent of the 1900 joint ventures established in East Germany from January to June 1990 being with West German firms. A unified Germany has about eighty million people and an economy nearly double the size of France's.

The trend within the Americas is also toward integration. At the very least, Canada, Mexico, and the United States are headed toward economic integration in the near future. The United States–Canada Free Trade Agreement went into effect on January 1, 1989, and both countries have agreed to negotiate a similar pact with Mexico. At present, United States two-way trade is about $167 billion with Canada and about $52 billion with Mexico. The combined North American bloc would have a population of 362 million and a GNP of $5.9 trillion, with integration stimulating an estimated 0.5 percent in extra annual growth.[11] North-South links at the state or regional levels, or both, are already in place, and long-term basic economic forces seem to favor economic unification. Naturally labor unions and less efficient industries are lobbying against such a free trade zone. Although on the surface it appears that United States jobs may be lost to low-wage Mexico, many believe these jobs would be lost anyway to Asia or elsewhere. Pressure is building to expand the trade pact to include South American countries. Preliminary groundwork was evident during President Bush's trip to four such countries in December 1990.

Large companies such as General Electric are already developing North American strategies, as well as worldwide strategies. Smaller companies, such as Mattel, Inc., maker of the Barbie doll, are also beginning to think in terms of a world market. For example, Mattel has introduced the "Friendship Barbie" to be sold in Eastern Europe, and it has set up offices in East Berlin and Budapest. Firms of all types are seeking international linkages. Firms in any particular nation can expect to see foreign competitors.

The most difficult trading bloc to evaluate properly is the Pacific Rim. Asia has six of the world's ten largest ports and the six largest banks. The combined GNP of the Pacific Rim equals that of Europe and is three quarters of the total of North America.[12] In resources and markets, Japan, Korea, Indonesia, Malaysia, the Philippines, and Thailand could be dominant in the world economy. Regarding alliances, these Asian nations do not demonstrate the same clear commitment to negotiate free trading as do the European and North American alignments. Japan is a world target because of its competitive attitude toward exporting, its financial resources, and its restricted position toward imports and joint ventures. In early 1990 the United States alone was running more than a $50-billion trade deficit with Japan. The collapse of social reform in China has cast a cloud over what appeared to be the awakening of the world's giant. Likewise, recent evidence suggests that Korea may face the challenges of reunification in the not-too-distant future. No one can question the economic potential of a Pacific trading bloc. The question is: When will it emerge? Many feel the 1990s will be the "Pacific Decade."

Mergers, acquisitions, and strategic alliances that transcend national boundaries are increasingly commonplace. Indeed, some believe that a new type of firm is emerging: the stateless corporation.[13] The characteristics of a stateless corporation are as follows:

- They operate within a particular country as if they were locals, unlike the classical multinationals which retained a national identity;
- They shift factories, research facilities, and technologies around the world, making their decisions without reference to borders, unlike the classical multinationals which usually designed and engineered products at "home" and which had a strict chain of command leading back to the "home" corporate headquarters;
- Key positions within the company are held by executives of various nationalities unlike the classical multinationals in which key positions were usually held by nationals of the "home" base.

Among companies ranked by percent sales from foreign countries in the "stateless world of manufacturing," the top United States firms are

Gillette, Colgate, IBM, NCR, CPC International, Coca-Cola, Digital, and Dow Chemical.

Of course, this phenomenon raises many questions. For one, are accounting rules outdated? When a United States company manufactures a product abroad for domestic United States consumption, should it count in the trade deficit? Taxes are another issue. Are "foreign" companies paying a fair share of taxes? Are tax breaks being used unfairly to attract businesses to a particular nation, region, or city? International politics add another layer of complexity. Has economic warfare replaced military warfare? When governments have a trade dispute, on whose "side" will the stateless corporation be? Is Japan observing the Arab embargo of Israel when it ships Honda Civics to Israel from Ohio, but not from Japan? Finally, the existence of the stateless corporation raises important national policy issues. Is it ethical for firms to shift operations to countries with fewer legal obstacles or environmental controls? When sales or operations abroad top a certain percentage, say 40 percent, should that firm be eligible for preferential tax treatment, subsidization, or research grants from the "home" government? Will stateless decisions be made consistently in favor of those nations with low "overhead" in terms of mandated social benefits or low wages, or both? Is global competition the result of the final word in economies-of-scale decision making? How does logistics fit?

☞ TREND 3: Market Concentration in the United States
The middle is squeezed.

The competitive arena is changing not only because of increased globalization, but also because of consolidation within the United States. The carpet industry, for example, faced a decade of consolidation during the 1980s.[14] Because of high shipping costs, international competition has traditionally played a limited role in the consolidation in this industry. In 1980 there were 350 carpet mills as compared to 170 today. Leaders in the industry used to be West Point-Pepperell and Armstrong. They are now both owned by Shaw, which in 1980 ranked sixth. Shaw, the current market-share leader with 18.4 percent, is trailed by Burlington Industries with 5.3 percent. Although concentration has increased the size of the remaining players, it is important to realize that size alone is no protection against foreign competition. Neither is high shipping cost! Recently the Beaulieu Group of Belgium opened a mill in the United States. Called Beaulieu of America, it is now ranked thirty-first in the industry. The editor of *Carpet and Rug Industry,* however, named it as Shaw's biggest threat. This example illustrates that no industry is safe from globalization. A firm's most dangerous competitors in the long run may not be the current industry giants. In fact, the firm's most dangerous competitors may not even be in the industry currently!

A 1991 *Business Week* cover story on the age of consolidation pointed out the effects of megamergers in the banking, appliance, airline, tire, and software industries.[15] The concentration of markets tends to leave either large or small firms operating, while the number of midsized firms is significantly reduced.[16] For example, in 1987, 9 percent of the wholesalers conducted 60 percent of the wholesale transactions. An increase in company size can have profound effects; it can be the driving force behind reorganization. Furthermore, size can drive strategy. In many industries, the low-cost producer is large because of economies of scale. On the other hand, flexibility and customization are sometimes characteristics of smallness. For small companies, living under the shadow of the giants presents both problems and opportunities.

Arm and Hammer is an example of a small company that must frequently do battle with giants such as Procter & Gamble (P & G), Unilever, and Colgate-Palmolive.[17] At the end of the 1980s, the company was being run with a highly personal management style and a "small firm" strategy. It had $318 million in revenues in 1987, however, and wanted to expand to a billion-dollar business. The company hired executives from major competitors such as P & G, Chesebrough-Pond, and Johnson & Johnson. They began to license their trademark, which had a 92-percent recognition factor, and establish strategic partnerships with both United States and European companies. They regularly raised prices in markets they dominated and became price followers in markets dominated by the giants. They revamped and consolidated their logistics system, reducing the number of distribution warehouses from twenty-one to fourteen. In addition, they invested in an electronic reporting system and increased the scope of their consumer surveys. By 1989 net sales had topped $400 million—a step in the right direction.

☞ TREND 4: The Computer Revolution's Effects Are Everywhere
The mechanization of management?

Because the computer revolution is so pervasive in its effects, it is sometimes difficult to remember how recent it is. A 1990 survey of 8,000 computer users in the workplace found that only 28 percent of these personal computers were in use in 1986, while as many as 24 percent of them were purchased in 1989.[18] The "office in a briefcase" is rapidly becoming common. Computers that recognize either voice or handwriting, or both, and that can handle video images are emerging. Using artificial intelligence, computers have the capability to sort through massive amounts of data and extract information tailored for a specific user. A proprietary software program that accomplishes sorting of this kind can provide a significant competitive edge. The owners of such a program can be expected to guard its secrets jealously. One firm destroys obsolete equipment rather than selling it and risking that its competitors learn even old "secrets." Indeed, protecting both data and software is rapidly becoming a major issue, especially since so many computers are networked together. For example, Oliver North did not know that IBM's PROFs mail system had an automatic backup and therefore erasing the memos did not erase the trail he left in the Iran-Contra affair.

The computer revolution rests on the following tripod: (1) *hardware,* such as personal computers in an office or data-entry devices on delivery trucks; (2) *software,* such as spreadsheets or database management programs; and (3) *interconnectedness,* such as electronic data interchange (EDI) or internal networking. These three attributes form the essence of the new information technology, with the last of the three becoming increasingly critical because of how the technology enables connections among people, among machines, and from people to machines.[19] Indeed, networking was a cover story in *Business Week* in 1990.[20] One of the main effects of implementing the new information technology has been to empower control systems of all types.[21] Another effect has been to increase customer service responsiveness. Still another has been to reorganize the way in which people and machines work together. The effects have been pervasive at every level of the channel. Several examples follow.

At the retail level, the effects of universal product code (UPC) scanning in association with automatic price lookup systems have already had a dramatic effect. The benefits are many.[22] Increased checkout speed means consumers spend less time waiting in line, which in turn decreases the probability of abandoned shopping carts and irritated customers. Shopping carts and parking places also turn over faster. Cashiers are more productive, easier to train, and fewer are needed at peak times. Point-of-sale terminals can be reduced in number, freeing up sales space. Errors in price, quantity, and stock keeping unit (SKU) are reduced, making sales information far more reliable. Fewer stock counts are required, stockouts are easier to avoid, and better assortments can be provided. The potential of using scanner data for the modeling of promotions, trade dealing, pricing, inventory replenishment, and forecasting is being exploited by many retailers.

For manufacturing, the effects of the computer revolution are equally dramatic. One area is in marketing and sales force management. For example, the President and CEO of Frito-Lay specifically highlighted the following benefits of the decision support system that feeds 200 managers information from 10,000 route salespeople, each of whom is equipped with hand-held computers: (1) helps track new products and allows for midcourse corrections; (2) enables faster, more accurate decision making; (3) permits "management by walking around" via electronic mail memo; and (4) helps in implementing decentralization.[23] Such quick, reliable information is becoming common among industries. Hanes Hosiery, for example, have equipped their sales representatives with (1) computers, UPC wands, and printers (all of which fit into one carrying case), and (2) a laptop computer for generating and transmitting orders. Using the new technology has cut time to take in-store inventory in half, leaving representatives more time to work on point-of-sale displays and to gather competitive benchmarking data.

Even more revolutionary results have resulted from computer-integrated manufacturing (CIM). CIM integrates factory machines being scheduled by the factory floor computers with databases from sales, logistics, and accounting. Outside vendors may also be connected through electronic data interchange (EDI) so that they coordinate their production to achieve just-in-time delivery of components. The goal is reduced cycle time—in product development and engineering, in procurement, in processing customer orders, in manufacturing, in shipping, in billing, and in practically every activity. For example, a computer-integrated Motorola plant, using the same machines as other United States factories, produces pagers at the same cost as a Singapore plant which has less expensive labor cost. Custom-produced pagers, which used to require six weeks for delivery, are now available within twenty-four hours.[24]

Computers, however, do not *necessarily* mean efficiency. The Japanese use far fewer computers than either Americans or Europeans, and yet no one claims that the Japanese are less efficient. Indeed, computers have the potential to decrease efficiency by causing information overload. Electronic mail enables people to send memos to everyone who may be interested, but which recipient has time to sort through it all?

Confusion over which software is becoming "the industry standard" in any particular industry is reaching new heights. Horror stories abound about expensive but useless bells and whistles, machines still sitting in boxes because too little was budgeted for training, software packages that are instantly obsolete or that cannot talk to one another, and confidential mail sent at electronic speed to the wrong person.

Some have said that the new information technology is the way in which white collar jobs can be "mechanized," thereby achieving productivity increases comparable to those experienced on the factory floor. Indeed, the lack of office productivity seems to lie at the core of American productivity problems, not any failure in factory productivity. Buying hardware and software without re-engineering the way in which work is done will not achieve these goals, however. For example, flexibility may decrease as the rules inherent in software "take over." Is customer satisfaction enhanced if the customer can track a package but never speaks to a human being?

☞ TREND 5: Many Organizations Are Flatter Than Before: Tasks and Functions Are Also Being Reorganized
Doing things right

The new organization is no longer "coming," it is here.[25] In the 1980s at least a million management jobs were slashed in the United States. One out of four jobs in Fortune 500 firms disappeared.[26] Among manufacturing employees, 47 percent are in nonproduction jobs as contrasted to 23 percent in the 1950s, which leads many to believe that there is lots of fat left to trim. And without doubt, "trimming fat" is one motivation for flattening organizational structures. The leveraged buyouts and takeovers of the 1980s were contributing factors. Well-publicized examples such as the Kodak restructuring (begun in December 1988) and the massive restructuring at AT&T have a rippling effect. Indeed, restructuring has been the focus of at least one advertising campaign! (See Exhibit 2-1.) Comparisons to foreign competitors have also encouraged companies to reduce organization layers. For example, Ford has fifteen layers of management while Toyota has seven! Finally, restructuring is not limited to United States firms. Many European firms are undergoing the same massive trimming of layers of organization and the reorganization of tasks. Steven Schlosstein, author of *The End of the American Century,* and others think that the United States is a clear leader in the change from rigid, centralized bureaucracies to organizations based on the new information technology, decentralized

EXHIBIT 2-1 Key Points from Wang Advertisement

Bureaucracy can kill a company

It can also cripple its customers. Today, no one can afford to work with a maze of corporate buck-passers.

So at the new Wang, we're attacking bureaucracy head-on.

We have 21% fewer vice-presidents today than on July 1, 1989, 25% fewer directors, 36% fewer managers, 55% fewer supervisors.

What you find today is the muscle, working muscle.

Over 20,000 people with the power and the willingness to act for you. People with answers for you.

For example, within 48 hours of placing an order, you'll now know exactly when your order will be delivered.

No if's, and's, and I-don't-knows.

Moreover, now no product will take more than eight weeks to arrive.

Most will take less than four. And many will be at your office within 24 to 72 hours.

Fast work, not fast talk.

Source: New York Times Magazine, June 3, 1990, p. 61. Wang Laboratories, Inc.

structures, individual autonomy, and teamwork.[27] Being leaders in this change could be a competitive advantage for United States companies.

For restructuring in an organization to achieve increased flexibility and faster decision making, the following principles are usually adhered to:

- It must be decided what does *not* have to be done;
- Employees and managers must be trained in new skills;
- Employees must be empowered to make decisions;
- Employees and managers must be rewarded during the transition period and after restructuring;
- Managers and supervisors can no longer be rewarded just because they manage lots of people or because they follow orders well;
- Neither dependency on the rulebook *nor* maverick individualism encourages the type of teamwork necessary;

- Departments and functional areas must learn to operate interdependently, not independently. This may require rethinking of how work is actually going to be done. Must physical layouts of offices, work stations, and so on, be changed? Should certain functional areas be dissolved and the functions and tasks be assigned elsewhere or perhaps dispersed throughout the organization?
- The hierarchical command and control organization must be abandoned in spirit as well as in fact. Internal political structures will be shaken and corporate management must assume new leadership roles.
- Efficient and effective use of the new information technology is both an enabler and a motivation for restructuring.[28]

For example, in manufacturing plants one motivation to reorganize is computer-integrated manufacturing (CIM), which is a new way to organize tasks and functions around information flows and requirements. Thus tasks and functions must be integrated similarly to the way in which information is integrated. Islands of automation are *not* enough. In fact, such islands may mask or even accentuate fundamental problems. CIM usually requires that departments not be run as fiefdoms. Rather, departments need to be structured as teams that guide a product from order to delivery—perhaps even from conceptualization to delivery. CIM properly implemented means JIT delivery from suppliers, JIT manufacturing, and JIT delivery to customers. CIM means computer tracking of every step in the process and making relevant information available to a wide variety of other computers, machines, managers, and employees.

Reorganization into flatter structures has a potential downside. Lines of authority become fuzzier and lower-level managers may have difficulty suddenly making strategic decisions. Workloads and responsibilities can dramatically increase. All of this change is in an environment that appears to offer fewer chances for promotion. Pressures to increase productivity per employee can significantly increase stress, especially if the primary motivation for reorganization is to reduce payrolls. Many such cutbacks are not well thought through, with little or no identification of essential tasks or personnel. The wrong jobs may be eliminated. Blanket deals to encourage early retirement or quitting may actually encourage the best people—those with other options—to leave. The goal of speeding up decision making may be unattainable if lower-level employees are not given real authority and if control is actually pushed up a decimated hierarchy instead of down. The remaining managers may have to work far longer hours and may quickly burn out. Work weeks of 60 to 70 hours can become common. Electronic hookups to homes mean no end to the potential for work-related responsibilities. Overall, 24 percent of full-time employees today work more than 49 hours per week compared to 18 percent ten years ago. Median leisure hours have dropped from about twenty-five in the mid-1970s to approximately sixteen at the end of the 1980s.[29]

Many fundamental questions related to organizational structural change remain unanswered. Is flattening caused by the replacement of human command and control with computer command and control—is it merely the mechanization of management? How will managers be developed in flat organizations? How will differential pay be justified when all employees are supposed to be equally valued members of the team? Is the formation of hierarchies inherent in human nature? The often-cited "orchestra" analogy is actually a very poor one, since all musicians play from notes—will computers write the notes?

The net result of reorganization may be chaos and a discouraged work force. The McDonnell Douglas Corporation's Aircraft Unit, which makes commercial jets and military transports, offers an interesting example. Work teams were set up and four management layers were cut, resulting in the layoff of 5,000 managers. These idle managers could then apply for about half as many positions in the reorganized company. The goal of the 1989 overhaul was profitability. The result was demoralization and confusion. Production rates slowed. On July 16, 1990, further layoffs of 8,000 jobs were announced at the Douglas Aircraft Unit. Capital spending, advertising, travel, and the use of consultants were cut in an effort to target savings of $700 million. The radical change was required in spite of record level firm orders for 157 MD-11s, a DC-10 descendant costing over $100 million apiece.[30]

☞ TREND 6: Supplier-Customer Strategic Alliances Are Being Formed: Are Corporations Becoming Hollow?
Recognizing common interests.

Strategic alliances are distinctly different from simple exchanges. In many ways they represent the opposite ends of a continuum.[31] Key features are illustrated in Table 2-2. The formation of strategic alliances has had a profound effect on all members of a channel. Major shifts in

TABLE 2-2 *Comparative Features: Transaction and Alliances*

Transaction Exchange	Alliances
▪ shorter term	▪ longer term
▪ multiple suppliers, who are played off against one another for concessions	▪ fewer suppliers (maybe even one) who are treated as valued partners
▪ price dominates	▪ value-added services dominate
▪ little dedicated investment from supplier	▪ specialized investment can be high for both partners
▪ little information sharing (no EDI interconnectedness)	▪ much sharing of product, production, and logistics information
▪ firms are independent	▪ firms are interdependent; joint decisions common
▪ formal, infrequent communication	▪ frequent formal and informal communication
▪ little interaction between respective functional areas (except logistics)	▪ many functional areas may interact across the partners (e.g., product development)

the channel paradigm are causing dramatic changes in the nature of management within the firm. Some examples follow.

In retailing, the benefits of scanning are more obvious than the impact of scanning on the supplier-retailer relationship. Many stores want to increase customer service through decreased stockouts and increased assortments while at the same time decreasing inventory investment and related expenses. Inventory velocity is key for retailers. LeviLink, a proprietary system of the Levi Strauss company, is an example of how scanning information can be used to directly link sales at retail with reorders and production scheduling at the factory. Many retailers are giving preference to suppliers who are willing to factory-install the UPC code because at the very least it helps in automating reordering. But the potential impact can be more far-reaching than that. For example, bar coding and EDI interconnectedness may have a major impact on the role of the retailer's distribution center, making it potentially obsolete if alternate methods of delivery become the rule.

If CIM in manufacturing is to become a reality, suppliers must be connected to the relevant information system. For decades, the relationship between supplier and customer in the United States has been more adversarial than fraternal. Suppliers were played off against one another and squeezed for lower prices. Now, both product and production information as well as associated technologies must be shared in order to achieve the necessary quality coordination. This close coordination can raise red flags in purchasing as well as in the legal department.[32] The end result, however, is a form of extended enterprise integration.

Companies engaging in extensive strategic alliances, in the form of outsourcing, for example, can even become "hollow." The purpose of the firm may become to coordinate and control, to organize and to develop and implement strategy, but not necessarily to manufacture or distribute products directly. As an example of a corporation that is approaching the hollow state, consider Conner Peripherals, Inc.[33] In the hard disk business, low-cost, high-quality manufacturing and constant innovation are essential for survival. Conner became the fastest growing company in American history by consistently launching and riding waves of new products. Listening to customers, identifying their needs, and then fulfilling them is one focus. Another is getting a firm order from a large customer and then designing the product, bringing it out first so that premium selling prices can be captured. However, a third secret of success is that Conner buys almost all its disks, heads, motors, and chips rather than making them. This permits flexibility to change products rapidly and avoid deep fixed-cost commitments.

☞ TREND 7: The Knowledge Era and the Value of Innovativeness
Knowledge and newness pay off.

Innovation in products, services, and processes is a hot topic worldwide. Even for mundane products in mature industries such as shaving instruments, a new product such as the Gillette Sensor can create quite a splash (and a logistical nightmare). Innovation is thought to be crucial to long-term prosperity for companies and for countries.

Innovating costs money. Such investment may not be recouped for many years. The top three spenders on industrial research and development in descending order are the United States, Japan, and Europe. Table 2-3 provides a comparison of the top companies in these three areas. The relative position of the United States in this intense competition has been widely debated. Some arguments are summarized below:

TABLE 2-3: *Top Ten Companies in 1989 Research and Development Expenditure in the United States, Japan and Europe*

	Spending (U.S. $Billion)	Spending (As % Sales)
Top United States Companies		
General Motors	5.25	4.2
IBM	5.20	8.3
Ford	3.17	3.3
AT&T	2.65	7.3
Digital Equipment	1.53	12.0
DuPont	1.39	4.0
General Electric	1.33	2.5
Hewlett-Packard	1.27	10.7
Eastman Kodak	1.25	6.8
United Technologies	.96	4.9
Top Japanese Companies		
Hitachi	2.19	9.9
Matsushi Electric	2.14	7.9
Toyota	1.90	3.9
NEC	1.78	10.2
Fujitsu	1.74	12.8
NTT	1.52	4.2
Toshiba	1.46	7.6
Nissan	1.36	5.4
Honda	1.13	5.0
Sony	1.01	6.0
Top European Companies		
Siemens (West Germany)	3.68	11.2
Daimler Benz (West Germany)	2.93	8.2
Philips (Netherlands)	2.15	8.0
CGE (France)	1.81	8.4
Bayer (West Germany)	1.40	6.1
Hoechst (West Germany)	1.38	5.9
ABB (Switzerland)	1.36	6.6
Fiat (Italy)	1.24	3.6
Ciba-Geigy (Switzerland)	1.23	10.2
Volkswagen (West Germany)	1.20	3.5

Source: Reprinted from June 15, 1990 issue of Business Week by special permission, copyright © 1990 by McGraw-Hill, Inc.

- The United States is losing the edge in innovation and consequently its ability to compete;
- Until recently, United States companies have been maverick innovators and independent of government support;
- The United States cannot compete because capital is relatively too expensive;
- The United States labor force is not educated enough and is too expensive;
- The ability of the United States to compete is reduced by the lack of an industrial policy.

These points are debatable. However, it is more difficult to dismiss the predictions of the Department of Commerce, which recently completed a study of twelve emerging technologies. It predicts that the United States will be behind Japan in most of them and behind Europe in several.

The percentage of science or technology PhDs working in the United States has dropped. By the mid-1980s, Japan surpassed the United States in the number of scientists and engineers per 10,000 workers. Japan succeeds well at developing and commercializing ideas that originated in the United States—fuzzy logic being a significant example. Europe has also entered the race in a major way. European venture capital spending rose 25 percent in 1989 to $5.5 billion, surpassing the all-time United States peak of $4.2 billion in 1987. Both Japanese and European companies are buying out high-tech firms based in the United States. The most famous (or infamous) example is Hoffman-LaRoche's $2.1 billion acquisition of 60 percent of Genentech. Competition for markets is global. As a result, competition in innovation is also global.

For any firm, innovation is a risky business. Innovation can be extremely expensive, and competition for the top researchers, applied scientists, test mechanics, and so on, can be fierce. People with the necessary knowledge for innovation may perceive themselves to be "independent contractors," and as a result they may be difficult to manage in the traditional sense of the word. New product failure rates are very high. The transition from concept to manufactured product is fraught with difficulty, especially when design and factory personnel are isolated from each other. In addition, *process* innovations are also risky. For example, during the 1980s, many companies invested millions of dollars in highly advanced factories and ended up with little of the projected automation benefits. CIM proved more difficult to implement than many companies had envisioned, and the "factory that runs itself" proved an elusive goal.

The General Electric compressor disaster captures many of the complex trends listed so far. GE bet its $2-billion refrigerator business on a revolutionary new compressor, and the company constructed a futuristic factory to supply it. In their vintage 1950s plant which was producing the old compressor, it took an additional forty minutes and double the cost to make a compressor that compared to its Italian and Japanese rivals. The new product decision was based (1) partly on the desire to build in America (and be a world leader in manufacturing) rather than purchase from abroad, (2) partly to reverse the appliance division's slide in market share and profits, and (3) partly to leapfrog the Japanese in new product design. Consumers were initially delighted with the new product, resulting in an increase of 2 percent in market share. The new product failed because of a design flaw. Inadequate testing, especially in longer-term field testing, meant that the fatal flaw was not discovered until the compressor was in widespread distribution. Technicians who did the actual testing were ignored, while executives six or more layers removed heard only positive reports about the compressor. The result was a $450-million pretax charge in 1988 alone. Over a million compressors had to be replaced, each replacement taking at least ninety minutes with the associated logistical costs. Compressors are now purchased from six suppliers, five of whom are foreign. GE had to convince one United States manufacturer to get back into a business they had previously quit. Without doubt, new product or process innovation is a risky business.

☞ TREND 8: Strategy in the Competitive Environment: Implementation Has Strategic Value
Doing the right things right.

In the turbulent environment of the 1980s, strategy became an overwhelmingly important concern—and it will become more crucial during the 1990s. In addition, the experiences of the 1980s have made it abundantly clear that brilliant implementation has immense strategic value. This is true whether the firm is a small player among giants or whether the firm has a virtual monopoly. Two examples follow.

■ The movie theatre business is dominated by four chains—United Artists, General Cinema, AMC, and Cineplex Odeon. The late

1980s were characterized by empire building, with some acquisitions being bought at more than twelve times earnings. By 1990, Carmike Cinemas, Inc., a relative unknown, was paying six times earnings and had expanded to 915 screens in 175 markets. Their secrets of success in turning box office returns into operating profits consisted of (1) sticking to small cities where competition was minimal, thus avoiding bidding wars for new releases and enjoying lower construction costs, and (2) computerizing ticket and concession-stand sales and linking them electronically to the corporate headquarters. Surprisingly, the latter feature had not been implemented by the giants in the industry. Control at Carmike is tight, and overhead costs are low. Only minimal corporate staff additions have accompanied the tripling in the number of screens.[34]

■ The strategy for reducing costs at the United States Postal Service is clear: labor accounts for 83 percent of expenses. However, annual costs for 1989 came in $1.34 billion over budget. This was partly due to the changeover to a $1-billion electronic mail handling system, but is this an indicator of hope for the future? A December 1989 audit showed that the high-tech sorting machines had delivered only a third of the expected savings, mainly because they weren't being used so that clerks and mail handlers could be kept busy.[35]

Michael Porter defined competitive strategy as a combination of the *ends* (goals, objectives, mission) and the *means* (operating or functional policies, tactics, implementation strategy).[36] Strategic success is associated with (1) the firm's environment—consisting of its markets, suppliers, competitors, and so on; (2) both the product and the process technologies the firm employs; and (3) the organizational structure of the firm, both its internal hierarchies, rules, and culture, and its cross-firm interrelationships. Strategy may be implicit or it may be explicitly developed through a formal planning process. Dimensions of strategy include decisions as to what business the firm should be in, how the firm will compete, what goals should be pursued, and so forth.

SUMMARY

It appears clear that today's logistics managers must be concerned with more than the management of warehouses and trucking. Indeed, with the advent of flat organizations, strategic alliances, and hollow corporations, the very concept of independently managing a narrow function of a business is obsolete. In one sense, logistics managers may be better prepared for the management of the future than managers in other functional areas because of the traditional importance of integration and boundary spanning to their discipline. Logistics managers have always managed a buffering activity between manufacturing and marketing. Logistics management has always needed to span boundaries. However, the nature of the new organization, whether the internal organization of the firm or the interorganization relationship between firms, is significantly different in a qualitative way and is not merely "more" of something that existed before.

The new organization—the new way of doing things—is based on new paradigms. Satisfying the customer marginally better than a competitor may be a dangerously myopic goal in a turbulent competitive environment because it focuses attention on the actions of current competitors rather than on the desires of future customers. The most important competitor may not be the largest current competitor, but rather the one that is currently creating a gestalt of technology, innovativeness, and organization to delight tomorrow's customer. That competitor may come from anywhere in the world.

The new organization is also based upon assumptions about the capabilities for interconnectedness of information technology. Never has it been more true that "information is power." This old saying about information has traditionally been cast and interpreted in political, military, or monetary senses and these of course remain valid. However, it is not *only* the possession of information that is the chief source of power. Rather, it is the speed of information dissemination to the relevant players that is critical. Once the relevant players have the necessary information, it is the ability to act that becomes critical. For example, making information available to lower-level employees without empowering them to act means missing the true potential benefit.

The "power of information" has another meaning for logistics managers. In today's universe, it is no longer enough to "know your job." "Knowing your job" means knowing today's job. Tomorrow, it will mean "knowing yesterday's job" unless an ongoing program of knowledge enhancement is undertaken. A lot has been written about a better trained work force—what is a better trained manager? One could give a simple answer: a manager who is *doing* today's job and is *thinking* about tomorrow's job, a manager who is thinking about change management.

Notes

1. Bernard J. LaLonde, Martha C. Cooper, and Thomas G. Noordewier, *Customer Service: A Management Perspective* (Oak Brook, Ill.: Council of Logistics Management, 1988).

2. Stephen Phillips and Amy Dunkin, "King Customer: At Companies That Listen Hard and Respond Fast, Bottom Lines Thrive," *Business Week* (March 12, 1990): 88–94.

3. David Wessel, "Sure Ways to Annoy Consumers," *Wall Street Journal* (November 6, 1989): B1.

4. George Stalk, Jr., and Thomas M. Hout, *Competing Against Time* (New York: The Free Press, 1990).

5. Stephen Phillips and Amy Dunkin, "King Customer."

6. Michael E. Porter, *The Competitive Advantages of Nations* (New York: The Free Press, 1990).

7. Bill Javetski and John Templeman, "One Germany: The Whole European Equation Has Changed," *Business Week* (April 2, 1990): 47–49.

8. William Matheson, "Japan: World's Leading Investor," *Wall Street Journal* (July 26, 1990): A12.

9. *Business Week,* "The Global 1000—The Leaders" (July 16, 1990): 112.

10. E. S. Browning, "Europe Still Finding Resistance to Efforts to Enter West German Market," *Wall Street Journal* (July 24, 1990): A8.

11. William J. Holstein and Amy Borrus, "Inching Toward a North American Market," *Business Week* (June 25, 1990): 40–41.

12. *Business Week,* "The Pacific Century: Europe Can't Stop It" (December 17, 1990): 126.

13. William J. Holstein, "The Stateless Corporation," *Business Week* (May 14, 1990): 98–105.

14. Josh Kurtz, "After a Decade of Consolidation, Hard Times Await Carpet Makers," *New York Times* (May 27, 1990): F11.

15. Brian Bremmer, "The Age of Consolidation," *Business Week* (October 14, 1991): 86–94.

16. Donald J. Bowersox, Patricia J. Daugherty, Cornelia L. Droge, Dale S. Rogers, and Daniel L. Wardlow, *Leading Edge Logistics: Competitive Positioning for the 1990s* (Oak Brook, Ill.: Council of Logistics Management, 1989).

17. Barnaby J. Feder, "Baking Soda Maker Strikes Again," *New York Times* (June 16, 1990): 17.

18. Laurence Hooper, "Future Shock," *Wall Street Journal* (June 4, 1990): R22–23.

19. Charles M. Savage, *5th Generation Management* (Bedford, Mass.: Digital Press, 1990).

20. Keith H. Hammonds, "Software: It's a New Game," *Business Week* (June 4, 1990): 102–106.

21. William J. Bruns, Jr., and F. Warren McFarlan, "Information Technology Puts Power in Control Systems," *Harvard Business Review* 65 (September-October 1987): 89–94.

22. Gary Robins, "Faster Checkouts," *Stores* 70 (December 1988): 65–66.

23. Robert H. Beeby, "How to Crunch a Bunch of Figures," *Wall Street Journal* (June 11, 1990): A10.

24. Stephen Kreider Yoder, "Putting It All Together," *Wall Street Journal* (June 4, 1990): R25–27.

25. Peter F. Drucker, "The Coming of the New Organization," *Harvard Business Review* 88:1 (January-February 1988): 45–53.

26. Thomas F. O'Boyle, "From Pyramid to Pancake," *Wall Street Journal* (June 4, 1990): R37.

27. Steven Schlosstein, "United States Is the Leader in Decentralization," *New York Times* (June 3, 1990): F13.

28. Charles M. Savage, *5th Generation Management.*

29. Carol Hymowitz, "When Firms Out Middle Managers, Those at Top and Bottom Often Suffer," *Wall Street Journal* (April 5, 1990): B1.

30. James E. Ellis and Eric Schine, "On a Wing and a Prayer at McDonnell Douglas," *Business Week* (July 30, 1990): 23.

31. Gary L. Frazier, Robert E. Spekman, and Charles R. O'Neal, "Just-in-Time Exchange Relationships in Industrial Markets," *Journal of Marketing* 52, 4 (October 1988): 52–67.

32. Stephen Kreider Yoder, "Putting It All Together."

33. Andrew Pollack, "A Novel Idea: Customer Satisfaction," *New York Times* (May 27, 1990): F1.

34. Chuck Hawkins, "The Movie Mogul Who Thinks Small," *Business Week* (July 2, 1990): 37.

35. Mark Lewyn, "The Post Office Wants Everyone to Pay for Its Mistakes," *Business Week* (March 5, 1990): 28.

36. Michael E. Porter, *Competitive Strategy* (New York: The Free Press, 1980).

Logistics: 1990s Style

CHARLIE knew he had to get up to speed quickly on what was going on in logistics—he wanted the details, the particulars. It is one thing to sense the overall picture. It's quite another to have an appreciation of what the leaders in the field are doing. Charlie decided that the quickest way to get up to speed was to attend an intensive week-long logistics seminar at a major midwestern university. At the very least, such a seminar would give him a good overview of what it takes to get things done in logistics. Thought Charlie—"such a seminar should give me an idea of what should be done!"

Charlie was skeptical about how well the program would integrate the macrotrends he had identified. Charlie knew that his mission was not to reorganize the trucking routes!!! He had to have broad-based information and knowledge that would enable him to implement major changes in basic practices of management. He had to convince others that drastic revamping was essential.

When Charlie arrived at the university seminar, he was surprised at the number of executives from other firms attending. In fact, the exchange of "war stories" alone almost made the trip worthwhile! For the first time, Charlie felt that he was not the only person that was pursuing this particular road. All of the people at the seminar seemed to be seeking the right way to improve overall logistics performance. His original expectations of what he'd get from the seminar were more than fulfilled. Three key concepts emerged as essential ingredients to launching a logistical orientation: formalization, technology adoption, and continuous performance measurement. At the end of the week, Charlie was anxious to get started on improved performance measurement. By measuring and evaluating his firm's performance, Charlie could potentially gain the ammunition necessary to institute real change. The reason was simple: the "right" performance measurements and the "right" benchmarking would enable Charlie to demonstrate not only *that* change was necessary, but also *what* change was necessary.

While at the seminar, Charlie heard about the upcoming meeting of the Council of Logistics Management. He decided to attend the professional meeting in order to learn more and to hear different perspectives. Charlie was one of 4,000 business executives and academics in attendance. It was during the meeting that Charlie became totally committed to the potential of logistics. After he arrived back home, Charlie felt he had a good grasp of how all the things he had been reading about and learning about fit together. Charlie remembered the intense conversations with Bob—and with others. It all fit now. Charlie looked in his desk and found his original list of "what logistics was all about":

> *transportation*: trucks? planes? Somehow materials had to be moved into the plants, they had to be moved around inside the plants, and they had to be moved out of the plants. Somehow the final product had to reach the customers.
> *warehouses*: to store supplies? to store finished goods?
> *inventory*: the company sure had a lot of raw materials and finished goods!!
> *documentation*: everything moved or stored had to be documented.

He remembered having laughed at the list because it seemed pathetically incomplete. Now he laughed at his own list because it seemed incredibly naive, even incorrect!!

This chapter presents an overview of the best practices of logistics management and develops a framework for the pursuit of excellence. The intent is to describe briefly the conclusions of previous leading-edge research and to sketch the likely direction that best logistics practice will take during the 1990s. The audience targeted is the manager who understands the basics of what constitutes leading-edge performance and now seeks guidance about how to implement quality logistical practices.

The essential starting point in revitalizing a firm's logistics is for the managers leading the initiative to become fully aware of where the discipline is and where it is headed. The forerunner to this book, *Leading Edge Logistics: Competitive Positioning for the 1990s,* reported research which examined leading companies and identified their managerial and operational commonalities.[1] Comparisons were made between leading-edge firms and a group of more typical or average companies.

Most firms fall short of being leading-edge logistics performers.

In this section, results of continuing research into best logistics practices are summarized. Out of 695 firms studied in the baseline research, only 117 qualified as being at the leading edge, which is approximately 17 percent. For firms in general, it is estimated that about 10 percent perform at the leading edge. This estimate is based on continued research of management practices subsequent to the baseline research. Similarities among leading edge firms emerged, particularly similar structures, behaviors, and strategies.

Leading-edge firms were found everywhere regardless of their place in the channel or industry group. Channel position was not related to a firm's logistical competence. Wholesalers, manufacturers, and retailers were all included in the set of leading-edge firms. Leading-edge performers also were identified in all industries. This general result serves to discount the long-standing paradigm that logistics is primarily a manufacturing concept. Rather, it is a professional management concept.

Firm size also fails to predict the likelihood of being a leading-edge performer. Logically it may seem that larger firms commanding extensive resources would be more apt to gain leading-edge status, but that was not necessarily the case. Some large firms may, in fact, suffer from inertia and thus be more resistant to change. Many leading-edge firms were identified to have sales under $100 million.

LEADING-EDGE ATTRIBUTES

The main attributes of leading-edge performers boil down to management practices in terms of: (1) formalization, which includes structure; (2) measurement; and (3) technology. Each of these categories represents a group of variables. The essence of each focused practice is briefly reviewed. In tandem, these three sets of attributes determine logistics flexibility. Flexibility is the fourth attribute of leading-edge performance. It is a result of the previous three attributes rather than a management practice.

Formalization

Formalization as used here refers to specific management practices related to logistics. Formalization is represented by the presence of written rules, plans, goals, and procedures. These descriptors offer insight into the extent to which logistics is treated as a fundamental or core process within a firm.

Formalization is a strategy of control. It provides a structure for directing logistics operations. Traditional organizational behavior research literature suggests that a high level of formalization may inhibit initiation of innovation particularly in command and control organizations. This was not found to be the case in terms of logistical performance. In logistics, formalization improved operating flexibility. Logistical formalization also helps in the achievement of operating efficiency.[2] Efficiency is improved because formal rules and procedures eliminate the need to treat every event as a new decision. Systemic thinking replaces event-oriented thinking. Formalization allows the logistics manager to avoid continuously operating in "crisis mode." With well-defined rules and procedures, the logistical organization is in position to react to special requests in a highly flexible manner. Formalization in logistics comprises the seven key attributes listed in Table 3-1.

Three groups of formalization descriptors are: (1) logistics planning, which includes the mission statement and the strategic plan; (2) empowerment, which reflects the extent to which logistics is formally treated as a strategic concern; and (3) structure, which refers to formal organization. Each aspect of formalization is discussed in the following subsections.

Logistics Planning

Outstanding logistics organizations are compulsive planners and implementers. They know that strategic planning is a key element of attaining

---

TABLE 3-1 Formalization Variables

Logistics Planning
1. Mission Statement
2. Strategic Plan and Frequency of Update

Empowerment
3. Title Level
4. SBU Planning Participation

Structure
5. Years Formally Organized
6. Frequency of Reconfiguration of Logistics Organization
7. Span of Control or Number of Logistics Functions

success. Two aspects of overall planning stand out: (1) the mission statement and (2) the strategic plan.

The formal logistics mission and logistics strategic plan are written statements outlining the purpose, role, and goal of the logistics organization. By virtue of being endorsed by senior management, these documents convey expectations to the remainder of the organization. These formal statements, although with the potential to stimulate positive practices, are not without pitfalls. Management must understand that a major adjustment in the culture of a firm is not as simple as issuing a mission statement. Business historians have documented that up to ten years may be required before a totally new culture pervades an organization. Most quality initiatives plan a minimum of five years continuous attention prior to achievement of desired performance levels. A formal mission statement and plan ignored by senior management may actually be detrimental.

The mission statement initiates the formal planning process by assuring that logistical resources are focused to create maximum customer impact. Without the clear overall direction and the widespread understanding of objectives that a mission statement provides, logistics organizational goals run a risk of becoming fragmented and misunderstood by both logistics personnel and other areas of the business unit.

Creating a formal mission statement is typically a laborious task. Whereas the first draft may be easy, subsequent review and ownership by key executives may prove to be tedious.[3] Different managers may have traditionally operated under different assumptions that formed their perception about what constituted acceptable performance. They may have legitimate differences of opinion concerning appropriate customer service levels and which components are critical. Since a formal logistics mission may place emphasis on one logistics activity over another, managers may feel a need to protect their "turf." Thus, constructive debate can be expected as management hammers out the prescribed strategic role of logistics.

There are direct benefits associated with the presence of a formal logistics mission statement. A formal mission statement is expected to serve as an integrative device around which organizational members and departments unite. When a logistics mission statement is shared with customers, employees frequently exhibit a heightened sense of responsibility.[4] The statement should facilitate the management trade-offs critical to strategic logistical performance.

Not all efforts to create a logistics mission statement are successful.

The debate that surrounds the development of a mission statement may serve to water down its content. Such dilution can lead to a weak, self-evident, and trivial mission statement that fails to serve the integrative intent behind its creation. A vague mission statement fails to provide critical leadership. For example, "We want to be the best" or "We want to be number one" may be appropriate cheerleading statements, but they are not mission statements.

The mission statement provides a performance ideal or target. Senior logistics management and employees of leading-edge firms continuously communicate to make certain that everyone understands the organization's mission and capabilities. A serious mistake is to dictate a mission statement and then assume that it is well understood. The process of mission definition and refinement is continuous in a leading-edge organization. The mission statement serves to communicate an organization's purpose and overall plan to trading partners, suppliers, and other segments of the business. The logistics mission statement sets the objectives for the logistics organization and communicates that mission beyond firm boundaries to the firm's channel partners and customers. *Conclusion—leading-edge firms use the process of developing and refining their mission statement to focus and communicate their commitment to high-level logistical performance.*

The mission statement becomes the focal point for the logistics strategic plan. A logistics strategic plan in a leading edge firm is far more comprehensive than a typical operating budget. The plan implements the mission and serves to guide the logistics organization in positively impacting the business unit's market share and profitability while maintaining cost control.

The formal logistics strategic plan represents the blueprint an organization is following to deal with the future. It sets future objectives and goals with respect to performance, technology adoption, employee attitudes, and overall culture. A logistics plan consists of much more than "next year's budget." A good logistics strategic plan is not purely cost-oriented. Cost control is important, but it is not the only focus of a logistics organization.

A comprehensive logistics plan usually spans a five-year horizon and details human, material, informational, and financial resource requirements. The plan is typically updated at least annually and often more frequently. Naturally such plans detail operating objectives along the planning horizon. However, the essence of strategic logistics is utilizing operating competency to gain competitive advantage. Thus the strategic plan should state clearly and concisely how logistical performance will impact customers.[5]

The formal logistics strategic plan serves to link logistics with overall business unit planning. Furthermore, the logistics strategic plan is typically presented in a published format. The formal planning procedure assures that activities have top management endorsement.

Leading-edge firms are considerably more aggressive in the use of logistics strategic plans than are average companies. More than 90 percent of leading-edge firms had strategic logistics plans as compared to less than 60 percent of the comparison group. *Conclusion—preparation and dissemination of a formal logistics plan is an essential aspect of leading-edge performance. Such plans serve to specify objectives and facilitate coordinated behavior.*

Empowerment

Empowerment refers to the extent to which logistics is formally acknowledged as an important process. Empowerment mirrors the image of logistics. The importance that senior management places on logistics varies significantly across firms. If logistics has a low level of empowerment, it follows that a fair share of resources may not be invested in the design and implementation of basic technological and administrative systems. Failure to empower logistics raises the odds that inherent logistical strengths and weaknesses may be overlooked when organizational strategy is formulated. Failure to empower logistics may result in a permanent reactive mind set.

Two types of empowerment were typical of leading-edge logistics organizations: (1) title level and (2) business unit strategic planning participation. The baseline research indicates that the formal title level of the senior logistics executive can range from CEO (or president) through intermediate title levels such as senior vice president, vice president, and director, to titles such as manager. The title level of a senior logistics executive is typically assigned by the chief executive officer. The use of a vice president or someone with a higher title means that logistics is headed by an executive at officer level. Executives at this level typically report to an executive who is part of the inner circle of senior management or they may themselves be members of the operating or executive committee. The title of the senior executive is an important descriptor of exactly where a logistics organization fits into the hierarchy of an organization.

A second indicator of logistical empowerment is the extent to which the senior logistics executive participates in overall business unit strategic planning. An involved senior logistics executive can bring to strategy sessions intimate knowledge about the logistical capabilities of the firm and its trading partners. For example, a strategy revolving around new deployment of an existing or altered product may involve servicing new customers. The senior logistics executive may be able to help calibrate the feasibility and desirability of such a venture in terms of inventory, material handling, transportation, and communication requirements.

The key to empowerment is that the firm's senior executives are being exposed to logistical input when making strategic commitments. Just as the existence of a formal logistical mission statement and strategic plan indicates that a formal logistics-based planning program exists, the title level and involvement in business unit strategic planning indicate that logistical competency is an important consideration in selecting business initiatives. *Conclusion—logistics organizations that are clearly empowered within the overall structure of a firm are more likely to achieve leading-edge status than those who are not.*

Structure (Organization)

Three structural descriptors are important in the identification of a leading-edge logistics firm. *First* is the number of years that logistics has been formally organized. The more longevity a formal logistics organization has, the greater the probability that various technological and administrative systems have been implemented. Longevity of a logistics organization is a reflection of staying power and commitment. Stability can signal that a firm has gained significant competitive advantage as a result of integrating logistical activities. It takes significant time to create fully integrated logistics. Once established, it is difficult for a competitor to quickly duplicate or neutralize a differential advantage built around logistical competency.

The *second* dimension of structure is the frequency of modifying the logistics organization. Today's business environment is one of constant change. Organizations that adhere to rigid structures may miss opportunities arising from change, such as new technologies or new services being offered by third parties. It is important to stress that this form of accommodation means regular modification of organizational structure to adjust to change. It does not mean that the commitment to logistics wavers or is in any way diluted.

The *third* aspect of structure is the span of control. A broad or wide span of logistics control implies the management of diverse activities. For example, a logistics organization that manages both inbound and outbound material and finished goods distribution is better positioned to coordinate the full materials flow process than one that does not. The span of control of logistics is sometimes an indicator of the degree of integration within an organization. An organization with a wide span of control is potentially better positioned to achieve integration than one with a narrow focus. However, the baseline research clearly indicated that *how* an organization manages is far more important than *how many* functions it manages. While span of control is an important indicator of integration, it is not conclusive. Many leading-edge organizations achieve high levels of functional integration without having accountability as manifest through formal structure. Such integration is achieved through information networking and performance measurement.

Table 3-2 presents the functional areas typically included in the logistics span of control. The most frequent functions directly assigned to firms engaged in basic manufacturing are outbound transportation, finished goods warehousing, intra-company transportation, finished goods inventory management, and inbound transportation. For firms engaged in retail and wholesale trade, the five most common areas of functional responsibility assigned to logistics are outbound transportation, warehousing, inbound transportation, materials management, and logistical engineering (or facilities design). *Conclusion—how a firm formally organizes its logistics is directly related to leading-edge status. Logistical organization in leading-edge firms has longevity, plasticity, and significant span of functional control.*

Measurement

The second major category of leading-edge attributes focuses on measurement. Increased pressures on business for greater productivity within a compressed time frame have made the logistics manager's job increasingly difficult. To meet shorter deadlines with improved execution, logistics systems have become more complex. Sophisticated measurement systems are required to monitor and direct the increased complexity. Logistics managers have adopted tools such as statistical quality control to monitor performance and eliminate practices that create variations. Leading-edge managers regularly use a benchmark to measure systems against the very best performers to maintain an understanding of best practice. Without measurement, operations can

TABLE 3-2: Activities Reporting to Logistics

Activity	Percent of Firms in which Logistics Controls Function	
	Manufacturers	*Merchandisers*
Sales forecasting	34.4	29.6
Purchasing	46.2	41.9
Inbound transportation	72.0	62.1
Outbound transportation	84.9	69.3
Intra-company transportation	73.5	56.0
Finished goods inventory management	72.8	54.2
Raw material/WIP inventory control	51.9	n.a.
Finished goods field warehousing	74.2	69.0
Order processing	56.3	44.0
Customer service	53.0	39.7
Logistics systems planning	67.7	54.2
Facilities design	44.9	56.7
Materials management	52.2	61.0
Logistics administration	66.7	54.9
International logistics	41.2	22.0
Capital equipment procurement	40.2	54.5
Computer processing for distribution applications	25.0	44.8

n.a. = not applicable.

quickly spin out of control. Performance measurement focuses attention on quality.

Many North American businesses learned the hard way about the impact of continuous process improvement. In many industries, Japanese managers demanded higher performance than their American counterparts. They emphasized process flow, which led to higher quality levels. In several cases, they achieved a level previously not thought possible. Often the reason for improved quality was the attention to detail that results when management is committed to continuous performance measurement. The quality process forces managers to continually assess their products and processes and to focus relentlessly on problems to eliminate their causes. Although many American managers have understood the importance of using performance measurement to control operations, competitive benchmarking is a relatively new phenomenon among logistics organizations.

Leading-edge firms are compulsive performance measurers. They continuously measure performance in a number of operational areas. These firms expect high-quality logistics performance to be the standard service.

Performance measurement is a critical activity in logistically sensitive firms. Measurement means monitoring all facets of performance. The key aspects of logistical performance measurement can be divided into internal and external focuses.

Internal Performance Measurement

Internal performance measurement consists of the monitoring of several specific costs and services. It includes the measurement of the total cost of logistics as a percentage of sales and the associated trend analysis. The measurement of total cost permits executives to gauge how well tradeoffs are being managed.

In addition to total costs, major logistical functional cost components must also be monitored. These include warehousing, order processing, inbound and outbound transportation, inventory, and administrative costs. It is through the measurement of specific activity-based functional costs that long-term efficiency improvements can be calibrated. The quantification of individual activity-based costs allows the degree of tradeoff to be measured in terms of the efficiency of the overall process.

A third area of internal performance measurement concerns asset management. Asset management in logistics typically focuses on inventory levels, velocity, and obsolescence. However, all assets deployed in the logistics operation must be regularly evaluated in terms of return on net assets and return on investment.

A fourth category of internal measurement monitors service performance. Service performance typically means monitoring such operational achievements as fill rate, cycle time, on-time delivery, and back orders. These performance measures are usually related to minimum objectives or standards as specified in the mission statement and logistics plan. The ultimate standard is perfection, because anything less means that at least some customers will be disappointed. Measurement of service performance should be augmented by regular feedback from customers: How meaningful are accomplishments in the eyes of those being serviced? This type of measurement deals with customer satisfaction. Firms that focus on performance regularly use surveys to ascertain opinions and attitudes about how well they are doing.

Comprehensive measurement of internal performance also includes productivity analysis. Productivity is the ratio of output divided by inputs. An example of a productivity ratio is units shipped divided by the number of employees over a specified time period. Through productivity ratios, organizations can track how assets are deployed over time.

A final form of measurement of internal performance is quality. This measurement is one of the most difficult to pin down, but it is also one of the most popular ways of assessing logistical performance. A new way of assessing quality performance starts with the expectation of zero defects. The notion is simple—do what you told the customer you were capable of doing. Taken to the extreme, zero defects means doing the right things in the right way every time. In the eyes of a quality-oriented organization, any firm that plans for a predetermined number of failures is designing a system to fail. In contrast, the firm that attempts to attain zero defects is designing for success. Although zero defects may not in fact happen, the firm is committed to continuous improvement toward perfection. *Conclusion—comprehensive measurement of internal performance is essential to gaining and maintaining logistical leadership.*

External Performance Measurement

Measurement of external performance is a key aspect of logistical situational analysis. It is sometimes referred to as benchmarking or competitor analysis or environmental scanning.

Many writers make a distinction between the various methods by which information about competitors is obtained. Obviously, clandestine methods such as industrial espionage, theft, and bribery are illegal in most countries. However, many legal means of collecting information about competitors exist. Several market research companies specialize in legitimate information collection. Speeches given by corporate executives and annual reports are two other legitimate sources of information. The company's sales force, vendors, and customers can be tapped as important sources of information about competitor performance and activities and can be used as sources of comparative information and data.

Two types of benchmarking are important.[6] The first is called performance benchmarking. It describes the process of comparing major indicators of logistics such as total logistics cost, customer service, asset management, quality, and productivity achieved by key competitors and the very best of all performers. The focal point is on the end result of the logistical process. Management seeks to answer basic questions that revolve around: How well are we doing? Comparing performance is the key goal.

The second type of benchmarking considers *how* logistical activities are being conducted as contrasted to *how well*. Focus on how activities are conducted is aimed at specific work practices. This is called operations benchmarking. The concern is with how the firm delivers time and place utility in the form of order-processing operations, transportation, warehousing, and the overall deployment of various technologies. Firms that use benchmarking to measure the operations of competitors and of leading organizations in other industries are likely to spot new technologies and market opportunities early.

One of the most important potential benefits of benchmarking is the early detection of "bad news." Some firms are prone to ascribe competitor gains to luck rather than to superior attitude, technology, strategy, management, or other controllable factors. A firm that seriously uses benchmarking cannot help but identify specific methods by which competitors have made financial and market share gains. Many can be emulated, copied, or tailored to a firm's specific needs.

A firm that does not use benchmarking may be prone to internally creating "good news." A "don't worry, be happy" attitude may permeate the firm. Everyone feels good about operations, management, or strategy since negative or critical statements are rarely made. When negative statements are made, a "kill the messenger" attitude prevails. A firm may slowly lose market share and never know why.

Both measurement of internal performance and benchmarking are important because they help management justify reinvestment. The development and execution of comprehensive benchmarking is a universal feature of leading-edge logistics organizations.

Leading-edge firms often measure a wide variety of performance indicators. They are able to use benchmarking to measure operations against other good performers both within and outside their industry. They can identify good performance and emulate it. *Conclusion—external benchmarking is a key indicator of leading-edge performance. Unless a firm knows fully where it stands, it is unlikely it will know where to go.*

Technology Adoption

The third major category of variables important to leading-edge performance is related to technology adoption, particularly information technology. Leading-edge firms are large consumers of information. They are often leaders in identifying and implementing relevant technologies. Among the most significant technologies in logistics are those related to information. Information accessibility is often the difference between excellent and unacceptable logistics performance.

The success or failure of logistics organizations is directly related to how effectively they use available information resources. There has been an explosion of new software and hardware technology in the last few years. For the past ten years, Arthur Andersen, in conjunction with the Council of Logistics Management, has compiled a list of available logistics software.[7] Over that period of time, the number of logistics software packages increased from 67 to over 1,000. It is difficult to keep up with fast-moving advances in information technology, but logistics managers of leading-edge companies know that they cannot afford to be left behind. These managers also know that they cannot rely on Management Information Systems (MIS) departments to be logistically literate!

Technology has been recognized as a major factor that contributes to competitive advantage. Logistics technology is process-related. Logistics process technology includes such things as electronic data interchange (EDI), the computerization of logistical operations such as inventory control and vehicle routing and scheduling, and various hardware such as bar coding and robotics, for example.

The selection of technology is complicated. A decision to postpone the acquisition of new information technology can have catastrophic long-term implications. Conversely, innovating too quickly can create serious problems.[8]

The trend in logistics organizations toward increased reliance on information is clear. Information is the critical factor in maintaining a leading-edge competency in logistics. Because of the technological explosion of the last few years, logistics managers find it increasingly difficult to maintain their current position. Significant decisions about acquiring and implementing new technology are required. The future success of logistics organizations will to a significant degree depend on how well they are able to evaluate, adopt, and implement emerging information technologies. Firms must be able to find relevant technology, evaluate it, and install and implement it at a faster pace than ever before. The baseline research identified the following indicators: (1) computer applications; (2) Electronic Data Interchange; (3) hardware installed; and (4) information quality.

Computer Applications

Leading-edge firms currently have more computer applications installed and plan to install more in the future than the average company. Leading-edge logistics management information systems compare favorably to MIS support systems in other areas of the business.

The computerization of operations offers organizations the ability to improve productivity. Applications software is also critical to the attainment of high-quality customer service. The availability of computer applications supported by high-quality data is critical to all types of performance measurement. *Conclusion—leading-edge firms are deeply involved in a wide variety of computer applications and plan to expand adoption of these applications in the future.*

Electronic Data Interchange (EDI)

A key logistics technology is EDI, and several brief observations about EDI technology are in order. EDI technology refers to electronic data transfer between organizations.

Many organizations that have implemented EDI technology to receive orders electronically have failed as yet to connect such information directly to their order processing system. Firms anticipated that adoption of EDI would reduce human resource requirements, but such has not been the case. The special benefit associated with implementing EDI is the establishment of a platform on which to build improved relations with key customers and vendors. Many firms are mandating that suppliers become EDI-capable as a prerequisite to doing business.[9] Such mandates are likely to increase in the future. An appropriate assessment of EDI is that it represents a step toward increased efficiency in interorganizational information flows that will become increasingly valuable over time.

The baseline research examined two types of EDI linkage: one with primary trading partners and the other with service providers. Leading-edge performers are generally more involved in electronic data interchange (EDI) than other firms. They also are more likely to develop EDI applications designed to make an impact on the market. Leading-edge firms in all channel categories had more EDI applications than other companies. Examples of EDI in action are presented in Chapter Seven and Appendix D. *Conclusion—EDI in its advanced form is a prime ingredient of leading-edge performance.*

Hardware Installed

A number of hardware technologies are directly related to logistical performance. Two types of hardware were examined: operational hardware, which refers to such items as robotics, bar codes, and automated storage and retrieval equipment; and computer hardware, which refers to such items as personal computers and local area networks (LANS).

Operational hardware serves two basic functions. First, a technology such as bar coding helps perform and improve the efficiency of many routine operations such as checkout, receiving, and inventory control.[10] The second function of hardware technology is to provide management with access to large amounts of transactional data. For example, a computerized inventory system can track the quantities of inventory stored at specific warehouses. Part of the key to utilizing these voluminous data is to have software and computer hardware capable of assembling, aggregating, and combining data, thereby distilling information for the measurement of performance. Among the firms reviewed in the baseline research, those identified as leading edge were involved in more overall applications of various forms of hardware and were testing new and innovative technologies. *Conclusion—installed hardware, whether operational hardware or computer hardware, offers a useful way to help determine leading-edge status. Leaders are committed to using state-of-the-art hardware.*

Information Quality

A key factor in logistical performance is the quality of information available to management. Five dimensions of the quality of information were examined: timeliness, accuracy, availability, whether it was formatted on an exception basis, and whether it was appropriately formatted to facilitate use. The quality of information available to manage the logistics process is a reflection of commitment to an information system. Leading-edge firms typically receive high-quality data in a highly usable format. They have made a major commitment of their resources to assure the best possible presentation of accurate and timely data. High-quality information is an integral part of their logistical competency. *Conclusion—leading-edge firms have taken care to assure they will be supported with the best information possible.*

Flexibility

A key variable in leading-edge performance is how firms react to unexpected operational situations that impact on their logistics plans. A typical situation might be a bad sales forecast, a special request by a key customer, or an excessive end-of-period sales surge. Flexibility is not a management practice per se, but rather a result of formalization, measurement, and adoption of technology. Although all logistics organizations are affected by unexpected events, leading-edge firms demonstrate remarkable flexibility in meeting the challenges of such a situation. Firms that are committed to planning typically build in contingencies to resolve problems. Firms that truly plan well are better positioned to handle unlikely and unpleasant situations. Leading-edge firms plan to more than merely accommodate unexpected events. They expect to gain superiority. Although the timing of many logistics problems may be hard to predict, many of the problems themselves can be anticipated. The situation is somewhat analogous to the emergency earthquake response system in California. When an earthquake occurs, crews can respond quickly because they have a formalized plan in place, they are empowered to make decisions, and the organizational structure is in place. Extensive measurement systems are ready to go. These range from "measurement" of which roads are open to which hospitals are incapacitated. The information technology for coordination is also in place. The quake is unexpected only in the sense that its timing is uncertain. Similarly, in leading-edge firms, logistics problems are "unexpected" but anticipated, and creative response is encouraged.

Leading-edge firms increase flexibility through the use of outside service providers. They utilize outside service firms in an innovative manner and often form strategic alliances. In general, leading-edge firms included in the baseline research intend to expand the use of outside services. Leading-edge firms have an above-average capability to handle special customer requests and to accommodate a wide range of extraordinary operating demands. Whereas they typically have a highly productive routine way of doing things, they have established easy procedures for accommodating unexpected situations. *Conclusion—leading-edge firms thrive on their ability to maintain a balance between routine and flexible operations. The end result is an above-average capability to satisfy their customers. Such flexibility is the essence of being leading edge.*

BUILDING LEADING-EDGE STATUS

The essential attributes of leading–edge logistics boil down to integrated performance that results in maximum capability to satisfy customers. A general model of desirable logistical attributes is illustrated in Figure 3-1. The model integrates the underlying constructs of excellent performance. Development of these attributes is essential to achieving leading-edge status. The model offers a framework for building upon the experience of others to significantly improve overall logistical performance. The linkage of these key variables is discussed in Chapter Six and supported in Appendix C.

The simultaneous achievement of formalization, significant technology adoption, and continuous performance measurement is what creates flexibility. These attributes enable a firm to react quickly and appropriately to unexpected situations.

At first glance, it may seem paradoxical to suggest that greater formalization results in increased flexibility. This is a unique feature of logistical operations which are characterized by the need to manage massive detail over a large geographical area. If the firm has a structure in place to automatically accommodate routine events, logistics managers can focus on strategic opportunities and mobilize logistics more quickly and with greater accuracy. *This is a key conclusion.*

The adoption of technology enables logistical flexibility. Superior

FIGURE 3-1: Leading Edge Attribute Model

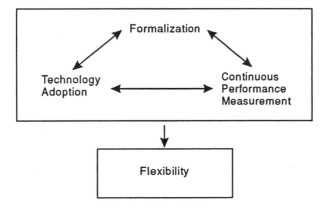

information systems allow better situational assessment. Timely, accurate information stimulates responsiveness. With superior information, the logistics group can not only respond more quickly, but also the probability of success is increased. Direct linkage provided by EDI or satellite communication to customers, suppliers, and other operating units of the firm reduces cycle times. Concurrent response replaces sequential response. A commitment to information technology increases a firm's ability to satisfy customers. The ability to accommodate special situations is crucial to superior logistical performance. In most highly competitive business environments, change is constant. The capability to quickly evaluate and adopt information technology can help firms in those highly competitive environments achieve superiority.

Continuous performance measurement enables managers to reduce logistics process variability. A clear understanding of costs, of customer service strengths and weaknesses, and of quality levels results in greater flexibility. The benchmarking of logistical practices allows a firm to observe how other organizations handle similar situations. If a logistics organization can learn to manage difficult situations through the analysis of other firms, resources and time are conserved. There is no reason to reinvent the wheel. Flexibility can be increased through good benchmarking.

With flexibility comes improved quality and speed. Flexibility grants the firm the ability to accommodate special situations. The flexible firm can exploit opportunities to realize substantial cost reductions or to maximize customer satisfaction. It can take advantage of unexpected opportunities to go beyond the routine and impact the bottom line through innovative behavior. Leading-edge firms excel at accomplishing the unexpected. They rise to their highest performance when faced with difficult challenges. Improved flexibility is the leading edge that enables these firms to customize services and capitalize on logistics strengths. Table 3–3 lists ten basic propositions that are integral to a leading-edge firm.

CHANGE MANAGEMENT MODEL

A management group that decides to launch a logistics initiative has a great deal of work to do before its implementation. Table 3–4 provides a four-step change management model to guide the process. This model forms the structure and focus for the next four chapters.

TABLE 3-3: Leading Edge Organizations—Ten Propositions

- Exhibit an overriding commitment to customers.
- Place a high premium on basic performance.
- Develop sophisticated logistical solutions.
- Emphasize planning.
- Encompass a significant span of control.
- Have a highly formalized logistical process.
- Place a premium on flexibility.
- Commit to external alliances.
- Invest in state-of-the-art information technology.
- Employ comprehensive performance measurement.

Source: Donald J. Bowersox, et al., *Leading Edge Logistics: Competitive Positioning for the 1990's* (Oak Brook, Ill.: Council of Logistics Management, 1989). Reprinted with the permission of Council of Logistics Management.

TABLE 3-4: Four-Step Change Management Model

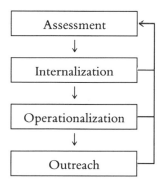

The change management model is a framework for continuous improvement and hence the feedback loop. Even if a firm is able to move through the process sequentially, the requirements and commitment associated with each step are never totally complete. Because of the dynamic nature of the competitive business environment, firms must continually reexamine themselves, internalize the assessment, revamp operationalization programs, and modify outreach or boundary-spanning efforts.

Assessment (Chapter Four)

The first phase of managed change is assessment. During assessment, a thorough examination of the firm's current logistics practices and structure is required. This internal assessment should be supplemented by the benchmarking of current practices to outside organizations.

The assessment phase of the change process is an exercise in sharpening focus. Key measurements are taken and examined. At this time preconceived notions or paradigms about traditional logistics performance are frozen and a careful "no holds barred" look as to how the organization really operates is completed. The process is designed to zero in on the ways and means of current operations and to compare them to the best available practice.

During this assessment phase, key and sometimes difficult questions are asked and answered to the best of a firm's ability. Some key questions are listed in Table 3-5. A particular concern is the level of logistical knowledge existing among key management personnel. The fact of the matter may be that a firm's current management does not have the formal training or experience necessary to mount a successful logistics initiative. The lack of fundamental understanding can result in a great deal of lip service to the idea without any real progress. The result may be a decline in current operating effectiveness if in fact leadership to bring about real change is lacking. Understanding the basic concepts of logistics at an in-depth level is essential to the change process. The fact that logistical performance areas are well established parts of all businesses makes the concepts of integrated and strategic performance somewhat elusive. Appendix A provides a listing of sources that a management group can use to quickly upgrade basic

---

TABLE 3-5: Examples of Key Management Questions

1. Where is the firm relative to its strategic objectives?
2. Where is the organization heading?
3. What opportunities exist for strategic redirection?
4. Do we have the overall management knowledge to lead a successful logistics initiative?

understanding of the fundamentals of logistics. The ultimate goal is to find new ways to perform old functions more efficiently and effectively. Because management is familiar with the traditional treatment of the parts, the danger exists that the new concepts of integration will be overlooked. The end result of the assessment is an implementation plan.

Internalization (Chapter Five—Moving the Mountain)

A second step in the change process is internalization. Inevitably, the assessment stage leads to a call for change. Whatever change is proposed, it can be expected that it will be met with resistance. Barriers to change must be identified and overcome. Change champions must be found and recruited to the cause. Because the process requires revamping long-standing and deeply entrenched practices of management, change may appear to be like "moving a mountain."

Operationalization (Chapter Six—The Keys to Success)

The third thrust in the management of change process is operationalizing the implementation plan. Once widespread acceptance of the necessity for change has occurred, the real work begins. A firm must carefully take steps to implement the attributes of leading-edge performance. Such operationalization requires that the entire organization take ownership of bringing about the desired change. Operationalization means moving from concept to performance. It requires an in-depth understanding of the relationships and linkages among formalization, technology adoption, and performance measurement as they combine to achieve logistical flexibility.

Outreach (Chapter Seven—Developing Strategic Alliances)

The last step in effective change is the outreach to and impact on customers and suppliers. In today's world, this often means the creation of strategic alliances. Managers must span company borders and make logistical connections with key customers and suppliers seamless.

THE CHANGE MODEL: CONCLUSION (CHAPTER EIGHT— THE DAY AFTER SUCCESS)

The final chapter summarizes the change model's implications in eight propositions. The propositions are oriented toward the future—a future of challenges and opportunities.

Notes

1. Donald J. Bowersox, Patricia J. Daugherty, Cornelia L. Dröge, Dale S. Rogers, and Daniel L. Wardlow. *Leading Edge Logistics: Competitive Positioning for the 1990s* (Oak Brook, Ill.: Council of Logistics Management, 1989).

2. D. S. Pugh, D. J. Hickson, C. R. Hinings, and C. Turner, "Dimensions of Organization Structure," *Administrative Science Quarterly* 13 (June 1968): 65–105.

3. Peter F. Drucker, *Management: Tasks, Responsibilities and Practices* (New York: Harper and Row, 1974).

4. For discussion of the content of what constitutes an ideal mission statement, see the analysis of 88 U.S. manufacturing firm mission statements from the Leading Edge Research in James R. Stock and Cornelia Dröge, "Logistics Mission Statements: An Appraisal," *Proceedings of the Nineteenth Annual Transportation and Logistics Educators Conference* (October 7, 1990): 79–91; and also see John A. Pearce, "The Company Mission as a Strategic Tool," *Sloan Management Review* 23 (Spring 1982): 15–24.

5. Bernard J. LaLonde and Paul H. Zinszer, *Customer Service: Meaning and Measurement* (Chicago: National Council of Physical Distribution Management, 1976); and Bernard J. LaLonde, Martha C. Cooper, and Thomas G. Noordewier, *Customer Service: A Management Perspective* (Oak Brook, Ill.: Council of Logistics Management, 1988).

6. For further details, see Robert C. Camp, *Benchmarking* (Milwaukee: Quality Press, 1989); Robert Hershey, "Commercial Intelligence on a Shoestring," *Harvard Business Review* 58 (September-October 1980): 22–30; William L. Sammon, Mark A. Kurland, and Robert Spitalnic, *Business Competitor Intelligence* (New York: John Wiley and Sons, 1984); Jerry L. Wall, "What the Competition is Doing: Your Need to Know," *Harvard Business Review* 52 (November-December 1974): 22–24; and George M. Zinkham and Betsy D. Gelb, "Competitive Intelligence Practices of Industrial Marketers," *Industrial Marketing Management* 14 (November 1985): 269–275.

7. Richard C. Haverly, Douglas McW. Smith, and Deborah P. Steele, "Logistics Software 1989 Edition," *Proceedings of the Annual Conference of the Council of Logistics Management* 1 (1988): 263–427.

8. Shoshanna Zuboff, *In the Age of the Smart Machine: The Future of Work and Power* (New York: Basic Books, 1988).

9. Kate Evans-Correia, "EDI: The Future Frontier," *Purchasing* 106, 3 (February 1989): 44–47.

10. Harry E. Burke, *Handbook of Bar Code Systems* (New York: Van Nostrand Reinhold, 1985).

Assessment

CHARLIE felt he had progressed sufficiently along the learning curve to start making some real changes. However, before moving forward he had to know three things:

Where are we now?
Where are we headed?
What opportunities exist for strategic redirection?

In fact, Charlie felt that he had a pretty good grasp of the *answers* to these questions. He constantly had to temper his enthusiasm for immediate action by the knowledge that he couldn't do it without the substantial support from the entire organization—top management as well as key personnel throughout middle and lower levels. Charlie knew he had to have a comprehensive and credible assessment of costs, benefits, and risks. He realized it was necessary to develop a believable rationale for change supported by a systematic implementation plan. He knew that he not only had to convince others that things could not continue the way they were, but that he also had to propose and defend a particular course of change. He was aware that there would be substantial obstacles and resistance. He knew it was essential to provide leadership. Charlie set out to build his case.

First of all, Charlie assembled as much information as possible. He wanted to look at historical trends—What did the sales pattern for the last five years look like? How volatile is any particular product line—how frequently are new products added or old products dropped? How does the company's business pattern compare relative to the industry norm—is the company an industry leader or is it relegated to being a "follower" that is constantly trying to catch up? Charlie also knew he needed to be able to evaluate the company's efficiency and productivity—are costs within an acceptable range as compared to the competition or should this be a top priority?

Once he had developed a comprehensive overview of past and current operations, Charlie began to look to the future. Where does the company want to be five years from now? A review of the strategic plan and discussions with key personnel provided Charlie with a vision of the company's long-term objectives and goals. Briefly, management's vision was to move out of the second tier of competitors and become an industry leader. Talk about a challenge!

Now Charlie knew what had to be accomplished, but not how to do it. What opportunities are there for improving overall competitive positioning? He began to make another list—what are the company's strengths? weaknesses? After spending considerable time on the list, he turned his attention to the marketplace and the industry. What do the customers really want in terms of customer service? What are the most likely changes anticipated in the future? How could he use logistics strategically to provide better service than the competitors? Charlie had become convinced that service was the key issue—he needed to outline a plan for gaining a competitive edge by offering superior logistical service.

The starting point in the change process is assessment. Assessment is the process of an organization examining itself—its current reality—while at the same time looking outside to evaluate the success or failure of logistics operations in other firms.

Regular assessment of a logistics organization is healthy. Routinized logistics procedures and operations can quickly become unmanageable or misdirected if they are not carefully scrutinized. As the span of control increases and managers are spread thinner, formalized assessment becomes more important.

Assessment is not merely measuring productivity, cost, or customer service. It is a careful examination of how business is conducted, that is, looking at which operations require adjustment and figuring out why they should be changed. Assessment is properly viewed as a process of renewal. It can be painful, but it is crucial to the attainment of leading-edge status.

Examination of leading-edge firms has resulted in an assessment methodology that is a synthesis of several techniques firms use to accomplish systematic review. Although assessment can be traumatic, leading-edge performers continually examine the impact of logistical operations to determine what if any changes are required to upgrade their performance.

ASSESSMENT OBJECTIVE

The goal of the assessment is to create value for the firm and its customers by redefining the logistical systems and processes. The assessment should quantify a firm's current operational capability, spell out where it is heading, and define what opportunities exist for strategic redirection. Consistent with the lessons learned from the leading-edge research, in the assessment process the firm should identify how it can improve its flexibility through examination of formalized control, define its ability to adopt and implement technology, and determine how to measure performance. The goal of continuous improvement in flexibility is to achieve closer relationships with customers and suppliers.

ASSESSMENT PROCESS

The assessment process can be summarized in a few key steps. The basic methodology should lead to a comprehensive understanding of the costs, benefits, and risks associated with system modification. The methodology presented in Table 4-1 is a synthesis of the best practices of leading-edge firms.

Decision to Assess (Step One)

The first step is to generate widespread acceptance for the decision to assess logistics proficiency. This part of the process may appear easy, but widespread acceptance is a hurdle that many firms never accomplish. The time and resources required to complete an adequate assessment may not be authorized without overall acceptance of the need for and the importance of regular assessment. In most situations, logistics personnel are likely to be doing all they can to move the product out the door and typically they are performing fairly well. The focus of the assessment is improvement. Nervousness over turf can restrict the depth of the examination. If an organization seeks to achieve leading-edge status, it must be willing to answer tough questions honestly and to investigate causes no matter where the answers lead.

Organizational assessment is similar to visiting the doctor. No one likes to hear that they are sick, but it is best to know specifically what

TABLE 4-1: *Assessment Process*

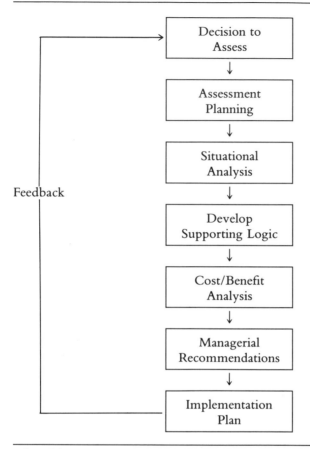

Adapted from *Logistical Management*, 3/e by Donald J. Bowersox, David J. Closs and
Omar K. Helferich. Copyright © 1986 by Macmillan Publishing Company. Reprinted by
permission.

is wrong if one wants to get well. A patient not only needs to know
why he or she is sick, but also the degree of illness and how to get
well.

Many firms become trapped by inertia. They become unwilling to
change or to critically examine traditional procedures and practices.
This attitude can lead to a dangerous complacency.

The one certainty in all organizations is that they are facing constant change. New technological breakthroughs can drastically alter a firm's appropriate organization and how it relates to its environment. A dramatic example is in the history of weaponry. The swordsman had to devote many years to attaining the level of skill necessary to use a sword competently. The introduction of the gun enabled warriors with far less skill and training to kill much more effectively. The gun required less direct physical participation in the act of injuring. Whole classes of specialists were eliminated as a result of such innovations. The gun destroyed the special role of the samurai warriors; the introduction of the crossbow eliminated the need for a class of knights.[1]

Assessment Planning (Step Two)

Once the organization has decided that it is willing to expend the time and resources required to examine the need for potential change, extensive planning is required before a successful assessment can be launched. Time and resources have to be allocated for the assessment. An assessment team must be assembled. Specific tasks have to be identified and prioritized. Successful completion of the assessment process depends a great deal upon the quality of the preparation.

Although it is important to complete the assessment as rapidly as possible, it is more important to evaluate operations thoroughly. Because of day-to-day business pressures, the temptation is to put band-aids on problems rather than to carefully examine the causes and plan corrective action.

Top Management Support

A key to comprehensive assessment is the involvement of senior management. Top management needs to understand fully the potential benefits of improving the logistical system. Customer service and competitive leverage are the most powerful issues in obtaining the support of top management. Without the support of top management, it is likely that recommended changes will be less than fully successful. Dr. W. Edwards Deming, who is generally credited with successfully revitalizing Japanese industry after World War II, found that his earlier efforts to improve quality in the United States were supported by technical people, but rejected by senior management. This rejection resulted in failure to adopt his philosophies in the United States.[2]

If senior management is deeply committed to implementing whatever change is required, employees at lower levels of an organization will be more receptive. Top management enhances an organization's ability to successfully complete an assessment. Greater overall cooperation is likely if senior management leads the initiative.

Assembling a Team

Networking in the assessment process begins with the selection of the right team. Senior logistics management must select a team leader capable of managing the process and possessing a track record of getting things done. The team should be comprised of people who are willing and able to isolate opportunities for improvement. They need to be aggressive; they also need to be people with vision.

Innovations can often come from the most unexpected sources. Although the assessment process needs top-level approval, it cannot be completely driven by senior management. Employees who best understand potential problems and inefficiencies in any department are the people who deal with such frustrations on a daily basis.

The members of an assessment team also need to be assured that they will not suffer repercussions if they discover problem situations. They require political immunity. People sometimes fail to expose problems because they fear punishment or harassment. If the team is responsible for evaluating people or existing processes in areas in which members of the team are regularly assigned, the entire assessment could be jeopardized unless the proper mechanism for protection is established in advance.

An assessment team typically consists of several different levels of employees and it may also include an outside consultant as a facilitator and messenger. One challenge for the team leader is to make certain that management will listen to its recommendations. Care is required to staff the assessment team with members who have the respect of senior management. A typical problem in assembling an assessment team is that the ideal members are typically the busiest employees. They are the same people who everyone thinks of when new assignments are handed out.

The assessment team should feature cross-functional expertise. For example, the participating employees from sales, marketing, finance, and, if appropriate, engineering or manufacturing, can offer valuable insights during the assessment process. In some situations, the assessment team would ideally include customers and even suppliers. Customers and suppliers typically view the logistics process from the perspective of daily interactions. Their perspective puts a new light on what is or is not important to increasing satisfaction and efficiency.

Task Specification and Prioritization

Once the assessment team is assembled, a critical step is to specify and prioritize assignments. The team must determine the appropriate scope of the assessment. Specific assessment tasks are unique to each situation and depend upon the original objectives established. If the assessment is directed to a total review of logistical operations, the specific tasks will be extensive and prioritization becomes critical.

The specification and prioritization of tasks should be outlined in a plan for the overall assessment. The initial cut at the assessment plan provides the framework for estimating the time and resources required to complete the process.

Planning Time and Resources

A critical aspect of logistics assessment is to complete the process as rapidly as possible in order to be able to start the actual change process. In most companies, only limited human resources are available to participate in the assessment. It is unlikely that many companies will be able to assign people to work full-time on the assessment. Since team members will probably have other duties, the allocation of time and resources must be flexible. A good rule of thumb is that the assessment should be carried out within a relatively short time, no longer than 90 to 100 days, for example. This will force attention to the most significant issues. If justified, a second or even third phase of the assessment can be scheduled to focus on new opportunity areas. The key to a successful assessment is timely results.

Framing Deliverable Results

The final step in assessment planning is to focus on expected deliverable results. Even this early in the assessment, the team can develop a working outline of the final report. The project plan should contain specific questions that will be addressed at predetermined times. For example, possible operational categories discussed in the deliverable results might cover such disparate topics as logistics computer applications, transportation resources and methods, and delivery performance. These topical presentations and their interrelations should be planned early in the process to assure that deliverable results are appropriately organized.

At the conclusion of the assessment planning phase, the stage should be set for the team to move forward in a coordinated manner.

Unless a tight and realistic plan is developed, the overall assessment runs the risk of getting bogged down and more or less pushed from the limelight. A safe generalization is that the most common causes of assessments failing to generate acceptable results can be traced to inadequate planning and unrealistic goals. Lack of time and lack of leadership are two other important causes of failure.

Situational Analysis (Step Three)

The situational analysis involves the collection and analysis of data about logistics operations. In many ways, analysis of the current internal and external impact of logistics is the guts of the assessment process. The primary purpose of the situational analysis is to identify opportunities for improvement, to isolate questionable practices, and to identify potential solutions to problems.

Identify and Prioritize Key Issues

The situational analysis consists of examining key questions about current operations. Based on identification and prioritization of tasks, it is now necessary to specify the logistics practices and processes that need to be examined and to identify the type of data that should be collected. The assessment team needs to focus on the high-impact variables involved in the various systems under review. Isolating key variables is the creative part of a situational analysis.

An important part of the situational analysis is to determine what information should be collected. Naturally the data need to flow directly from the key variables identified. Data collection can become the quicksand of an assessment because it gives the illusion that the team is making progress. Care must be taken to ensure that the data collected are essential to the assessment objectives. Collection of data must focus on fundamental applicable information and avoid the opinions or unsupported generalities of individuals. All data must be carefully verified for accuracy. Often, accepted beliefs or long-standing paradigms concerning a specific function or cost are false. The team needs to look for irregularities, uncertainties, and conflicts within the data. It is also important to indicate the source of the data in order to be able to recalibrate that information later.[3] The typical situational analysis must focus on the collection of both internal and external information.

Internal Review

The internal review seeks to establish a factual presentation of the existing logistical process. During the internal situational analysis, a profile of current performance, data, strategies, operations, and tactics is developed. This internal situation profile becomes the baseline from which to evaluate the desirability of change and to design the bench-marking practice to that of leading-edge performance.

Seven areas are identified as typical of a comprehensive review: (1) mission statement; (2) planning; (3) organization; (4) customer impact; (5) performance measurements; (6) technology adoption; and (7) flexibility. Just as tasks are specific to the individual firm, the internal situational analysis needs to focus on achieving the overall objectives of the assessment.

Mission Statement: Verification and examination of the mission statement that guides the overall logistical operations is the ideal place to initiate an internal review. Does a formal logistics mission statement exist? Is it widely distributed? Do management and employees understand the mission and do they support it? The mission should be reviewed to determine its level of comprehensiveness. Ideal mission statements should focus on customer satisfaction, identify the strategic importance of logistics, and highlight the importance of cost control. A mission statement should commit the organization to quality performance and continuous improvement. Table 4–2 suggests some specific questions related to the assessment of the existing mission statement. More specific discussion of the attributes of an ideal mission statement is presented in Chapter Six.

In the overall assessment of the logistics mission statement, it is essential to determine whether it provides sufficient foundation and

---

TABLE 4-2: Mission Review Questions

- Does a formal logistics mission exist? Is it widely distributed?
- How clear is the mission statement? Do logistics personnel understand it?
- Do people pay attention to the mission or is it ignored?
- Does the existing statement commit management to continuous quality improvement?
- Is the logistics mission linked to the business unit mission?
- What elements are specifically included and excluded in the mission statement?

guidance for managing the logistics process as an integral contribution to the overall business strategy.

Planning: A key to understanding overall logistical performance is often found by careful review of the existing planning processes. Does a plan exist? Is a formal planning process established? If so, the planning process should be mapped and critiqued. The length and currency of the plan are of prime importance. Is the plan comprehensive in terms of strategic and tactical considerations? Is the plan relevant to key business issues? The team should review linkages between strategic and operating plans. It is important to determine if the planners and the users are jointly involved in the development and maintenance of the plan. Some typical planning review questions are listed in Table 4-3.

The assessment team should also determine if the logistics organization maintains adequate input into business unit strategic planning. If upper management needs to be educated to the importance of linking the planning processes, the assessment should develop evidence to support this case.

Organization: The key organization issue is to determine if the existing structure hinders successful achievement of the logistics mission.

To many employees the topic of a systemic change immediately translates into "it's time to reorganize again." Reorganizations are typically disruptive and personally annoying. However, refocusing an organization can be therapeutic for the firm. The baseline research has disclosed that leading-edge firms reorganize functional areas frequently

---

TABLE 4-3: Planning System Review Questions

- Does a strategic logistics plan exist?
- Does a formal planning procedure exist?
- What is the planning horizon of the strategic plan?
- How relevant are the strategic and tactical logistics plans?
- How often are the plans updated? Is currency maintained?
- What elements are included in the plan?
- Is the logistics planning process linked to business unit planning?
- Does the logistics organization have input into corporate and business unit strategic planning?

---

to accommodate change and better position the firm to capitalize upon new opportunities. Reorganizations ideally reflect adaptation to a dynamic environment.

Of particular interest in an assessment is the level of integration of the logistics organization. A careful analysis should be conducted of the specific functions that are accountable to the logistics organization and the degree to which their performance and measurement are integrated. The potential expansion or contraction of the functional scope of logistics operations in terms of organizational trends and influences that impact on the overall firm is of special concern during an assessment.

The logistics organization's span of control should be sufficiently large to create a critical mass capable of achieving the logistics mission. In advanced organizations, functions can be networked to achieve integration without actual reorganization with its inevitable turf wars.

When reviewing the organizational structure, the assessment team must fully understand how the overall logistics process is managed. Peter Drucker suggested that American business is in transition from the traditional command and control organization structure to one based on information.[4] His concept of the information-based organization is a group of knowledge specialists linked in a network but functioning as independent agents. These specialists are viewed as interacting with customers and suppliers. This interaction occurs across internal functions on a networked basis rather than by formally reporting to a specific manager. The variety of trends highlighted in Chapter Two should be reviewed in terms of specific impact on the organization's appropriate structure, strategy, management processes, human resources, and technology. One clear indication of success in leading-edge firms is their commitment to managing the overall process, as contrasted to remaining loyal to a given organizational structure.

The ability of the logistics organization to interact with corporate management is another key concern. Access to senior management and to the overall strategic posture of the logistics organization is important. Typical questions related to organizational assessment are presented in Table 4-4.

Customer Impact: Firms do not achieve leading-edge status without spending a great deal of time and energy understanding their customers. The scope of customer analysis should appropriately include internal customers as well as external channel partners.

Specific questions centering on customer relationships all lead to

---

TABLE 4-4: Organization Structure Review Questions

- How integrated is the logistics organization? Where do logistics functions report?
- Are lines of communication open between functions? Across organization borders?
- What level of importance does the overall business unit place on logistics?
- What is the level of the senior logistics executive? Who does that executive report to?
- When was the last reorganization? How often does a reorganization take place?
- Does the current structure enhance or hinder completion of the logistics mission? How?

---

one assessment—are customers' needs being met? The quality of the relationship between customers and a firm's logistics organization should be carefully reviewed. For example, does the logistics group really understand customers or do they assume that a lack of complaints means that everything is okay? What is the frequency of direct customer contact? If the relationship between logistics and customers has an adversarial track record, it is likely that no real effort is being made to understand life from a customer's perspective. The baseline research suggests that about one out of five firms conducts a comprehensive and continuous analysis of how well it is serving its customers from the "customer's perspective."

Some measurements of customer service are easy to implement and assess. Most firms have some type of system to track delivery and inventory performance. The order cycle is also relatively easy to measure. The assessment needs to move beyond simple measurement and seek to identify underlying causes for specific performance. Bottlenecks and roadblocks that potentially reduce customer satisfaction need to be identified and alternatives explored. In many situations, it will be necessary to conduct customer service research to fully understand how well outside customers are being satisfied.

Many key customers are internal users of basic logistics services. Care must be taken to isolate how well customers are being serviced and what adjustments are justified. For both internal and external customers it is important to assess the quality and timeliness of information. Most customers would rather be told bad news immediately instead of being surprised later. Anticipated delivery dates should be realistic rather than too optimistic. Typical customer impact questions are listed in Table 4-5.

Performance Measurement: A significant portion of the internal review should focus on questions about measuring performance. Understanding current performance measurements and how they are used is critical to improving logistics practices. However, the firm cannot measure everything, so it needs to focus on "impact" measurements.

TABLE 4-5: Customer Impact Review Questions

- Does a formal customer service policy exist? Is the policy adequate? Is the policy adhered to and understood?
- How flexible are logistics operations? Can special customer service requests be adequately handled?
- What organization personnel have direct contact with customers? What is the nature of that contact? What controls over customer contact exist? Are employees handling contact with customers in a manner that will positively impact the customer's view of the firm? Are employees adequately trained to interact with customers? Are employees evaluated on how well they deal with customers?
- What level of responsiveness currently exists? What level of responsiveness should exist? What is the level of customer responsiveness in comparison to competitors?
- What internal information is shared with customers? Are customers dealt with honestly? Do customers believe what they are told? Are customers often disappointed when comparing actual performance to stated plan?
- What is the length of the order cycle? How long should it be?
- What are customer expectations? What variables impact customer expectations? Do customers expect similar performance from competitors?
- Do customers understand how they are expected to perform? Do logistics personnel provide unambiguous instruction to customers?
- What customer service measurements are used? Do current customer service measurements adequately measure performance? Do measurements address the central issue of customer need satisfaction?

In an earlier step in the assessment, key processes and variables were identified. When reviewing performance measurement, the internal review seeks to determine the impact of each process on the total system and, in particular, the combined impact on customers and profitability. Performance measurement offers a meaningful way to review specific logistics functions and the contribution each makes to the integrated system. Potential assessment questions for specific logistical areas are suggested in Tables 4-6 through 4-9.

The degree to which statistical tools are used should be evaluated as part of the measurement review. To understand the avalanche of performance data that exists in most firms, the ability to generate statistical summaries and graphical representations is necessary to create meaningful information. If used correctly, statistics can minimize confusion and offer significant insight. Statistical methods help people to understand processes and what is required to improve control.

TABLE 4-6: Transportation Audit Questions

- How much is spent annually on transportation? How are costs allocated? Are costs for carriers accounted for differently than for private fleets?
- What is the justification for the fleet? Does the firm really need to maintain a fleet or should transportation be outsourced?
- How many carriers are used? What level of business is given to each carrier?
- Who determines the carrier and the carrier instructions? How is that carrier selection made?
- Can freight bill audit and payment systems be improved?
- Can we improve consolidation of outbound and inbound shipments?
- How many miles do we deadhead? Are those miles necessary? Can we work with someone to reduce those empty miles?
- Can routing and scheduling be improved?
- Is freight being moved and handled too many times?
- Can transportation damage be reduced?
- Should freight negotiations focus on issues previously neglected?
- Can congestion at the dock be reduced?
- Should further modal analysis be performed?
- Can we position equipment better?
- How much does the firm rely on overnight package services?

TABLE 4-7: *Warehousing Audit Questions*

- How many warehouses are included in the network? What is the size of those warehouses?
- What is the total cost (per square foot) of each warehouse?
- What costs are included in warehouse expenses?
- What is the difference in cost between public and private warehousing? In level of control? In strategic positioning?
- Are the warehouses laid out adequately?
- From receipt to shipment, how many times is material handled?
- Are warehousing systems in place to reduce handling and streamline operations? Short-order scheduling? On-board terminals? Workload balancing? On-line receiving?
- How is performance measured within the warehouse?
- What system logic is used to lay out the warehouse and make product storage assignments?
- How fast does inventory move through the warehouse?
- What visibility level into warehouse inventory is available? Does the system always reflect what is actually in storage?

These lessons are not new. Many firms have been using statistical measurement to assess quality for years. However, American companies have been somewhat shy to apply statistical measurements. Leading-edge firms develop and use more statistical measurement than average organizations. Leading-edge firms spend considerable effort improving the product and process quality. A critical dimension of situational analysis is to determine the degree of application of statistical tools in day-to-day control of the logistics process.

The Shewhart cycle is an example of a methodological tool that has proven helpful for testing specific logistics variables. Named after Walter A. Shewhart, a statistician at Bell Labs, it is sometimes referred to as the "PDCA Cycle" for Plan, Do, Check, Act. It is illustrated in Table 4-10. The first step in this cycle is to study a process and decide what changes might be desirable. The second step is testing, or making a change. Such tests are usually implemented on a small scale. The third step is observing the effects of the test. Step four involves studying the results and determining what was learned. The cycle is a closed loop so that, following step four, step one is repeated with new knowledge from the previous completion of the cycle.[5]

TABLE 4-8: Inventory Audit Questions

- What is the average level of inventory in the system? In each location by SKU? By categories?
- How much inventory is in raw materials? Work in process? Finished goods?
- Are ratios between raw materials, work in process, and finished goods inventory appropriate given organization cost and customer service objectives?
- Are average supplier lead times on crucial materials reasonable? Are average processing times reasonable?
- How often is inventory handled?
- How is inventory performance measured? Do current inventory performance measurements adequately address key inventory issues?
- What function is responsible for maintaining inventory? Is authority for obtaining and maintaining inventory adequate?
- How is inventory replenishment handled? What logic is used to handle replenishment?
- What is the inventory record accuracy level? Does the firm always know how much inventory is on hand, allocated, en route, or in receiving at all times?
- What is the amount of obsolete or damaged inventory in the system? What level of shrinkage or unusable inventory is typical?
- What cost categories are included in measuring inventory carrying cost? Does management pay adequate attention to inventory carrying costs?
- How is inventory forecasting completed? How accurate are forecasts? How many adjustments to forecasts are made?

Statistical tools that are helpful during the measurement review are listed in Table 4–11. Such tools are described in greater detail in Appendix B.

Technology Adoption: The first step in a technology adoption review is to evaluate current applications. Because of the explosive rate at which technology is expanding, it is likely that areas for improvement will be identified. Operations personnel typically have long wish lists of desired changes.

After determining the gaps in the technology and systems, it is necessary to develop a prioritized list of potential adoptions. To fully

---

TABLE 4-9: *Logistics Information System Audit Questions*

- Is the system able to adequately address key logistics information requirements? What segments of the business does the logistics system encompass? What areas of the business still need to be computerized? What is the level of cross-functional integration?
- How old is the system and the system technology? Should the technology be updated? Have logistics information requirements changed much since the system was implemented? Has the minimum level of required information system performance increased since implementation?
- How seamless is the logistics information system? Can information move easily from material origin (suppliers) to material destination (customers)? Are system boundary-spanning capabilities adequate?
- Is information received by the logistics organization timely, accurate, readily available, and appropriately formatted?
- What visibility level into logistics processes exist? Does the system accurately reflect status and location of materials?
- How difficult is it to change systems to reflect current business requirements? Who makes changes to logistics information systems? What priority level do logistics system change requirements have within the total organization?
- Do logistics personnel have to improvise to complete everyday tasks? Is the formal system logistics personnel are supposed to use equivalent to informal systems actually used?
- How much flexibility is built into the system? Can the logistics system handle special customer requests such as unique shipping instructions or requests to expedite?
- How efficiently can new technology be implemented? What roadblocks for implementation exist?
- How often are information systems reviewed?

---

develop a technology plan, it may be necessary for a firm to undertake an in-depth study.

Technology adoption can lead to competitive advantage. The situation analysis should frame current and potential technology in terms of how it can be strategically leveraged. Technology is a strategic variable that can catapult an organization's logistics competencies forward.

Specific characteristics of the organization may enhance or inhibit

TABLE 4-10: Shewhart Cycle

Step 1: What could be the most important accomplishment of this team? What changes might be desirable? What data are available? Are new observations needed? If yes, plan a change or test.
Step 2: Carry out the tests, or change, on a small scale.
Step 3: Observe effects of the change or test.
Step 4: Study the results. What was learned?
Step 5: Return to Step 1 with new knowledge accumulated.

Source: Mary Walton, *The Deming Management Method* (New York: Perigee Books, 1986). Reprinted by permission of The Putnam Publishing Group from *The Deming Management Method* by Mary Walton. Copyright © 1986 by Mary Walton.

TABLE 4-11: Statistical Tools

Cause-and-effect diagrams (Fishbone)
Flow charts
Pareto charts
Trend charts
Histograms
Control charts
Scatter diagrams

Source: Mary Walton, *The Deming Management Method* (New York: Perigee Books, 1986). Reprinted by permission of The Putnam Publishing Group from *The Deming Management Method* by Mary Walton. Copyright © 1986 by Mary Walton.

the ability to adopt new technology. The identification of such characteristics and an examination of how they can be expected to impact on technology adoption is important. In an ever-changing technological environment, the logistics organization must assess, acquire, and implement new capabilities quickly. If a logistics organization continues to use old technology while its competition has moved forward, the ability to compete in an effective manner can be limited. Specific technology review questions are listed in Table 4-12.

Flexibility: The flexibility of the logistics organization is reflected by its ability to handle unusual or "unexpected" events. The assessment team should examine how a firm handles unexpected events such as a

---

TABLE 4-12: Technology Assessment Review Questions

- What technologies are available?
- How adaptable are new technologies?
- Can we install and implement technologies within a reasonable time frame?
- Are potential technologies finished or "still in development?"
- What impacts will implementation of new technology have on logistics organization processes?
- What impacts will implementation of new technology have on personnel?
- How can potential technologies be leveraged strategically?

---

product recall or computer breakdown to determine if an organization is able to respond appropriately. Key questions to help isolate the flexible capabilities of an organization are listed in Table 4-13.

External Review—Benchmarking

To supplement the internal review, attention should be directed to how current practices compare to other industry firms or admired performers. At this stage in the assessment process, management should have a good idea of significant areas for improvement. Benchmarking is a technique designed to help a firm's management understand what other firms are doing. Benchmarking input is crucial to a comprehensive assessment.

Benchmarking is an objective-setting process. It is important that the benchmarking portion of the assessment process focus on logistics practices worthy of study and emulation. It should focus on *dantotsu*, a Japanese word that means the best of the best practices.[6] Table 4-14 presents the basic benchmarking cycle.

Advantages of insightful benchmarking should be clear. It allows the firm to compare its performance to the best practices of other firms. It allows managers to view successful practices. Often, it is difficult for managers in a risk-averse environment to adopt a new technique or practice without a meaningful example to illustrate that it works. Benchmarking enables managers to see new ideas at work, and it prevents their "reinventing the wheel."

Benchmarking serves to reduce a firm's isolationism. Reviewing

TABLE 4-13: Flexibility Assessment Review Questions

- Are special customer service requests easily satisfied? Is the logistics organization able to customize service levels to specific markets or customers?
- Is the logistics organization able to respond adequately to special sales and marketing incentive programs?
- Does new product introduction or old product phaseout drastically reduce logistics organization efficiency? Is the logistics organization able to handle new product introduction or old product phaseout without building up too much inventory or having too little inventory on hand?
- What impact on the organization does a major computer breakdown have? Can the logistics mission still be accomplished?
- How do product recalls or returned goods impact the logistics organization? Does the logistics system work when run in reverse?
- Does the logistics system allow for modification or customization of product if required?
- Is the firm able to utilize outside third party service vendors to handle overflow or excess demand during peak periods?
- How does a disruption in supply impact the organization? Can the firm smoothly shift from one vendor to another?
- Are contingency plans in place to appropriately respond to catastrophic events such as warehouse fires or floods?
- Are logistics personnel able to perform several different types of tasks and jobs? Is the labor force flexible?
- Is the logistics organization able to respond appropriately to competitive pressures or changes in competitors' logistics systems?
- Is the firm able to adjust the logistics system to respond adequately to global demands? As the firm moves toward a global market, can the logistics system support that move?

other companies and the way in which they develop and complete their logistics mission can be a rallying point for the total organization. In Table 4-15, a methodology for benchmarking is detailed.

Benchmarking can take several different forms depending on the degree of formalization of the process. The details cannot be simply adopted but rather must be tailored to the specific situation. There is no formula or exact process for benchmarking so that a firm can identify and simply copy the ingredients of another firm's success. Instead,

---

TABLE 4-14: *Fundamental Philosophical Steps of Benchmarking*

---

1. Know your operation.
2. Know the industry leaders or competitors.
3. Incorporate the best.
4. Gain superiority.

Source: Robert Camp, *Benchmarking: The Search for Industry Best Practices That Lead to Superior Performance* (Milwaukee: ASQC Quality Press, 1989). Reprinted with the permission of ASQC.

TABLE 4-15: *The Benchmarking Process: A Continuous Loop for Improvement*

 Planning Phase
  Identify what is to be benchmarked.
  Identify comparative companies.
  Determine data collection method and collect data.
  ↓
 Analysis Phase
  Determine current performance "gap."
  Project future performance levels.
  ↓
→ **Integration Phase**
  Communicate benchmark findings and gain acceptance.
  Establish functional goals.
  ↓
 Action Phase
  Develop action plans.
  Implement specific actions and monitor progress.
  Recalibrate benchmarks.

Source: Adapted from Robert Camp, *Benchmarking: The Search for Industry Best Practices That Lead to Superior Performance* (Milwaukee: ASQC Quality Press, 1989). Reprinted with the permission of ASQC.

benchmarking is a learning process during which managers observe practices and translate them to the degree that is practical.

Development of Supporting Logic (Step Four)

One of the most difficult yet important parts of the assessment process is the development of a supporting logic for logistics system changes. During this phase, the findings of the situational analysis are integrated and analyzed. Redesign tools such as flow diagrams, Pareto charts, and outlines are used to assist in the integration process. Knowledge accumulated from both the internal review and benchmarking are integrated, and redesign alternatives are developed. Cost–benefit analyses are performed, with care taken to determine both long- and short-term impacts on the organization.

Review Integration

Part of developing a supporting logic is the integration of internal and external reviews. This phase calls for the successful blending of internal improvements and the best external practices. The findings that come out of the benchmarking process provide new options for the logistics organization. The results of the internal review are measured against the findings of the benchmarking process. Team members pick and choose from among the best practices found at other firms and potential improvements developed during the internal review. Areas of weakness pointed out by the internal review are built up by borrowing the best of the benchmarked practices. This integration provides a foundation from which strategic logistics system changes can be made.

Redesign Alternatives

The objective of the situational analysis is to assess logistical processes and practices and identify system strengths and weakness, risks, and opportunities. The internal review identifies areas of improvement. Benchmarking current practices against leading-edge firms provides a factual basis for change that can be presented to upper management with the knowledge that actual practices put into place elsewhere can be borrowed and adapted for use.

The integration of the internal review and benchmarking results provides the firm with redesign alternatives. These alternatives are catalogued and closely examined. Alternatives are measured for strategic fit with the firm. Some alternatives that come out of the benchmarking process may not be usable because they do not fit with the overall company mission or firm culture.

Next, the redesign alternatives are prioritized. These alternatives can be prioritized by cost reduction and avoidance, customer service impact, competitive advantage potential, ease of implementation, system effectiveness, or other criteria. The prioritized redesign alternatives must be pared down further to identify the best options. These options are then evaluated as to their impact on costs and benefits.

Cost–Benefit Analysis (Step Five)

The best options identified during the supporting logic development phase are then subjected to a thorough cost–benefit analysis. Potential benefits are carefully catalogued and quantified. Benefits can be summarized into categories such as increased formalization, technology adoption, and improved measurement and flexibility.

All relevant costs for each of the best options are identified and compared. The assessment team should be careful to consider both visible short-term costs and hidden long-term costs. These options should be considered both for their quick impact and their viability over the long run. It is crucial to the success of the assessment that results are visible quickly. However, long-term viability cannot be sacrificed in order to make short-term gains. Quick fixes often have a negative impact over time. The assessment team should think carefully about what actions will result in the most value to the organization both now and in the future. Too often firms make choices that are based only on improving quarterly or period results without thinking about long-term costs and benefits. These choices merely lead to the postponement of what will become inevitable later. For example, bad choices cause firms to put patches on logistics systems instead of carefully reexamining the entire system. The firm does not run as efficiently as it might in the short term, and the cost of overhauling the entire system is postponed until later when the price of a system reconfiguration has increased.

By now the assessment team has a thorough comprehension of logistics systems and processes. They understand the firm's strategies and the role of logistics in accomplishing the firm's mission. They have developed new ideas and options. They have carefully critiqued those options. They are now in a position to make recommendations that should be acceptable.

Cost projections should be as realistic as possible. These cost projections should be methodically analyzed to ensure accuracy and reasonableness. Care should be taken not to be either overly optimistic or pessimistic. As with most logistics operations, more planning up front will result in better outcomes.

Managerial Recommendations (Step Six)

Once the best options are subjected to a thorough cost–benefit analysis and the results are carefully verified, the final recommendations are developed. The assessment team has quantified each of the options and determined their impact on the logistics system and the entire firm. All project results are presented to top management. Care should be taken to format the recommendations appropriately. Information presented to top management should be clear and easily understood. The structure or method of presentation should not detract from the substance of the presentation. It is important that top management view the team's efforts as being helpful. Inappropriately formatted recommendations may consist of good ideas, but they could end up being rejected if the substance of the recommendations is not easily accessible to management. The assessment team should try to hit top management's "hot buttons." If the recommendations fully address the current concerns of top management, it is much more likely that they will be adopted.

Before any tentative or final recommendations are presented, management should be kept informed and continually updated about the assessment process. This strategy will help to ensure that management is not "blind-sided." It will also allow the team to better channel their efforts. If some recommendations are likely to be rejected because of management perceptions about their inability to fit in with the strategic mission or planned actions of which the assessment team may not be aware, those recommendations should be adjusted after learning of these discrepancies.

Establishment of Implementation Plan (Step Seven)

After the recommendations have been developed, a managerial plan is put together. The purpose of the managerial plan is to guide the implementation of the recommendations produced by the assessment team. The managerial plan should include a statement about the project objectives. The objectives should be stated clearly and typically they include specific cost and service goals to be accomplished within a set period of time. Clear objectives should result in a well-planned logistics system that can be executed.

A statement of time and resource constraints is also contained in the managerial plan. An understanding of time and resource constraints defines the boundaries of the implementation process. This understanding assists in ensuring that implementation of overly optimistic plans is not attempted. A statement of constraints allows the team to have a grasp of the overall effort required. It provides a sense of perspective on the project.

Another important aspect of the managerial plan is the development of measurement standards to be applied to the project throughout the implementation process. These standards apply structure to the implementation process and will provide regular information about the success of the process. Measurement standards should be held constant throughout the implementation process. Adjustment of measurement standards halfway through the project is likely to disrupt the implementation process.

The managerial plan includes a breakdown of the implementation tasks with anticipated resource usage and time commitments. Milestones by which progress is measured are set. Failure to reach a milestone by a specified date results in that milestone being flagged and the reasons for failure examined. A commercial project management software package may be helpful at this point. Many project management software packages designed to run on microcomputers are available at a reasonable cost (see Appendix A).

Feedback Loop

A comprehensive assessment is really never complete. It is a dynamic process that should become a regular part of ongoing logistics management planning. A continuous feedback loop provides a mechanism by which the assessment process can be updated.

NEXT STEPS

Following a comprehensive assessment, the logistics organization is faced with having to get the rest of the organization to accept its recommendations. It may also be necessary to gain support from customers and suppliers. Unfortunately, the change process is not easy.

The type of skepticism that can be expected as one tries to implement change is discussed next. Change management is a difficult process, but good ideas that should be adopted can be implemented if the innovation diffusion process is executed correctly.

Notes

1. Shoshanna Zuboff, *In the Age of the Smart Machine: The Future of Work and Power* (New York: Basic Books, 1988).

2. Mary Walton, *The Deming Management Method* (New York: Perigee Books, 1986).

3. William P. Leonard, *The Management Audit: An Appraisal of Management Methods and Performance* (Englewood Cliffs, N.J.: Prentice-Hall, 1962).

4. Peter F. Drucker, "The Coming of the New Organization," *Harvard Business Review* 66:1 (January–February 1988): 45–53.

5. Mary Walton, *The Deming Management Method*.

6. Robert C. Camp, *Benchmarking: The Search for Industry Best Practices That Lead to Superior Performance* (Milwaukee: ASQC Quality Press, 1989).

Moving the Mountain

CHARLIE was convinced something had to be done—and he had a pretty good idea of what it was. Charlie thought back to what Bob had said: ". . . the numbers tell you that Universal is our main rival. Every guy in the office will tell you Universal is our main rival. But I'm telling you that they're not." Charlie recalled that when he had spoken with "every guy in the office," it had indeed been the case that everyone had named Universal. In fact, only one other person had even alluded to Special. If we can't even agree as to what is going on, thought Charlie, how are we going to agree as to what to do about it? Charlie grimaced as the thought occurred to him that the various departments in his own company probably spent more time competing among one another than they did competing with either Universal or Special!

Charlie knew that a few largely cosmetic changes would not suffice. It was going to take major change to position the company for the future. A truly revolutionary and fundamental change was going to be necessary. Charlie thought of the feedback he had received so far to what he felt were modest ideas and suggestions. He reflected on the "red flag" words he had spoken unwittingly, and on the reactions he had encountered.

"we have to be faster . . . we have to be more flexible . . . we have to get it right the first time"

When this comment was floated, everyone agreed! In fact, many were positively enthusiastic! However, the more Charlie thought about it, the more he realized that people were merely agreeing to a "motherhood and apple pie" kind of statement. Every time Charlie had tried to put some number, some measurement parameter on the statement, the conversation quickly disintegrated.

Different departments had substantially different criteria to determine what was "fast," "flexible," and "right." Furthermore, being "fast" in one department could automatically create an enormous bottleneck in another department! Charlie worried about what each of these key words *meant* to the people involved. Nowhere did "fast" mean *today,* "flexible" mean *no problem,* and "right" mean *100 percent.* Indeed, on-time perfectionism seemed to be frightening and irritating to many—or, at least, what it took to be an on-time perfectionist seemed to be perceived as irritatingly aggressive nitpicking.

Charlie recalled the stories he heard about this production manager that had been brought in a while back. "He was never satisfied" was the comment Charlie heard the most, and that comment was always said in a derisive fashion. Apparently, he had pushed other managers for changes— pushed too hard. He was never in his office, and once he showed up at a meeting with grease on his hands. Apparently, he was unsuccessful at getting things done. "Can you imagine? That aggressive SOB tried to tell me what to do. I told him to get his own place fixed up first. When he can fix his own numbers, then he'll have proved that he has something to tell me." So went a common story. No one liked him, except, Charlie recalled, some of the guys who actually worked on the floor. Even they didn't so much seem to like him as one would like a buddy, but rather they seemed to talk with a great deal of pride about *themselves* when they talked about *him.* No one knew whether the guy had left or whether he had been told to leave. Bob seemed to be the only one who knew where the guy was now—in charge of production at Special. The guy was one of the five guys who ran that company.

"we have to delight our customers . . . satisfying them is not enough"

This comment also led to an echo of widespread agreement and enthusiasm! The only trouble was that most managers seemed to think that customers *were* satisfied. Indeed, stories about "delighted" customers were frequently offered for consideration. Bob's comments were extremely pessimistic in comparison, yet Charlie knew that Bob was not a pessimist. And Bob *was* the top account manager! Also, Charlie recalled, there seemed to be quite a proportion of "unreasonable" customers who were always on the phone complaining. "These guys are always on the phone: where's their order, how come this and that was missing, this carton arrived damaged, and so on and so on . . ." was what Charlie remembered hearing.

Charlie began to wonder why no one was tracking complaints. The sales representatives were expected to handle some of the complaints, but complainers were also calling shipping, production, accounting, in fact, virtually all departments. What was their total number, and what were the complaints about? No one seemed to know exactly. Charlie did know how many reached the CEO's office because it was a secretary's job to answer letters with one of six form letter replies and then pass the complaint on to the "correct" department. This secretary had actually kept a record of the people to whom letters had been sent, but had no compilation of what the complaints were about or what was done to correct them. Charlie began to wonder if "unreasonable" customers were simply going elsewhere with their business.

Another problem was that different people seemed to believe that different actions were required to satisfy customers. Production thought keeping the price low through long runs was the most important aspect of servicing customers. Sales, on the other hand, never gave a thought to production runs and according to production seemed to think that inventory would appear from nowhere. Sales complained that production just didn't understand customers: "They're not the ones who have to talk to these guys." Logistics often found themselves in the middle.

"change the way we're organized"

This one really got people's goat. "Not again" was a common reaction, followed by long horror stories about what happened "last time." Charlie heard endless stories about what "my department" had gained or lost. Invariably, what was gained was now being handled much better than before and what was lost was being handled much worse than before by others. However, Charlie got the impression that what happened "last time," or, as many had specified, "the last six times," was only part of the story. The rest of the story, which was never spoken, concerned individual power and careers.

People were afraid of losing power! Managers had their little fiefdoms, and the bigger they became, the more power they had. And the more they got paid. Charlie thought hard if anyone had ever been promoted to a position where he or she had fewer people or fewer functions to "manage." Moving up the ladder—what did it really mean? A bigger office? An office with a corner window? An office that was furthest removed from the actual value-added activities performed by the company? A private secretary? A better parking space?

People were also concerned about their careers. Some seemed afraid of losing their jobs. Rumors about what had happened at other companies spread throughout the firm. How can you move up if you've lost your job and are now competing with hundreds of others who have also lost theirs? Even if you keep your job, how can you move up, when the "up" has been reduced by 50 percent?

And it was not only the way people were organized that caused an uproar! Suggestions as to hooking up computers caused some problems, too. It seemed that each department's computer requirements were so unique that others couldn't possibly "understand." In fact, according to several departments, even MIS didn't "understand." In any event, it appeared that MIS worked only for accounting, or so other departments complained: "They're real good at payroll and billing . . . well, most of the billing gets out in a reasonable time." Meanwhile, accounting wasn't too happy with MIS either. And MIS complained that it was grossly understaffed, and couldn't possibly keep up with the numerous "special" requests. Such special requests represented about a two-year backlog of work.

Departments didn't understand why MIS had all the data, and yet couldn't produce the information *they* wanted. Certainly, MIS had records of every transaction—why couldn't they produce a list of all customers of a certain type in Atlanta? The net result was that departments created their own information. Indeed, some individuals created software which they didn't even want to share with others in the same department! Charlie began to really understand what the old saying "information is power" meant in the computer age. Charlie tried to get a handle on what the obstacles really were.

In many companies, it is an open secret that things are not quite right. Managers and employees may be very aware that the firm is being beaten by the competition in one or more areas measured by benchmarking. Everyone may even agree that "something has to be done!" Then why is it so difficult to institute real change?

When a firm decides it is time to revamp its logistical system, management can anticipate that the plan will be met with resistance. Following the situational analysis, chances are pretty good that senior management will endorse and support the proposed changes. However, approval of top management alone is not sufficient to institute major changes in a process as comprehensive as logistics. The manager of change can expect resistance.

This chapter addresses six major obstacles to change that one can expect to confront. In fact, these obstacles are interrelated, and addressing any one of them while ignoring the others will probably lead to less than satisfactory results.

The first major obstacle is the *lack of real focus on the customer.* Sometimes, lip service is paid to the customer mission, but somehow this mission is forgotten in the day-to-day activities of the firm. Some managers have not listened to a real customer in years! Dissatisfied complainers are labeled fusspots—and the goal somehow becomes to "get this guy off the phone." Sales representatives' reports are carefully filed in the "black hole," never to be seen again. Many employees have no idea why their job is important in servicing customers.

The second major obstacle is *lack of information that has strategic value*. Many kinds of data are collected—some would say too much for the human mind to comprehend!—but somehow these data are not transformable into the kinds of information that are valuable in decision making. The firm may have vast data sets containing accounting information, and yet the simplest question concerning customers cannot be answered. Somehow customer profile data—other than purchase history—are not collected. Opportunity costs are ignored, and cost accounting data may be incapable of answering today's critical questions.

Related to the lack of the right information for today's environment is the third obstacle: even if the "right" data are available, these data are not always *organized and distributed to facilitate strategic usage*. Traditional hierarchical organizations encourage information hoarding because information is power to a functional area or to an individual. The *least* informed members are often those at the bottom of the hierarchy—and they are often the very people who interface with the customer the most!

The fourth obstacle is the difficulty in *revamping organizational structure and tasks*. A flattening of structure too often means everyone has twice as much of the same work as they had before. Sometimes pay is cut simultaneously. It is no small wonder that reorganizations often result in bitterness! Often, a reorganization of personnel is not accompanied by the reorganization of technology—especially information technology—that would enable people to do a redefined job better.

The fifth obstacle is the *lack of a clear and appropriate strategy and mission*. At least three major dimensions are involved: (1) the "correctness" of the strategy and mission; (2) the clarity with which the details are communicated; and (3) the degree to which the firm rallies. Often, the rationale behind the strategy is disbelieved, the details of the implementation are left to competing functional areas, and the reward structure is such that everyone pretends to rally while actually protecting their own turf.

The sixth obstacle is overcoming the deadly inertia created by the *accepted way of doing things*. Fundamental paradigms about the way things are and the way things should be tend to be dearly held and enduring. The manager of change is *not* starting from zero, but rather from a base of an accepted set of "rules of the game." These rules are often outdated and even dangerously counterproductive in the new competitive environment. Nevertheless, people cling to these rules because a sense of security and certainty is derived from rules that worked in the past.

In the following sections of this chapter, each of these obstacles is discussed in detail, and examples are given. It is important to keep in mind that not each of the six obstacles is equally applicable in every firm. Some may be more important than others, depending on the circumstances. However, all of them *are* interrelated, and thus completely ignoring one will probably be counterproductive. Systematic thinking is necessary!

OVERCOMING A LACK OF CUSTOMER FOCUS

Many companies say they are focused on customers and that they are interested in customer service—but how many act as if they really are? Focusing on the customer means that everyone *in* the firm realizes that the most important person in the firm is the customer *of* the firm. In a customer-focused firm, customers are not an interruption of some other activity. They are the purpose of all activity. This is true for manufacturers, wholesalers, retailers, and for service firms. This is true for profit-oriented firms as well as nonprofit organizations. No firm survives without customers.

In a customer-focused firm, a complainer is not a pain in the neck who is shuffled around until he or she gives up. "The customer is always right" is *not* just a slogan, wearily uttered when convincing the customer that the firm is right has become futile. Some complainers do not give up! Instead, a complainer is looked upon as an important source of feedback—as a spokesperson for the dozens of other people who do not complain to the firm but rather who complain to other customers or who silently withdraw themselves from ever doing business with the company again. Complainers are an *opportunity*—they are telling you what is wrong with the product or service. They may even tell you what you can do to fix it. Anyone who is motivated enough to take the trouble to complain deserves at the very least to be listened to.

Firms that think that complainers are nothing but "fusspots" might do well to remember that one of the reasons that Japanese and German firms pay so much attention to quality is that their domestic customers are among the "fussiest" in the world. The quality and service specifications that are demanded by these firms often stun potential suppliers. Some have charged that such specifications are designed to keep certain suppliers out of the bidding. Suppliers can complain that the specifications are unnecessarily stringent if they so choose, but there is little to be gained by complaining in this case—contracts will go to the suppliers who can perform.

In a customer-focused firm, customer satisfaction and dissatisfaction, as well as other forms of customer input, are measured in a multitude of ways.[1] Customer input during the design of a product or service can limit the need for expensive changes at later stages in the development cycle. Complaints and other communications from customers should be tracked and compiled for cross-reference. The results of such tracking can be used both to stimulate continuous improvement of the product or service and to evaluate how well the firm is doing in terms of customer satisfaction. Customer surveys should be conducted regularly. The objective is to make it easy for customers "to reach out and touch" the firm. Service firms that provide "disguised" customer contacts can be commissioned to find out how customers are being treated on a variety of specific fronts.

Sales representative reports should not merely be filed. Once again, cross-referencing information from the men and women "in the trenches" can provide valuable information. And in a customer-focused firm, the sales representatives are not the only ones "in the trenches"! Managers at all levels and from every area of the firm need to spend time with real customers. If product researchers and technicians spend time in the customers' plants, they will develop a clearer idea of the problems and opportunities facing these customers. For example, consider the case of Detroit Diesel Corporation, long a money-losing maker of truck engines under General Motors. In 1987, a new management instituted a policy requiring that all managers and distributors contact at least four customers per day. The distributors' employees were invited to visit the new parts distribution center in Ohio. The result was 250 suggestions for improvements. Delivery time was cut from 5 to 3 days and 24-hour emergency delivery was instituted. By 1989 Diesel's market share doubled from 3 to 6 percent and profits were $21 million on sales of $971 million.

In customer-focused firms, customers buy what they really want.

They are not sold what a firm desires to sell them. Customers are delivered goods according to their schedules, not when it is convenient for the firm to deliver. Finally, customers are not "abandoned" once a sale is finalized. Rather, all members of a firm recognize the responsibility for after-sales service. The customer should be delighted at every interface with the firm—before the sale, during the sale, and after the sale. Customers buy a product or service in order to use it, and thus the firm has a stake in the entire usage experience. It is one thing to ask the customer if he or she is satisfied with the new car one month after buying it, but it is another thing to ask the same question when the car is being sold or traded in. Customers, potential customers, and anyone else with whom the customer-focused firm happens to come in contact, all should be treated with courtesy and respect, because that is the way a business is built in the long run.

In some companies, the stated mission of customer service is "accepted," and everyone pays lip service to this ideal. However, when it comes to actual implementation of this mission, the results are far less than ideal. For example, say the words "customer service," and invariably the idea of a toll-free number comes up. In theory, an 800 number appears to be a good idea: operators can help customers assemble or use the products, they can answer customer questions and generate sales leads, they can take orders for customers, they can track the location of the customers' orders in the logistics pipeline, and so on. Indeed, operators can do lots of things, depending on the purpose of the 800 number. Or can they? In many cases, a customer calling an 800 number is disappointed. The result is a recorded commercial, or an operator who cannot answer basic questions about the product or service. Such a situation may be worse than not having an 800 number. The customer's expectations can be raised and then dashed. The first interface with the firm can be, *from the customer's point of view,* an extremely negative experience. "If they can't even answer that simple question," asks the customer, "what will happen if I actually deal with them?"

Although most of this discussion about the importance of customers should be obvious to an experienced executive, the fact of the matter is that firms can lose touch. Managers at all levels can become so involved in the day-to-day problems of running an enterprise that they fail to remember why the firm exists as well as the importance of maintaining deep involvement with their customer base.

The first obstacle to instituting logistical change is to reverse this mind-set of neglecting the customer. All managers and employees must revamp their thinking about how customers are satisfied. Careful analysis can clearly delineate the important role that logistics plays in a customer service delivery system. Data collected during the situational analysis will help in benchmarking just how well the firm is doing in comparison to its main competitors. It is essential that a new spirit of commitment to customers be instilled throughout the organization as a prerequisite to instituting meaningful change.

COLLECTING THE RIGHT INFORMATION: WHAT INFORMATION HAS STRATEGIC VALUE?

In many companies, basic information about customer satisfaction or dissatisfaction, including complaints, is not compiled. In fact, only one out of five firms conducts a regular assessment of its performance as viewed by its customers. But the problem is far more serious than the failure to compile data. In many companies, basic profitability profiles of customers or groups of customers are essentially unavailable. Managers may have no idea how much money it costs to lose a customer, although they often can predict what will be lost in terms of sales. On the flip side, managers often do not know how much it is costing them to hold on to a customer! Not all customers are profitable! Finally, how much does it cost to obtain a particular customer or a particular segment of customers?

In general, much of the data collected by firms is intimately tied to their accounting systems. However, the type of data collected in such a system, such as accounting cost data, is essentially backward accounting. Cost data and such measures as return on investment (ROI) do not capture the essential dimensions underlying success in today's competitive environment. For example:

- What is the return on a "delighted customer"? What is the value of a repeat customer? What is the value of an absolutely loyal customer?
- What is the return on "being first"? What is the comparative return of being second? Third? Last? What is the return of cutting new product (or new process) development time from, say four to two years?
- What is the value of a lost opportunity?
- What is the value of quality in a product or service? What is the comparative value of being perceived as second in quality? Third? Last?
- What is the value of "being the cheapest"?

To these general questions one could add an endless list of specific concerns. What is the value of "we can deliver Monday" versus "we'll be there at the beginning of the week"? What is the value of 90-percent correct orders versus all perfect orders? To every one of these questions beginning with "What is the value . . .", a corresponding question can be constructed beginning with "What is the cost . . . ?".

Another problem with accounting data is that costs are often arbitrarily assigned.[2] Thus, even if an attempt is made to answer fundamentally important questions using such data, one is apt to get the "wrong" answer.[3] The principles of current cost accounting were established following passage of the Securities Exchange Act of 1934. For example, during the 1930s, labor was the most significant component of variable cost. Today labor typically accounts for anywhere from 4 to 12 percent of total production cost. Some companies have eliminated labor as a separate major cost category.

The major problem is that various manageable costs are lumped together under "overhead." Overhead in some situations ranges from 50 to 55 percent of production costs. Across a product line, the various items that a firm manufactures are priced by averaging the costs of all items in the line. This leaves the firm vulnerable to any competitor who produces a limited line of the most popular products, because large volumes can then be discounted. Moreover, because of accounting conventions, firms frequently have no idea what any particular product costs to produce or what logistics costs are associated with a particular product. Assigning all relevant and direct costs to specific products is the only way of knowing which products contribute which profit margins. Assessing cost estimates over the life of a product may provide a better picture of what is really happening than assigning costs over a prespecified payback period. Assessing activity-based costs (ABC) to the services performed or assessing costs on the basis of time spent might so radically change the "perceived cost structure" of a firm that management may consider the newly developed accounting guidelines as competitive weapons. Revelations can identify average production costs that are off by as much as 60 percent, resulting in outsourcing that was not justified or the failure to outsource products or services that should have been.

Are inventories assets or liabilities? The "accountant's" answer is well known, but large inventories can be liabilities even if they are not obsolete. Large inventories can mask inefficiency and delay the detection of defects. Inventories tie up money and absorb time. They are sunk costs.

Furthermore, the costs of keeping large inventories do not include the opportunity costs of *not* investing in the information technology that has the capability of reducing inventory because it can provide superior information to the firm without detriment to customer service levels. What is the value of faster flow-through? How should the investments in process technology or other assets be costed? One of the main areas of potential time savings is in the time spent in storage, handling, transportation, packing, and so on. It is a growing reality that more critical time can be saved in the logistics process than in most production processes.[4]

To illustrate, consider the case of the $80,000 laser that was projected to save $4,000 per year in labor costs.[5] At Rockwell International, the decision to implement this laser was "sold" on the basis that the laser would save $200,000 per year in inventory-holding costs by reducing a two-week bottleneck to a ten-minute process. This costing does not fully credit improvements in product quality and faster overall work flow. Many process innovations, such as automation, show up as easy-to-measure costs. Their benefits are difficult to measure because they transcend many areas in terms of increased speed, flexibility, and quality.

Even the accounting practices related to an item as basic as a personal computer or a piece of software are suspect. How much should a firm be willing to pay to join the information age, when the price of *not* joining may be the very survival of the firm? How much should a firm pay for *speed*? For *flexibility*? For *quality*? For *customer service*? How much is substantial competitive advantage worth? How much does it cost to halt production, or to rework, or to scrap a product or a process when other costs such as interest expenses continue regardless?

Actually, managers were not trained to think in terms of total cost and systems technology. The fact that the traditional accounting procedures and systems fail to capture critical information is a real obstacle to implementation of logistical change. It is essential that those proposing change be able to demonstrate what the true total cost of current logistics is and what the cost reduction and containment opportunities really are. Only if total cost is fully understood will a firm's management be able to address the more difficult questions related to benefits and risks associated with innovative logistics practice. Whereas stimulating a renewed commitment to customer satisfaction involves revitalizing a mind set (Obstacle 1), knowing what the right information is in terms of accurate process accounting is an educational process. Unless this educational mission is accomplished, meaningful cross-functional change will not occur.

ORGANIZING AND DISTRIBUTING INFORMATION

One significant gap in many firms is that even available data are not organized into information to facilitate decision making, to enable enhanced customer service, to empower employees with greater responsibilities and ownership of their role in the firm, or to do anything but permit customer billing and other accounting functions. The fact of the matter is that even customer billing falls short of being a high-quality process. Manufacturers of grocery items, for example, are generally experiencing nearly 50-percent error rates on customer invoices. A related problem is that data organized for the use of one functional area may not even be accessible by the computers in another functional area. The reasons vary from structuring data files in ways that discourage data sorts to computers that cannot talk to one another. The overall problem is compounded when the firm tries to set up electronic linkages with suppliers, customers, service providers, banks, or with an other parties of interest.

Another problem concerns the distribution of the information to the people who need it for day-to-day management. Exactly who needs to know the time that a particular product spends in a particular manufacturing process, the time a product spends in a particular part of the logistics stream, or the characteristics of the customers that a particular product is targeted toward? The traditional answers focus on the identification of the appropriate function because the firm was typically structured around functional areas that were organized hierarchically. Information was often collected and jealously guarded by functional areas, with little sharing across areas and even less sharing across firms. Information enhanced the power of a functional area or of an individual. Management and unions were often on opposing sides of information "wars," with unions frequently complaining that management was withholding crucial facts. Salespeople often spent much time tracking down information on customers' orders—it helped to know "someone in production." Often, the people at the bottom of the organizational totem pole had the *least* information, and they were the people who interfaced with customers the *most*—or who *actually* assembled the product—or who *actually* had to locate products in warehouses. In today's flat organizational structures, such an organization of information can be suicide.

A fact that all managers must understand is that the purchase of high-powered computer programs will not guarantee high-quality information that is appropriately organized and distributed throughout the firm. The history of technology adoption has been dominated by installing particular devices to help people do traditional jobs better. As a result of this job focus, databases tend to mirror the "smoke stack structure" of a typical enterprise. Data are not organized and distributed to facilitate cross-functional process management in such areas as logistics. And data are not organized, formatted, and distributed to facilitate the implementation of a customer service mission in today's flat organization. For example, how quickly can a trend be identified from a 100-page printout?

Where a firm stands in terms of its information system capability should be well documented following the logistical situation analysis. In most cases, the situational analysis will highlight deficiencies that confront implementation of strategic logistics. Obstacle 3 is real and involves much more to overcome than revitalizing attitudes toward customers (Obstacle 1) or even educating management and employees concerning costs (Obstacle 2). Even if everyone agrees what should be done to upgrade the quality of correctly organized information, the development time may span years.

Given a realistic assessment of the firm's information system competency, an implementation plan for logistical sophistication can be developed that does not get the "cart ahead of the horse." All executives must fully understand the time required to develop the systems necessary to support leading-edge logistical performance. A safe rule of thumb is to double the time estimates of systems development personnel and then to avoid underestimating training and organizational changes necessary to implement the new information technologies.

REVAMPING THE STRUCTURE OF THE ORGANIZATION AND OF WORK TASKS

Organizational structure is a subject near and dear to most managers. The reason is simple: a manager's span of control and organization level are directly related to his or her personal compensation. Many aspects of technology adoption require that the structure of the organization and the content of tasks be modified to fully exploit the new potential. Organizational change is a difficult process. However, every day we hear about flatter, leaner, and meaner organization structures. Many experts feel that more than adequate technology exists to drive continuous improvement of business processes well into the twenty-first century.[6] The real barrier or obstacle is to change the way in which organizations are structured in order to facilitate technology implementation, and to reap the real benefits thereof.

In many firms, the organizational chart that appeared as a tree diagram was always a fiction. Most managers understood that the real sources of power, and the real reward system, were hidden. The tree often implied that tasks were organized along distinct hierarchical functional areas. However, a flat organizational structure does not necessarily mean that the real sources of power or the real reward system suddenly become transparent. Nor does a flat structure mean that the basic activities of the firm are integrated rather than separated. Furthermore, the real power structure, the real reward system, and the deep-seated traditions of organizing tasks in certain ways frequently act to make the transformation from a tall hierarchical organization to a flat organization extremely difficult. Finally, a reorganization of structure without the corresponding reorganization of information (and a rethinking of its distribution) will probably be counterproductive.

There are many motivations for reorganizing organizations or activities (and often the two go together):

- refocusing on customer service;
- cutting costs by cutting labor;
- reducing raw materials, work in process, and finished goods inventories;
- faster cycle times (in order processing, in billing, in production setup time, in flexible manufacturing, in logistics, in product or process development, etc.);
- higher productivity;
- preempting or responding to the competition;
- improving quality.

Reorganizations can also be driven by such forces as technology advances or fear of bankruptcy. Reorganizations can be all-pervasive or they can be minor in effect on the prevailing status quo. For example, one seemingly minor effect of Statistical Quality Control systems is that they invariably increase the number of machine operators and decrease the number of people who "fix" mistakes, such as inspectors.[7] Finally, reorganizations can be implemented in an abrupt, discontinuous manner or they can be introduced step by step. Radical changes such as switching the currency of an entire country (East Germany) or switching the driving lane from left to right are best accomplished in an extremely short time period. However, moving toward a completely automated factory usually involves first simplifying and restructuring the shop floor, which is not necessarily related to technology at all. This first step must be done right if the ultimate automation is going to achieve its expectations.[8]

Regardless of motivation, restructuring often results in two things. First, organizations become flatter because fewer managers are needed to command and control and to gather and process information in the information age. Second, lower-level employees are empowered with decision-making responsibilities that they did not have before. Of course, these are the "ideal" results, as stated by top managers. Realistically, this is often not achieved in all cutbacks—often managers and employees just work longer and harder at the very things they were doing before the so-called reorganization. Past experiences of this type often harden the resistance to change, and make the attainment of the ideal restructuring results more difficult. Under true reorganization, the tasks and authority of both managers and lower-level employees will change. Thus, the goals must be clearly communicated, and training at all levels is essential. For example, some of the traditional control functions can be taken over by computers rather than being performed by managers, and more authority can be vested in lower-level employees who are backed by these same computers.

Many of the trends highlighted in Chapter Two boil down to reorganizing the basic way in which work is done. If in fact we are experiencing the "coming of the information age," it is essential that managers begin to think in terms of process management.[9] Logistics as a process is boundary spanning in that it cuts across an organization and facilitates product and material flow from vendors to customers.[10] When customer service is the real focus and new technologies are implemented to facilitate the logistical process, it is likely that traditional ways of working will need to be rethought and changed. This is true for *all* members of the firm. Failure to accommodate the requirements of the new technology will tend to reduce the level of obtainable benefits. Obstacle 4 is concerned with changing how a firm manages a process to fully exploit new concepts and technology. If a firm retrofits a new technology to an old procedure, it is possible that some benefits will result. However, if the procedure is modified to exploit the technology, it is more likely that significant breakthroughs will occur in terms of effectiveness and efficiency. Obstacle 4 is concerned with developing a widespread change in mind-set about how to do things.

CLARITY IN STRATEGY AND MISSION

One of the main problems that underlies all of the first four obstacles is that top management often does not have a clear sense of strategy and mission, or if it does, the strategy and mission are not clearly communicated to employees, suppliers, and customers. Furthermore, strategies and missions are often devoid of statements as to how they are to be implemented or realized. Brilliant implementation has enormous strategic competitive advantages, and yet the "how to" is often left to managers or employees in various functional areas to figure out as best they can. If these functional areas are individual fiefdoms, the actual implementation of even the most appropriate strategy could be disastrous. Each functional area can "ride off furiously," and indeed even meet its individual targets, but the overall effect could be one of four (or more) horses reined together and pulling in four (or more) different directions.

An important problem occurs when the strategy, mission, or implementation strategy is not communicated or is miscommunicated or outright disbelieved. It is pointless to "reorganize for efficiency" and to communicate the slogan "lean and mean fighting machine" to employees if they believe that the only thing that is going to be mean is the company attitude toward them and the only thing that is going to be lean is their paycheck. Under such circumstances, "protecting our markets" will be translated as "protecting my job or my career" and "expanding our markets" will be translated as "keeping my eyes open for a new job opportunity."

Once a strategy, mission, or implementation strategy is communicated to all employees, and is correctly understood, it is important that the total organization rally round the strategy. One way to do this is to structure the reward system to encourage movement toward the desired end results. This type of reward or incentive restructure is easy to talk about but difficult to mobilize. Likewise it is difficult for function-oriented expenditures to result in a commitment to integrative management. Getting the job done faster, getting it done right, and being flexible in doing it cannot be accomplished if pieces of the strategy are implemented in such a manner that momentum is lost.

The above assumes that top management is already behind the strategy, mission, and implementation strategy. A completely different problem is faced by a top manager who is the lone voice in championing a radical departure from the status quo—the more radical the departure, the more difficult it will be to get others to agree to it. Sometimes, when the firm is facing a crisis that threatens its very survival, it is easier to convince middle managers that radical change is necessary. But most of the time, even in crisis situations, people tend to prefer familiar paths. Why would what worked in the past not work in the future? "Don't fix it if it ain't broke." This type of built-in resistance is the prime reason that the ratchet effect can frequently be observed in organizational change histories. The typical pattern is long periods of stability followed by brief bursts of radical change until a new equilibrium is established. Brief periods of radical change are often characterized by outsiders being brought in during crisis situations. For example, consider the influence of Lee Iacocca at Chrysler and David Johnson at Campbell Soup Company.

A problem of a different sort occurs when the strategy itself is wrong. For example, Wickham Skinner, Professor of Manufacturing at the Harvard Business School, estimates that no more than 20 percent of a manufacturer's competitive advantage derives from cutting waste and inefficiency, replacing people with machines, and other traditional cost-cutting measures.[11] In an interview in the *Wall Street Journal,* W. Edwards Deming claims that the very goals of most American firms are wrong.[12] These misguided goals include "staying ahead of the competition." Deming points out that the most crucial mistakes cannot be fixed with automation. For example, plants close because they were producing products with insufficient markets and savings and loans close because their officers were making bad loans. Whether one agrees or disagrees with all of what Deming is saying, he does reemphasize that doing things *right* is virtually pointless if the *right* things are not being done.

The question of clarity and full understanding of a strategy is the real issue in the implementation of logistical change. Following a successful analysis, the groundwork is complete for launching a revitalized logistics initiative. However, some doubt might still exist on the part of senior management concerning the full ramifications of the new logistics strategy. The key to overcoming this potential fifth obstacle is to be sure that the strategic perspective is broader than a drive to cut costs. Leadership is key. A logistics strategic initiative is properly positioned when it seeks to use logistics competency to gain and maintain customer loyalty and therefore competitive advantage. Failure to understand the focus of proactive logistics can result in widespread belief that the prime objective is to cut costs. This misconception will lead to a general failure to focus on the key elements of required change and to relegate emphasis to cost control. Care must be taken to assure that the thrust and mission of the strategy are fully understood and disseminated.

CHALLENGING THE "ACCEPTED" WAYS OF DOING THINGS

The accepted ways of doing things, and the motivations for doing them, permeate every type of organization. These include the accepted ways of saving costs, looking at competitors, managing workers, and managing change. For example:

Traditional Motivations	*The Not So Traditional*
■ automate to cut costs (especially labor costs)	■ automate to keep or win customers; to cut lead times; to reduce inventories; to increase flexibility
■ boost productivity by laying off workers or closing plants, or both	■ boost productivity by automating and computerizing; by retraining workers
■ cut waste; replace people with machines	■ improve control over flows; manage people better; invest in equipment and process technologies

Fully 80 percent of a manufacturer's competitive advantage comes from the list on the right, and yet many companies are focusing on the list on the left.[13]

Many of the rules of the game *have* changed. What do long production runs mean when "farm to table" is four months, of which less than seventeen minutes are spent in actual factory production? What does automation mean when the only thing that changes is that all the mistakes are automated and are now made a lot faster? Almost every office has a sign hanging somewhere which says, "to err is human, but to really screw things up you need a computer."

Generally, it is very difficult to change fundamental paradigms about the way things are and the way things should be. For example, many Americans believe that Japan only copies others and that the Japanese are neither "creative" nor innovators. Nothing could be further from the truth.[14] In fact this myth is extremely destructive, because as a consequence American companies frequently do not pay sufficient attention to new products and processes originating outside the United States.[15] Even worse, Japanese competitors or other foreign competitors are often not taken seriously. The president of Canon stated openly and directly that Xerox could have stopped the onslaught of Japanese competition—before it almost became too late. Many companies who believe that their industry is immune from foreign competition due to, for example, high transportation costs, are conceptualizing competition using obsolete assumptions. Transportation cost advantages can be nullified simply by transplanting production to the United States—and the Japanese have the perseverance to absorb years of losses from such initiatives until a beachhead in the targeted market is established.

The long-term view of the Japanese is well known. However, many firms in the United States do not seem to have learned from this lesson. For reasons as diverse as the demands of the financial markets to the desire of managers to make their mark as quickly as possible before they move on to another assignment, many companies have a very short-term orientation. At a recent seminar, a Japanese executive presented a 50-year "plan" for the Chinese motorcycle market. Related to the long-term view is the attitude that *small, constant improvements* lead to substantial advantages in the long run. Being patient, persistent, and striving for the constantly moving target of perfection is a stance that has little appeal to many managers with a "home run" mentality.

In many United States companies, workers are still considered as cogs in a wheel. In contrast, in many Japanese companies workers are constantly suggesting ways to improve products and processes—and they are much more frequently listened to and well treated as associates. The pay gap between top managers and workers is also far less than that in the United States. In the new flat organizations of tomorrow, workers will need to be trained—and retrained. The value of those who actually do the work cannot be underestimated or discounted. Everyone, including managers, will have to be constantly learning, because things will be constantly changing. Furthermore, new ways to motivate all members of the firm must be found. Greater control over the work done, raises or bonuses tied clearly to performance, and greater autonomy from hierarchical control can be motivators as well as business necessities in today's turbulent environment.

Logistics, one of the oldest and most traditional processes in an enterprise, has the potential to be stereotyped in terms of traditional work practices. The fact that every firm has always had to perform the basic logistics function to survive creates a real obstacle to instituting change. The manager of logistics change can expect to confront the "This is the way we have always done it" obstacle at many different points along the way. The only way to change the mind-set of others is to educate them and encourage patience, persistence, and a long-term perspective. This mind-set requires a dedication to fundamentals and a commitment to continuous improvement.

SUMMARY

Not only have the rules changed, but also the competitive situation today quickly punishes those who do not change. Change must be accepted. In some firms, change has been welcome. Leading-edge companies see in change not an enemy to be beaten, but a potential friend. Those who adopt new processes quickly have a distinct competitive advantage. Certain basics are likely to become even more important in the near future, especially the desire for speed, quality, and flexibility.

Why then is it so difficult to change things? It is difficult even if everyone agrees that things have to change! Several potential obstacles were highlighted in this chapter. It is difficult to obtain true commitment as contrasted to lip service. It is difficult to know what the right information is, how to collect it, and to whom it should be disseminated. Decisions about strategy and structure are difficult to make and difficult to implement. There is a great deal of entropy in most organizations when it comes to changing fundamental ways of thinking, and implementing change is inevitably met with resistance.

A serious crisis certainly helps to break through the inertia. However, managing crisis-induced change is not the desired way of managing change for obvious reasons. Yet, in the United States today, fundamental changes seem to come about primarily because of an internally or externally induced "crisis." Takeovers induce change! Recessions induce change! Change becomes a reaction to pain. Tomorrow's successful companies must realize that many potentially fatal diseases are initially painless, and that change is a preventative measure rather than a cure. Change should be proactively and creatively managed! The challenge of the logistics change agent is to dynamically induce new and better ways into one of the oldest and most traditional functional areas of a firm.

Notes

1. Stephen Phillips and Amy Dunkin, "King Customer," *Business Week,* (March 12, 1990): 88–94.

2. Otis Port, "How the New Math of Productivity Adds Up," *Business Week* (June 6, 1988): 103–105, 108ff.

3. Peter Drucker, "The Emerging Theory of Manufacturing," *Harvard Business Review* 68, 3 (May–June 1990): 94–102.

4. Gene R. Tyndall, "We Must Manage Change Before it Manages Us," *Marketing News* 24,3 (February 5, 1990): 14.

5. Gregory L. Miles, "Selling Rockwell on Automation," *Business Week* (June 6, 1988): 104.

6. Charles M. Savage, *5th Generation Management* (Maynard, Mass.: Digital Press, 1990).

7. Drucker, "Emerging Theory," *Harvard Business Review* 68, 3 (May–June 1990): 94–102.

8. Otis Port, "Smart factories: America's future?" *Business Week,* (May 8, 1989): 142–148.

9. Peter Drucker, "The Coming of the New Organization," *Harvard Business Review* 66, 1 (January–February 1988): 45–53.

10. Donald J. Bowersox, "The Strategic Benefits of Logistics Alliances," *Harvard Business Review* 68, 4 (July–August 1990): 36–45.

11. Port, "The New Math," pp. 103–105, 108ff.

12. "An Interview with Edwards Deming," *Wall Street Journal* (June 4, 1990): R39.

13. Port, "The New Math," pp. 103–105, 108ff.

14. S. Tatsuno, *Created in Japan: From Imitators to World Class Innovators* (New York: Ballinger, 1990).

15. David Montgomery, "Understanding the Japanese as Customers, Competitors, and Collaborators," *Japan and The World Economy: A Journal of Theory and Policy* (1991): forthcoming.

The Keys to Success

AS CHARLIE thought about the obstacles that confronted him, he sometimes got discouraged. He knew that he was perceived as power hungry by some, and just plain misguided or idealistic by others. The battle lines had been drawn, and Charlie found himself a target in everybody's rifle scope. Of course, everybody had a different reason for targeting him, but that alone was not very reassuring. Charlie seriously contemplated looking for another position. He didn't know how much longer he could take this level of frustration.

Suddenly things began to move. First, Randy Good started to throw his weight behind Charlie. This helped enormously because the levels of conflict and outright hostility were immediately reduced. Charlie began to feel that others were giving him a fair hearing and they were not actively trying to sabotage him. Glimmers of cooperation began to surface. Second, Super, their largest customer, wanted to jointly evaluate the potential of an operating alliance. They were talking about modifying how the two firms do business together in an effort to both benefit from a closer working relationship. This seemed nothing short of a miracle—what timing!!

Within days, a logistics steering committee was set up, and their mandate from Randy was to "get the show on the road." The composition of the committee sent a clear message to everyone in the firm. Top managers from key departments were chosen, and Randy made it clear that he expected both a blueprint for change and a time table for its implementation within each and every department. "Right now, we have to think in terms of departments, because that's what we've inherited," said Randy, "but when the dust settles, I want everyone thinking in terms of customers, in terms of what we can do to create value for customers. When we do things right, our customers don't think 'Wow, Joe Smith in manufacturing really did his job' and when things go wrong, our customers don't think 'Joe Smith really messed up.' Everything any of us does reflects on our company as a whole— our reputation—and in this dog eat dog environment, our reputation is all we really have. In manufacturing we *do* manufacture products and in accounting we *do* process orders and so on, but no one should ever lose sight of what it is we *really* do. Every second of every day, we either enhance our reputation by creating satisfied customers or we don't. We either deliver value to customers (*not* warehouses) or we don't."

Charlie's group started with a logistics mission statement and plan that were congruent with the company's overall business strategy. They specified a technology evaluation plan and developed a new logistics performance measurement program. In fact, once their mission was specified and the committee was empowered by Randy, Charlie found that it was not as difficult as he had thought to get a commitment to action. One breakthrough came when everyone agreed that value-adding processes had to be accomplished faster and with more accuracy. Then someone had said "Hey, our trucks can only go as fast as the speed limit, and there's a limit to how fast our machines and personnel can work!" Trucks, thought Charlie, we're back to my original list with those damn trucks! As it turned out, those "damn trucks" made everyone realize that they couldn't just do the same things the same way, but faster and more accurately, without hitting inherent "speed limits." Suddenly, everyone was forced to abandon the "faster and better" *platitude,* and deal with the fact that "faster and better" really meant a whole new way of accomplishing the core value-adding activities of the firm. For example, interrelatedness implied the necessity for integration in the timing of flows, in information systems, in performance assessment, etc. Most importantly, the final plan incorporated a way of institutionalizing logistics as a key business process—a way of ensuring that a logistics management mind-set was permanently implanted in "our way of doing our business." This way of looking at logistics as a business process, Charlie realized, was far more important than any particular change that could be made in organizational structure. If successful, it would begin what could amount to permanent change in the way "we do business."

Charlie reviewed the steps required to stimulate real change: CEO support, the composition of the change committee, the focus on customers and value-added processes, clear mission, a specific plan and programs, and so on. Charlie had obtained a commitment to action from the top managers from key departments, but he did not stop there. He realized that to sustain the difficult follow-through, *everyone* from the top down had to be thoroughly convinced that the correct and necessary steps were being taken. "The burden of proof is up to me and the committee," thought Charlie, "and I must dot every 'i' and cross every 't' in this endeavor. No matter how tedious, no one will ever be able to say that I didn't cover all the bases! I have to document every step in great detail." Charlie's goal was to convince even hard core skeptics and jaded survivors of previous attempts at change.

After thorough preparation, the task of building a new logistics initiative must be tackled at a basic level. Several key concepts set the foundation for reevaluating a firm's logistical process.

Organizational structure and practice, as treated here, refer to allocation of financial and human resources to meet specific operating objectives. In this chapter, three critical aspects of successful logistical performance are discussed. First, a number of descriptors of organizational structure are grouped under the heading of *formalization*. The second major design variable is the practice of *measurement*. The third element is *technology* adoption. The objective of this chapter extends beyond describing how formalization, performance measurement, and technology interrelate. These attributes of top-notch performance were introduced in Chapter Three, in which a basic model illustrating how these attributes combine for logistical leadership was presented (Figure 3-1). The three attributes have been isolated as the key contributions to a firm's logistical *flexibility*. The flexibility of a firm is the characteristic which research suggests is the key to achieving leadership. All elements of leadership are defined and described later in the chapter. In fact, the chapter is devoted to showing how and why these attributes are judged to be so important. This chapter is also devoted to assuming the burden of proof—a difficult and often tedious endeavor.

It is assumed that an organization is by and large rational, although to those involved this may not always appear to be the case. Turf battles, gamesmanship, and other political manifestations may affect organizational design and logistical performance of any firm in the short run. The nature of the competitive process dictates that select firms will be better at conducting some activities than other firms. The leading-edge research focused on firms that appeared to have mastered logistics as they entered the 1990s. Thus, the practices that this chapter builds upon are representative of North America's more progressive organizations as identified in the baseline research.[1] These firms include manufacturers, wholesalers, and retailers operating in many different industries.

LINKAGES AMONG FORMALIZATION, PERFORMANCE MEASUREMENT, AND TECHNOLOGY

This section illustrates how formalization, performance measurement, and technology are linked. The discussion is based on a continued analysis of 556 participants in the baseline research. Details about the sampling methodology, measurement of the variables, the statistical tests used, and the results are presented in Appendix C. The goal is to describe linkages among formalization, performance measurement, and technology that can be isolated in leading-edge logistical performers. In the first part of the section, formalization and performance measurement are discussed. In the second and third parts, formalization and technology linkages as well as performance measurement and technology linkages are discussed, respectively.

Formalization and Performance Measurement

Table 6-1 summarizes results of linking formalization and performance measurement. An "x" in this table, and in all subsequent tables, indicates pairs of related variables. If no x appears, the pair of variables is statistically unrelated.

Mission Statement and Plan

Columns 1 and 2 of Table 6-1 show that the existence of a formal logistics mission statement and strategic plan is associated with high levels of all seven types of internal performance measurement and both types of benchmarking measurement. In other words, if an organization has a formal logistics mission statement or strategic plan, it is more likely to be heavily engaged in performance measurement. Similar findings have also been reported for the existence of a formal customer service mission statement and internal performance in both industrial and consumer service organizations.[2]

Of course, this finding does not imply that performance measurement is unimportant to organizations lacking a formal logistics mission statement or a logistics strategic plan. Rather, the relationship is a matter of degree. A formal mission statement and strategic plan reinforce the objective of performance measurement and may actually legitimize the measurement process.[3]

Having a mission statement and strategic plan implies that an

TABLE 6-1: Linkage Between Formalization and Performance Measurement

Performance Measurement	Formalization						
	1	2	3	4	5	6	7
Internal Measurement							
Total cost	x	x		x	x		x
Cost components	x	x		x			x
Asset management	x	x		x			x
Service	x	x		x			x
Feedback	x	x					x
Productivity	x	x		x			x
Quality	x	x		x	x		x
Benchmarking							
Logistics components	x	x			x		x
Operations/strategy	x	x		x	x		x

The Formalization Variables are:
Mission statement and plan
1 = Mission statement
2 = Strategic plan

Empowerment
3 = Title level of senior logistics executive
4 = Level of participation by senior logistics executive in business unit strategic planning

Structure
5 = Length of time logistics formally organized
6 = Number of times logistics reorganized over past five years
7 = Total activities performed by logistics

x = statistically significant positive relationship

organization engages in formal logistics planning. Formal logistics planning is highly dependent on information generated by continuous measurement of performance. This circular effect reinforces performance measurement since such information is required to ascertain if formal goals are being attained.

Empowerment

Empowerment revolves around two variables: the title level of the senior logistics executive and the extent of the senior executive's participation in business unit strategic planning.

As illustrated in Table 6-1, columns 3 and 4, the relationships of these two descriptors of empowerment with performance measurement differ markedly. The title level of the senior logistics executive is not positively related to any of the nine types of performance measurement. Thus the title level of the senior logistics executive is relatively unimportant in terms of a firm's commitment to compulsive performance measurement. This finding highlights the critical need to measure performance as a vital aspect of logistical process control.

The previous result contrasts sharply with how the participation in overall business unit strategic planning by the senior logistics executive relates to performance measurement. Participation is related to six of seven types of internal performance measurement and one of the two types of benchmarking. Thus as the logistics executive is increasingly involved in the most senior strategic planning circle, more performance-related information becomes critical.

This linkage can be viewed in a broader organizational context. Senior executive participation in business unit strategic planning is related to the presence of a formal logistics mission statement and strategic plan. All of these activities imply that formal logistics planning exists in an organization. Participation by the senior logistics executive in business unit strategic planning indicates that the logistics planning process is integrated into an organization's overall planning program, all of which fosters performance measurement.

Structure

The descriptors of structure are the length of time that logistics has been formally organized, the number of times that the logistics organization has been recently modified, and the logistical management span of control (see columns 5, 6, and 7 of Table 6-1).

The number of years that logistics has been formally organized is related to only four of the nine types of performance measurement. This finding probably results from the simple notion that the longer logistics has been formally organized, and hence the longer that an integrated approach has been taken, the longer the firm has had to install performance measurement systems. The number of times that logistics has been reorganized during the past five years is completely unrelated to all nine types of performance measurement. Reorganization does not necessarily foster measurement.

These two variables are in sharp contrast with the linkage of span of control to performance measurement. Span of control is related to all nine types of performance measurement. As logistics line or staff responsibility is expanded, performance measurement becomes both more critical and more likely.

Formalization and Technology

The results of the statistical linkage between formalization and technology variables are presented in Table 6-2. The seven indicators of formalization are organized in seven columns similar to that used in Table 6-1.

Mission Statement and Plan

The existence of a formal logistics mission statement and strategic plan is linked to all technology and information quality variables. A formal mission and strategic plan serves to prioritize goals, create organizational unity, facilitate measurement of internal and benchmarked performance, and foster technology deployment and information quality.

That formalization facilitates adoption and implementation of technology may appear counterintuitive. Technology adoption and implementation require innovative and creative behavior on the part of individuals. Formalization, which is grounded in rules and procedures, could be viewed as creating a bureaucratic organizational climate that stifles individual risk-taking and innovative behavior. But such a chain of logic does not accurately reflect the underlying process that links formalization and technology implementation. The findings demonstrate that formalization fosters technology. The presence of a formal logistics mission statement and strategic plan promotes an organizational climate that is conducive to managers actively scanning the environment for appropriate distribution technology. In the absence of formal logistics planning, individual managers may very well feel a planning void that could ultimately result in an "it's not my responsibility" attitude.

Empowerment

The title level of the senior logistics executive does not appear to be strongly linked to formalization and technology. Title level is related

TABLE 6-2: Linkage Between Formalization and Technology

Technology and Information Quality	Formalization						
	1	2	3	4	5	6	7
Computer Software							
Basic installations	x	x			x		x
Other installations	x	x		x	x		x
EDI Linkages							
Links with channel members	x	x	x	x	x		x
Links with third parties	x	x		x	x		x
Hardware Technology							
Operational hardware	x	x	x	x	x		x
Computer hardware	x	x	x	x		x	x
Information Characteristics							
Timely information	x	x			x		x
Accurate information	x	x			x		x
Readily available information	x	x		x	x		x
Exception formatted information	x	x					x
Appropriately formatted information	x	x		x	x		x

The Formalization Variables are:

Mission statement and plan
1 = Mission statement
2 = Strategic plan

Empowerment
3 = Title level of senior logistics executive
4 = Level of participation by senior logistics executive in business unit strategic planning

Structure
5 = Length of time logistics formally organized
6 = Number of times logistics reorganized over past five years
7 = Total activities performed by logistics

x = statistically significant positive relationship

to three of the six technology variables. The title level of the senior logistics executive is unrelated to all five information quality variables.

In contrast, empowerment as a result of the participation of the senior logistics executive in business unit strategic planning is related to five of six technology variables and to two of five quality of information variables. Thus, empowerment through participation is a better stimulant of technology deployment and information quality than is executive title. A similar conclusion was previously drawn in linking empowerment to performance measurement. The senior executive's participation in business unit strategic planning was more positively linked to performance measurement than executive title.

The linkage of the senior logistics executive to business unit strategic planning suggests that logistics is an important component of the firm's overall strategy. This linkage in turn would typically facilitate the identification and implementation of various technologies.

Structure

The more longevity the logistics organization has, the greater the time available to implement complex information and transactional technologies. This is problematic for the firm that is just formally organizing logistics if key competitors have already done so for some time. A competitive advantage in process technology created by a more mature logistics philosophy may be difficult to compensate for, especially if a formal mission and strategic plan are lacking and if the senior logistics executive does not participate in business unit strategic planning. In terms of organizational structure, the number of times that logistics has been modified is linked to only one of six technology variables and is not positively related to any information quality variables.

The linkage between span of control and technology is best explained by role specialization. As the span of logistics control increases, so does technical expertise. This expertise should be focusing on finer and more unique types of problems. For instance, a logistics function with a broad span of control may be more likely to employ materials-handling specialists. Such specialists may be more likely to engage in benchmarking to identify specific technologies. They also have the expertise required to implement technology and may have been delegated decision-making power for technology adoption. In other words, a logistics function with a wide span of control may be particularly amenable to isolating, adopting, and implementing innovative process technologies.[4]

Performance Measurement and Technology

The third leg of the logistics triangle is the linkage between performance measurement and technology. The summary of the linkage analysis is presented in Table 6-3. The performance measurements are presented in the nine columns.

All but four of the ninety-nine relationships between technology and measurement are statistically significant. Clearly, as the level of technology in the organization increases, so does the level of performance measurement and vice versa.

Only in the case of EDI technology are the relationships not pervasive and indiscriminatory. Of the eighteen relationships between EDI technology and performance measurement, all but four were significant. As mentioned earlier, EDI technology is currently concerned primarily with the movement of data. EDI does not necessarily enhance performance measurement capabilities, unlike the other components of information technology included in the research.

The linkage between technology and performance measurement can be viewed in two ways. First, technology can be seen as an information creator. Second, performance measurement can be thought of as part of an organization's formal logistics planning program. The more extensive the performance measurement, the more a firm will be willing to invest in technology. Benchmarking can also play an important role in fostering technology levels. The organization that actively scans the environment may be better able to spot technology opportunities. Senior management knowledge of available opportunities may enhance their desire to implement logistics-based technology.

The positive linkage between technology and performance measurement is a reflection of the critical role information plays in logistics. Technology fosters performance measurement, and such results are a critical component of formal logistics planning and, especially, benchmarking, in facilitating technology implementation.

IMPROVING LOGISTICAL FLEXIBILITY

Achieving predetermined service levels and controlling costs associated with these service levels are of utmost importance to the firm's long-term performance. Performance, however, is often described in terms of three dimensions: efficiency, effectiveness, and flexibility. The key to logistical leadership is found in adding flexible competency to a

TABLE 6-3: Linkage Between Performance Measurement and Technology

Technology and Information Quality	Performance Measurement								
	1	2	3	4	5	6	7	8	9
Computer Software									
Basic installations	x	x	x	x	x	x	x	x	x
Other installations	x	x	x	x	x	x	x	x	x
EDI Linkages									
Links with channel members	x	x	x	x	x	x		x	x
Links with third parties	x	x		x			x	x	x
Hardware Technology									
Operational hardware	x	x	x	x	x	x	x	x	x
Computer hardware	x	x	x	x	x	x	x	x	x
Information Characteristics									
Timely information	x	x	x	x	x	x	x	x	x
Accurate information	x	x	x	x	x	x	x	x	x
Readily available information	x	x	x	x	x	x	x	x	x
Exception formatted information	x	x	x	x	x	x	x	x	x
Appropriately formatted information	x	x	x	x	x	x	x	x	x

The Performance Measurement Variables are:
Internal Performance Measurement
1 = Total cost measurement
2 = Cost components measurement
3 = Asset management measurement
4 = Service measurement
5 = Feedback measurement
6 = Productivity measurement
7 = Quality measurement

Benchmarking Performance Measurement
8 = Components benchmarking
9 = Operations/strategy benchmarking

x = statistically significant positive relationship

system that is very good at efficiently achieving basic customer service goals. Investigation into management practices suggests that firms that simultaneously achieve the attributes of formalization, performance measurement, and technology adoption are most likely to become leading performers. In the previous section, the constructs of each of these three attributes were examined and for the most part determined to be linked. In this section, the linkage analysis is extended to embrace flexibility. *The key to logistical leadership is the development of flexible competency.*

Previous research has identified long- and short-run aspects of flexibility. Long-run flexibility refers to the ability of the firm to alter its product offering and asset deployment in response to such challenges as changing customer requirements, new technologies, or increasing competitive pressure.[5] The role of logistics in determining long-run flexibility tends to focus on system design issues. For example, what configuration of warehouses will achieve the desired customer service performance at the lowest total cost? Logistical planning is critical to achieving long-run flexibility.

Short-run flexibility is the ability of a firm to alter operations to meet demand and supply fluctuations. In most logistical situations, short-run flexibility concerns a firm's ability to react to unexpected variations. From an operational perspective, short-run flexibility is more than adapting to unexpected performance failures. In many cases, logistical flexibility can be used to capture a favorable demand fluctuation and result in capturing increased sales and market share. In other situations, flexibility may be responding to a key customer request for customized logistical services. Regardless of the reason, a firm's ability to respond quickly is what superior performance is all about.

It is easier to say that a firm's goal is to increase logistical flexibility than it is to realize such performance on a daily basis. It is difficult to implement administrative and technological systems that enable logistical flexibility. The remainder of this section discusses how flexible capacity is related to achievement of high levels of formalization, performance measurement, and technology. The order of discussion is to first examine linkages between technology and flexibility and then linkages between flexibility and performance measurement and formalization, respectively.

In the baseline research, senior logistics managers were asked to rate their organization's ability in accommodating eight situations requiring short-run logistical flexibility. The eight operation situations were (1) special customer requirements; (2) sales/marketing promotions; (3) new product introduction; (4) product phaseout; (5) product recalls; (6) supply disruption; (7) special service requests; and (8) modification to products while in the logistics system.

Technology and Flexibility

The relationships between technology and flexibility are presented in Table 6-4. The flexibility indicators are presented in the eight columns of this table. It is clear that logistical flexibility is directly linked to information. As information becomes more available, accurate, appropriately formatted, formatted on an exception basis, and more timely, managers perceive their organization to be more flexible. Thirty-nine out of forty information characteristic variables were positively linked to flexibility. It is clear that flexible competency rests in information quality.

Basic software installations and computer hardware technology are the vehicles that place quality information at the disposal of management. From this basic notion it is expected that technology variables will be linked to flexibility. The actual process by which technology enables flexibility is quite complex. The implementation of basic computer software installations, such as the computerization of order processing, is required in order to achieve a high level of basic performance. It enables accurate, fast decision making. Organizations that have adopted high levels of basic computer applications and have made substantial progress toward the development of integrated data should be ideally positioned to handle nonroutine events that call for enhanced flexibility.

Computer hardware and basic software are positively linked to all types of logistical flexibility. The associations of flexibility with operational hardware and with specialized software applications show a generally positive, but not comprehensive, linkage. The computerization of the other applications is related to six of eight types of logistical flexibility. In terms of operational hardware, the linkage is positive to four types of flexibility.

The remaining technology variables, EDI links with channel members and EDI links with third parties, are related to five or fewer types of logistical flexibility. These aspects of technology are viewed as favorable to developing flexibility but do not seem to be prerequisites.

TABLE 6-4: Linkage Between Flexibility and Technology

Technology and Information Quality	Flexibility							
	1	2	3	4	5	6	7	8
Computer Software								
Basic installations	X	X	X	X	X	X	X	X
Other installations		X	X	X	X	X		X
EDI Linkages								
Links with channel members			X		X			
Links with third parties			X	X	X	X		X
Hardware Technology								
Operational hardware			X	X	X	X		
Computer hardware	X	X	X	X	X	X	X	X
Information Characteristics								
Timely information	X	X	X	X	X	X	X	X
Accurate information	X	X	X	X	X	X	X	X
Readily available information	X	X	X	X	X	X	X	X
Exception formatted information	X	X	X	X	X	X	X	X
Appropriately formatted information		X	X	X	X	X	X	X

The Flexibility Variables are:

1 = flexibility in accommodating special customer requirements
2 = flexibility in accommodating sales/marketing incentives
3 = flexibility in accommodating product introduction
4 = flexibility in accommodating product phaseout
5 = flexibility in accommodating disruption in supply
6 = flexibility in accommodating product recall
7 = flexibility in accommodating customized service
8 = flexibility in accommodating product modification while in a
     logistics system

x = statistically significant positive relationship

Performance Measurement and Flexibility

An analysis of linkages between performance measurement and flexibility is presented in Table 6-5. Again the flexibility variables appear in the columns.

Sixty-nine out of seventy-two relationships are significant. Performance measurement and flexibility are thus clearly linked. This result can be generalized in two ways. First, the more comprehensive the practice of performance measurement, the greater the absolute level of

TABLE 6-5: Linkage Between Flexibility and Performance Measurement

| | Flexibility | | | | | | | |
Performance Measurement	1	2	3	4	5	6	7	8
Internal Measurement								
Total cost	x	x	x	x	x	x	x	x
Cost components		x	x	x	x	x	x	x
Asset management	x	x	x	x	x	x	x	x
Service	x	x	x	x	x	x		x
Feedback	x	x	x	x	x	x	x	x
Productivity	x	x	x	x		x	x	x
Quality	x	x	x	x	x	x	x	x
Benchmarking								
Components	x	x	x	x	x	x	x	x
Operations/strategy	x	x	x	x	x	x	x	x

The Flexibility Variables are:
1 = flexibility in accommodating special customer requirements
2 = flexibility in accommodating sales/marketing incentives
3 = flexibility in accommodating product introduction
4 = flexibility in accommodating product phaseout
5 = flexibility in accommodating disruption in supply
6 = flexibility in accommodating product recall
7 = flexibility in accommodating customized service
8 = flexibility in accommodating product modification while in a
     logistics system

x = statistically significant positive relationship

information that management has at its disposal. Such information provides the basis for managing flexibility. Second, as pointed out earlier, the more extensive the practice of performance measurement, the more intense an organization's formal logistics planning process. An intense formal planning program requires extensive technology deployment and high-quality information. This leads to the same general conclusion: information provides the ultimate basis for logistical flexibility.

Formalization and Flexibility

Table 6-6 summarizes the analysis of the linkage between formalization and flexibility. In terms of linking formalization to flexibility, the key variables are a formal mission statement and a logistics strategic plan. Senior logistics managers in organizations with logistics mission statements ranked their organization's short-run logistical flexibility significantly higher than managers in firms without such statements. The linkage was even more striking regarding a formal logistics strategic plan. Firms that had well-established planning practices were judged as being more flexible with respect to all eight situations.

There are several ways in which a formal mission statement and strategic plan can foster flexibility. Mission statements in leading logistics organizations place a premium on achieving customer satisfaction. The plan provides resources for accommodating events that require flexible capacity. Note that formalized plans and goals are distinct from formal work rules and job descriptions, which might be viewed as potentially stifling flexibility by constricting individual creativity by limiting areas of responsibility. A formal mission statement and strategic plan can be viewed as stimulating flexibility by imbuing employees with a sense of organizational rather than individual responsibility. The corporate culture, in part influenced by formal missions and strategic plans, may establish the belief that flexibility is expected. Thus the first way in which a formal logistics mission statement and strategic plan encourage flexibility is by imbuing the firm with the attitude that flexibility is an expected routine event.

Other linkages of mission statement and strategic plan formulation to flexibility are through performance measurement and technology. As discussed earlier, a formal mission statement and strategic plan are reflective of extensive logistics planning. Flexibility is related to the practice of logistics planning. In other words, a formal mission statement and strategic plan facilitate performance measurement, which in

TABLE 6-6: *Linkage Between Flexibility and Formalization*

Formalization	Flexibility							
	1	2	3	4	5	6	7	8
Mission Statement and Plan								
Mission statement		x	x	x	x	x	x	x
Strategic plan	x	x	x	x	x	x	x	x
Empowerment								
Senior executive title level								
Senior executive participation in business unit strategic planning								
Structure								
Years logistics organized		x	x		x	x		
Reorganizations during past five years								
Total activities controlled by logistics	x		x	x	x	x		x

The Flexibility Variables are:

1 = flexibility in accommodating special customer requirements
2 = flexibility in accommodating sales/marketing incentives
3 = flexibility in accommodating product introduction
4 = flexibility in accommodating product phaseout
5 = flexibility in accommodating disruption in supply
6 = flexibility in accommodating product recall
7 = flexibility in accommodating customized service
8 = flexibility in accommodating product modification while in logistics system

x = statistically significant positive relationship

turn generates the information needed to manage flexibility. As illustrated in Figure 6-1, formal mission statement and strategic planning both facilitate flexibility by providing information related to anticipated performance.

Technology is also linked to the mission statement and strategic

FIGURE 6-1: Formal Logistics Mission Statement and Strategic Plan Both Directly and Indirectly Related to Flexibility

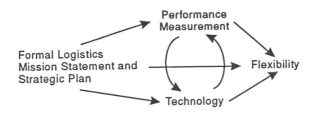

planning in terms of facilitating flexibility. Logistical planning stimulates technology adoption. The computerization of basic installations, fostered by the logistical planning, affects flexibility as described earlier.

The linkage of empowerment to logistical flexibility is at best indirect and flows through measurement and technology adoption. Table 6-6 points out that increasing the title of the senior logistics executive is not directly linked to any type of logistical flexibility. Earlier the general lack of title importance was pointed out with respect to performance measurement and technology. The lack of direct linkage to flexibility offers additional proof that the senior logistic executive's title is not nearly as important as other factors.

The active participation of the senior logistics executive in business unit strategic planning is not related to logistical flexibility. The lack of linkage between participation in business unit planning and flexibility means that actions required to accommodate special situations are tactical in nature. However, participation indirectly influences short-run logistical flexibility for the same reasons as a formalized mission statement and a strategic plan do. As noted earlier, participation in business unit planning promotes technology implementation and performance measurement. Thus, participation is indirectly related to flexibility. It is likely that empowerment also directly influences flexibility in the sense of front-line employees having the authority to take action to accommodate special situations. Figure 6-2, however, illustrates the indirect relationship of empowerment and flexibility. Note the lack of an arrow directly from participation to flexibility.

The relationships between structure and short-run logistical flexibility are also presented in Table 6-6. The longevity of the logistics

FIGURE 6-2: *Participation in Business Unit Strategic Planning is Indirectly Related to Flexibility*

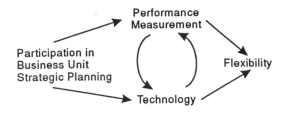

FIGURE 6-3: *Organization Longevity is Both Directly and Indirectly Related to Flexibility*

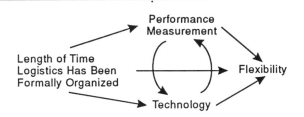

organization was linked to four out of eight flexibility variables. As specified repeatedly, the longer that logistics has been formally organized, the more likely is the implementation of sophisticated performance measurement and advanced technology. Therefore the linkage of longevity and flexibility is both direct and indirect, as shown in Figure 6-3.

The frequency of organization modification is neither directly nor indirectly related to any type of logistical flexibility. Since the frequency of logistical reorganizations is unrelated to performance measurement, technology, and flexibility, it is clear that this variable is unimportant to achieving logistical superiority.

The span of control of logistics is linked to five out of eight types of flexibility situations. Similar to the linkages of flexibility to the mission statement and the formalized logistics plan, longevity has both a direct and an indirect link to flexibility. Span of control was linked

FIGURE 6-4: Span of Control is Both Directly and Indirectly Linked to Flexibility

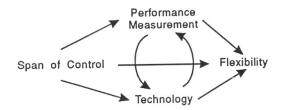

to a significant number of performance measurement and technology variables. The overall relationship indicates direct and indirect linkages as depicted in Figure 6-4.

All analysis suggests that flexibility is the key to logistics leadership. The statistical analysis has isolated the attributes that contribute to logistical flexibility. Table 6-7 provides an analysis in rank order of the formalization, performance measurement, and technology variables in terms of their linkage to the various forms of logistical flexibility.

This analysis is applicable only to variables that can be ranked on a continuous scale. Therefore the presence or absence of a formal logistics mission statement and a formal logistics strategic plan, are not included in the analysis because they are binary (yes or no) measurements. However, because these two variables are very highly related to performance measurement, technology, information quality, and flexibility, it is clear that their presence is extremely important and that they play a major role in facilitating logistical flexibility.

As illustrated in Table 6-7, sophistication in basic computer applications offers the most direct linkage to the eight flexibility situations. In other words, computerized application of basic activities stands out as the single most important practice leading to flexibility. Firms seeking to leverage logistical performance should expend significant resources to the computerization of basic applications. Basic computerization is followed in rank order by quality performance measurement, availability of accurate, timely, readily available, exception formatted, and appropriately formatted information. Aside from the quality measurement and basic software applications, five out of seven most significant predictors of logistical flexibility are information characteristics.

A pattern emerges from the rank ordering presented in Table 6-7.

TABLE 6-7: Rank Order of Flexibility Impact Variables

Rank Order	Variable for All Firms	Type of Variable
1.	Basic software applications	technology
2.	Quality performance measurement	measurement
3.	Accurate information	technology
4.	Timely information	technology
5.	Readily available information	technology
6.	Exception formatted information	technology
7.	Appropriately formatted information	technology
8.	Components benchmarking	measurement
9.	Operations/strategy benchmarking	measurement
10.	Total cost performance measurement	measurement
11.	Service performance measurement	measurement
12.	Feedback performance measurement	measurement
13.	Total activities controlled by logistics	formalization
14.	Productivity performance measurement	measurement
15.	Other computer installations	technology
16.	Asset management performance measurement	measurement
17.	Computer hardware technology	technology
18.	Cost components performance measurement	measurement
19.	EDI links with third parties	technology
20.	Operational hardware technology	technology
21.	Years logistics formally organized	formalization
22.	EDI with channel members	technology

No relationship

23.	Title level of senior logistics executive	formalization
24.	Participation of senior logistics executive strategic planning	formalization
25.	Number of times logistics reorganized during the past five years	formalization

Notes

1. Not included in analysis because questions were binary, but extremely important to flexibility:

   Formal mission statement
   Formal strategic plan

2. Rank order indicates the mean level of relatedness of the variable with all eight measures of logistical flexibility.

3. The variables listed under "no relationship" were not ranked since they were unrelated to all eight measures of flexibility.

Overall, the technology adoption aspects are most directly linked to logistical flexibility. Performance measurement, both internal and benchmarked, is the second most important linkage leading to flexibility. The least important direct linkage to logistical flexibility is formalization. The most directly linked aspect of formalization is logistical span of control, which ranks thirteenth. Three formalization variables are not linked directly to logistical flexibility.

The pattern presented in Table 6-7 supports direct and indirect linkages presented in Figures 6-1 through 6-4. The more indirect the linkage between a specific variable and logistical flexibility, the lower the rank ordering in Table 6-7. The role of formalization in flexibility is not direct. Formalization represents a commitment to basic operational requirements. It serves as the platform from which technology and measurement directly facilitate flexibility.

The generalized results provide in-depth support for the propositions about leading-edge logistics practices summarized in Chapter Three and abstracted from the baseline research. From the viewpoint of mobilizing an initiative to upgrade a firm's logistical performance, it is clear that formalization, technology, performance measurement, and short-run flexibility form a highly related set of variables. Over time these attributes can be incorporated into a firm's logistic management practices and can be expected to form the nucleus of efforts that lead to the reaching of leading-edge status.

Does Merchandiser versus Manufacturer Make a Difference?

As mentioned at the beginning of this chapter, the discussion of linkages among formalization, measurement of performance, technology, and logistical flexibility was evaluated without consideration of possible distinctions or differences between manufacturers and merchandisers (wholesalers and retailers).

At the outset there is no overwhelming reason to expect linkages to differ between manufacturers and merchandisers. In fact, the baseline research concluded that leading-edge practice was observed independent of size, type of industry, or position in the channel of distribution.

Several different analyses were conducted to isolate potential differences between manufacturers and merchandisers (see Appendix C for complete details). Table 6-8 summarizes a key analysis. The ranking is basically the same as that presented in Table 6-7, but was conducted separately for manufacturers and merchandisers. Table 6-8 presents the rank order of the average importance of the formalization, performance

TABLE 6-8: Rank Order of Flexibility Impact Variables Separate for Manufacturers and Merchandisers

Rank Order	For Manufacturers	For Merchandisers
1.	Basic software applications	Timely information
2.	Operations/strategy benchmarking	Quality measurement
3.	Accurate information	Accurate information
4.	Cost components measurement	Readily available information
5.	Readily available information	Service measurement
6.	Appropriately formatted info.	Feedback measurement
7.	Total cost measurement	Other software installations
8.	Timely information	Exception formatted information
9.	Quality measurement	Appropriately formatted information
10.	Components benchmarking	Total cost measurement
11.	Asset management measurement	Asset management measurement
12.	Total activities controlled by logistics	Total activities controlled by logistics
13.	Exception formatted information	Components benchmarking
14.	Other software installations	Computer hardware
15.	Productivity measurement	Basic software installations
16.	Computer hardware	Operations/strategy benchmarking (T)
17.	Operational hardware (T)	EDI links with channel members
18.	Feedback measurement	Productivity measurement
19.	Years logistics formally organized	Cost components measurement (T)
20.	Service measurement	EDI links with third parties
21.	Participation in strategic planning	Number of years logistics formally organized
22.	EDI links with third parties	Operational technology
23.	N/A	Participation in strategic planning
24.	N/A	Title level of senior executive

No relationship

	Number of reorganizations	Number of reorganizations
	Title level of senior executive	
	EDI links with channel members	

Notes

Rank order refers to the mean level of relatedness with the eight logistical flexibility variables.

T means that the variable listed immediately afterwards was tied in terms of rank order.

measurement, and technology variables in terms of their ability to predict logistical flexibility separately for manufacturers and merchandisers. For instance, on the average, the seventh best predictor of the eight flexibility variables among manufacturers is total cost measurement, while the seventh best predictor, on the average, of the eight flexibility variables among merchandisers is other computer software applications.

Several specific differences in the rank orderings are apparent. A statistical test was conducted to determine if the rank orders for the manufacturer and the merchandiser are significantly different. The test generated strong evidence indicating that the separate rank orders are not significantly different. The rank order correlation was .497, which is significant at the .007 level. Thus the average linkage between formalization, performance measurement, and technology, respectively, and logistical flexibility does not differ statistically between manufacturers and merchandisers.

This test in combination with other analyses presented in Appendix C offers substantial support that the linkages reported are equally applicable to manufacturers and merchandisers. This does not mean that there are no differences between manufacturers and merchandisers. Rather, it means that the relationships supported in this chapter are so fundamental that the commonalities among manufacturers, retailers, and wholesalers far outweigh the differences.

SUMMARY

The major objective of this chapter was to build proof concerning what needs to be done. The approach was to examine the management triangle and its linkage to logistical flexibility. The triangular relationship consists of formalization of the logistics process, performance measurement of operations and competitors, and technology adoption (see Figure 6-5). Each of these three foundations is related to flexibility in different ways. Formalization of the logistics process is at the same time a facilitator of performance measurement and technology adoption, and for some constructs it is a direct driver of flexibility. The other two points of the triangle, performance measurement and technology, foster each other, each creating an infrastructure amenable to the implementation of the other. Together, they represent primary drivers of flexibility. Flexibility is viewed as logistical leadership because it permits an organization to continuously improve customer satisfac-

FIGURE 6-5: Leading Edge Attribute Model

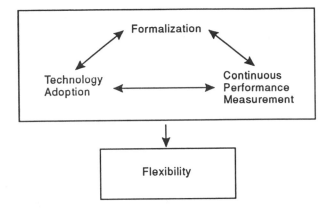

tion by leveraging routine performance to high levels of nonroutine compliance.

Organizational structure and practices do not always appear to be the design of rational processes. However, setting aside short-term and politically-driven ambition, logistics as a process is rational. Senior management can focus the course and performance of a logistical organization through rational design. This chapter has isolated what rational design is.

The linkages reported in this chapter are not the result of chance, serendipity, or happenstance. Instead they result from managers rationally linking and prioritizing components of organizational structure and strategy. For example, the fact that the presence of a formal logistics mission statement is linked to enhanced performance measurement is the product of design. Managers "fit" components of organizational commitments together because such linkages lead to improved performance.

Notes

1. For further details concerning sampling methodology see Donald J. Bowersox, Patricia J. Daugherty, Cornelia L. Dröge, Dale S. Rogers, and Daniel L. Wardlow, *Leading Edge Logistics: Competitive Positioning for the 1990s* (Oak Brook, Ill.: Council of Logistics Management, 1989).

2. Richard Germain and M. Bixby Cooper, "How a Customer Mission

Statement Affects Company Performance," *Industrial Marketing Management* 19, 1 (1990): 47–54.

3. Peter F. Drucker, *Management: Tasks, Responsibilities and Practices* (New York: Harper & Row, 1974).

4. Relationships between functional differentiation, which is somewhat similar to total activities, and technology have frequently been reported in the management literature. See, for example, Michael K. Moch, "Structure and Organizational Resource Allocation," *Administrative Science Quarterly* 21 (December 1976): 661–674.

5. Hans-Christian Phöfl and Werner Zöllner, "Organization for Logistics: The Contingency Approach," *International Journal of Physical Distribution and Materials Management* 17, 1 (1987): 3–16.

Developing Strategic Alliances

AT THIS POINT, Charlie felt he had learned a great deal about the relationship of key activities within his firm's operations. However, he realized that to build a truly successful alliance with Super, their number one customer, he needed to find out more about Super's business.

Charlie contacted Super's senior logistics person, Dan. During that conversation, Charlie detailed how he thought they should proceed. Charlie proposed that he spend some time—a minimum of two weeks, but more if possible—on the premises learning how Super operated. Charlie emphasized that it would be necessary to get exposure to a variety of areas such as Sales, Marketing, Logistics, and Store Operations. He wanted to be sure to come away with a comprehensive picture of what would be needed for a successful alliance based on an appreciation for the interactions and relationships within the company. Charlie knew he had to be in a position to realistically assess whether his firm and Dan's were good candidates for an alliance. Alliance partners must work closely together—not unlike a marriage—and he knew that it was critical that their two operations be "compatible." He also wanted to develop a greater appreciation for what Dan's people expected from a strategic partnering arrangement.

Dan was at first surprised that Charlie would be interested in such a wide variety of areas—after all, what was being proposed was a *logistics* alliance. However, he was impressed that Charlie was willing to make such a significant investment in terms of time and effort. He liked that "spirit of commitment." But before proceeding further, Dan said he needed to have at least some indication of how the proposed alliance would work and a good idea of "what's in it for us." They scheduled a meeting for the next week. Charlie's charge was to come in and "sell" Dan and his colleagues on the idea.

As Charlie prepared for the meeting, he knew there were some basic and important points he needed to get across if his plan was to have any chance for success. He didn't want to be perceived as self-serving. Sure, his company hoped for potentially significant improvement—but so did Dan's. The venture must be two-way. He had to make the point that each side would bring different, but complementary—even synergistic—capabilities to the party. By proper leveraging, the idea was to gain a competitive advantage for both sides.

Charlie was faced with a dilemma. To really convince Dan and the others to proceed, he needed to come up with concrete reasons and benefits that would materialize from an alliance. However, in order to be able to clearly define alliance-associated benefits, he needed to know more about Super's business.

Charlie had decided it would be necessary to compromise. He would need to do a "generic" selling job on the advisability of developing an alliance and ask for conditional approval to proceed. If he could sell Dan and his colleagues on the potential of an alliance, then he would ask if he could do an "internship" within their operations and use the information gained to tailor a long-term working arrangement.

During the actual meeting Charlie focused on the advantages to be gained by working cooperatively. This would allow each firm to specialize in select areas and result in subsequently more efficient overall operations. He highlighted the benefits of working together to increase flexibility and responsiveness. He tried to realistically assess the strengths of both firms and define expectations.

At the meeting, Charlie presented a strong case for further exploring the potential benefits of a strategic alliance. Dan and his colleagues became enthused about the possibilities. They were especially interested in Charlie's projections about the time that could be cut from their typical order cycle. They all agreed to go ahead. Arrangements were made for Charlie to spend time at the retailer's facilities. They formed a joint task force to work out definitive operating guidelines for the new alliance. The task force was eager to get to work.

What transpired was truly astonishing. Working together, Charlie's group and the retailer's people worked out a way to share information and revamp delivery times so that inventory turns in the channel went from seven to over forty times per year!! The result was a substantial reduction in inventory for both firms. Even more important, Charlie could clearly see that business gains were going to far surpass those projected to support the new arrangement. It was clearly a WIN-WIN situation.

A significant contemporary trend is the emphasis on developing partnerships and cooperative buyer-seller relationships in all types of business arrangements. Traditional adversarial practices have been replaced with a philosophy of cooperation. Buying situations previously dominated by bidding and price-only negotiations have been repositioned to take advantage of mutual commitment and a longer-term perspective. The objective of these cooperative relationships is not just to survive in today's market, but to improve the long-term competitive positioning of the involved parties. Such relationships are often referred to as strategic alliances. Strategic alliances focus on achieving, maintaining, and enhancing a firm's competitive advantage.

The *boundary-spanning* aspects of strategic alliances are of special interest. Boundary spanning involves increased cooperation among channel members or trading partners in order to decrease uncertainty and gain overall improvements in productivity or quality, or both.

In this chapter, attention is first directed to how and why alliances develop. Major factors encouraging alliance development are reviewed, the most common logistics-based agreements are illustrated, and then attention is directed to the rationale that leads firms to establish alliances. The second section stresses that a "new mind-set" must prevail within most organizations if they hope to develop successful alliances. This involves understanding the factors critical for success as well as the reasons why alliances fail. Since most alliances are dependent upon information exchange, it is not surprising that electronic data interchange (EDI) plays a prominent role in such arrangements. The role of EDI in its more sophisticated applications is reviewed in the third section. The fourth section examines the critical attributes of strategic linkage and presents a model illustrating their interaction. The final section generalizes risks associated with strategic alliances. Whereas Chapter Six developed an internally focused model of logistical leadership, Chapter Seven extends the conceptualization to leadership in a channel-based strategic alliance.

Attention is focused on domestic strategic alliances. A growing number of firms are entering into global strategic alliances. Many of the issues addressed regarding domestic strategic alliances also are relevant in a global perspective.

BUSINESS ALLIANCES

Traditional buyer-seller behavior is often based on an adversarial relationship. The goal in adversarial negotiation is to minimize purchase price. In order to realize the lowest price, a buyer (1) works with a large number of suppliers who can be played off against one another to gain price advantage and ensure adequate sources of supply; (2) allocates each supplier sufficient or fair share purchases to "keep them in line"; and (3) assumes an arm's-length posture based on short-term contracts.[1]

In contrast to an adversarial buying approach is the alliance. Longer-term, cooperative relationships between buyers and sellers are becoming increasingly common.[2] In a cooperative alliance, two or more independent organizations agree to work closely together in an effort to achieve specific objectives. The parties specialize in performing specified tasks in a jointly integrative manner.

Cooperative alliances provide an opportunity to achieve long-term stability through the sharing of resources and skills. Alliance participants position themselves to mutually pursue joint objectives in a manner that reduces each party's risk. Alliances typically extend over time, involve sharing of benefits and burdens, are based on extensive planning, include extensive information exchange, and implement cross-firm operating controls.[3] The parties to an alliance must proactively work to create and maintain its continuing success.

In previous chapters, the wide range of forces that are changing business practices were reviewed. The vast amount of change in the overall business environment has greatly influenced strategic choices. During the 1980s significant political and technological developments combined to create an atmosphere conductive to the formation of alliances, and these trends are expected to continue in the 1990s. In particular, regulatory trends, information technology development, better understanding of activity-based costs, human resource shortages, emphasis on quality, restructuring and downsizing of organizations, and increased attention to time-based strategies are factors that have encouraged the formation of alliances.

Types of Business Alliances

Although virtually unheard of a decade ago, alliances are now becoming a desired way of lowering logistics costs and increasing customer satisfaction.⁴ Alliances can be structured in a variety of ways. The following formats are fairly common throughout industry.

Between Product Marketer and Service Firm

A common format for a strategic alliance is one between a product marketer and a service firm. It involves coordination between a multifaceted service provider and one or more customers. A large number of integrated service arrangements among product marketers, carriers, and warehouse firms fit this format. More sophisticated examples involve customized facilities and equipment dedicated to meeting the needs of a specialized marketer.

For example, Itel Distribution Services and Sears Business Systems have a joint operation in Alsip, Illinois. Sears operates a reconfiguration room within Itel's warehouse to modify equipment to its customers' specifications. Itel provides a full range of logistics services which are tied into the Sears Information System. Basic orders are assembled by Itel, with equipment requiring modification being positioned in the reconfiguration room for customization. Itel then assembles the complete order and performs tasks required for timely customer delivery.

As a second example, consider Federal Express who through its Business Logistics Services division offers central warehousing and overnight delivery services. Electronic data interchange (EDI) capabilities allow them to act immediately on orders. They have established partnership arrangements with several companies and work to make boundaries between the two companies appear transparent to outsiders. One such partnership arrangement is with Jaguar. Prior to the operating agreement with Federal Express, Jaguar found that imported replacement parts took as long as eleven days to reach the United States. "Now by entrusting Federal Express to warehouse those parts in bulk at a Memphis location, cycle time has been cut to four days."⁵ Similar arrangements are provided by United Parcel Service as well as Airborne Express for key customers.

Between Service Firms

This type of alliance seeks greater efficiencies by linking resources. It may involve jointly providing an integrated service to a product marketer.

Recently established intermodal freight service between J. B. Hunt Transport Service, Inc., and the Santa Fe Railway Company is an example of this "end-to-end" format. Hunt provides transportation pickup and delivery while the Santa Fe provides line-hauling service. The combined offering will be advertised as the "Quantum Service" and is scheduled to operate daily between Chicago and Los Angeles. United Parcel Service and Ralston Purina are important participants in the new service. Their participation helps to maintain sufficient freight to assure daily viability of the service.

Between Vertically Aligned Product Marketers

This type of alliance joining two or more firms engaged in product marketing is very common. Inventory ownership is typically transferred between alliance partners.

A number of these alliances have recently been publicized. Alliances between Procter & Gamble and Wal-Mart; Kraft General Foods, Inc., and Shaw's Markets; and arrangements such as Owens-Corning Fiberglas Pink Link; Lithonia Lighting Light*Link; and Levi Strauss Levi-Link all represent examples of two-stage vertical alliances. Bergen Brunswig, McKesson Drug, and Alco Health Services alliances with health-care users and retail druggists also fit this format.

A more complex version is illustrated by the potential alignment of four firms each of which represents a different level in women's ready-to-wear apparel. The alliances involved DuPont (producer of the basic fiber), Milliken (who will convert fiber into fabric), Leslie Fay (manufacturer of women's garments), and Dillard's Department Store, a retailer. The objective of the alliances is to arrange channel structure in a manner that facilitates efficient cross-company alignment of resources in order to respond to the volatility of fashion demand. The alliances seek to implement quick response (QR) inventory replenishment and significantly reduce total time from fiber to the retail rack. Because of the expansiveness of the overall operation, multiple service companies may be involved.

Between Horizontally Aligned Product Marketers

This type of alliance seeks to collaboratively join two or more independent firms who sell to the same customers. It is one of the newest and most complex formats for an alliance. One of the major implementation decisions concerns which of the proprietary operations' resource base should be used to implement the alliance. Service providers such as carriers are often a part of the alliance.

Hospitals constitute the common customer base in one such alliance. Formed in October 1987 by Abbott Laboratories and 3M, the

Corporate Alliance now includes Standard Register Company (business forms), IBM Corporation (information network services), Kimberly Clark Corporation Professional Health Care Division (nonwoven disposable products), and C. R. Bard (Urological Division). This logistics alliance seeks to improve overall service to hospitals by offering frequent joint delivery of product assortments from member companies. The operations of these cooperative firms are coordinated by electronic data interchange (EDI) linkages.[6] The objectives of the alliance are to increase service and improve operating efficiency. A primary motivation behind the alliance was to more effectively compete with Baxter International Value-Link and Johnson & Johnson Hospital COACT capabilities.

Rationale For Alliances

Firms enter into cooperative alliances in anticipation of specific benefits. Although each situation is different, the following are some of the more commonly perceived benefits.

Cost Reduction Through Specialization

Alliances allow firms to exploit benefits associated with specialization. Each participating firm concentrates on tasks it can perform most efficiently and economically. This is often referred to as "core strength focusing." Firms focus on what they do best, and all other functions become potential candidates for outsourcing to alliance arrangements.[7]

The economic justification for the shifting of functional responsibilities is economy of scale. In any situation, selected activities are positioned to experience increasing returns while others are at the point of diminishing returns. Ideally firms should specialize in activities that have potential for increased return on investment and, to the extent possible, avoid functions with diminishing returns. From a cost perspective, alliance participation should be restricted to firms that are capable of offering a high level of expertise at a lower cost than a partner firm achieves internally.

Joint Synergy

Many firms are entering into alliances because they realize it is best not to continue functioning alone. Few firms have sufficient internal resources: "With enough time, money, and luck, you can do everything yourself. But who has enough?"[8] Cooperative efforts can reduce cost and time while improving competitive positioning. Firms involved in alliances can capitalize on joint synergism and reduce risk. Entering into alliances with other firms generally allows a firm to build competency rapidly at relatively low cost. Alliances can be structured to permit access to new technologies and markets. They offer innovative approaches to revamping business operations and can result in additional adaptability and flexibility. All of the above benefits flow from the synergism of working together. As the Japanese say: "Know when to cooperate and when to compete."

Increased Information To Support Planning

Partnership arrangements allow participants to engage in joint planning. Alliance planning is facilitated by the sharing of important information. Motorola has alliances with Hewlett Packard and Techtronics aimed at making maximum use of EDI. EDI and the resulting integration of systems have yielded significant benefits. The information exchange has given Motorola a better understanding of its partners' requirements because they share forecasts. As a result, the level of shared business has increased significantly.[9]

Customer Service Enhancements

The focus on increasing customer satisfaction has prompted many firms to seek new service approaches. For example, the Corporate Alliance formed by Abbott Laboratories and 3M to handle the distribution needs of hospitals was in response to the demand for more frequent, small quantity deliveries. Abbott and other hospital supply vendors were required to make frequent deliveries which necessitated numerous small shipments. In order to obtain economies associated with larger shipments, the participants formed a strategic distribution alliance.

Reduced or Shared Risks

Alliance arrangements may be motivated by a desire to reduce risk and uncertainty. Alliances can help firms avoid or offset some costs associated with entering new markets and product development. For example, under provisions of the Cooperative Research and Development Act of 1984, the big three United States automotive producers have agreed to jointly conduct research and development of composite materials. The big three also combined forces with a group of electrical utilities to form the United States Advanced Battery Consortium, which jointly with the United States Department of Energy announced plans to spend $260 million over four years to develop a new generation of batteries for electric vehicles.

The purpose of the National Cooperative Research Act of 1984 was "to promote research and development, encourage innovation, stimulate trade, and make necessary and appropriate modifications in the operation of the antitrust laws." The act modifies antitrust law to permit firms, even competitors, to work together on research. Parties entering into cooperative ventures must file written notification with the Attorney General and the Federal Trade Commission disclosing (1) the identities of the involved parties and (2) the nature and objectives of the cooperative venture. Review of the *Annual Federal Register Index* from 1984 through 1989 indicates that in excess of 150 cooperative research notifications were filed during that period.

In such cooperative situations, research and development costs and risk are shared. The objective is to reduce the elapsed time of product development from concept to commercialization. In the event of non-productive research, each firm's losses are lower. Such risk avoidance is a key motivation behind strategic alliances. The basic premise is that pooling knowledge and talent will result in significantly greater overall resources being committed to a joint project and thereby improving the odds for success. Of course, this is only true in situations where the involvement of multiple organizations does not have a multiplier effect on overhead and administrative costs.

The Bush Administration is currently drafting legislation that would amend the National Cooperative Research Act of 1984. The act would be expanded to permit firms to form informal partnerships to share manufacturing, equipment and plants, employees, research and development, and marketing and promotional programs. The modified legislation would permit firms to notify the federal government that they are working together, making no requirement for a formal certification process.[10]

Shared Creativity

The potential to share creativity is often the factor that stimulates alliance development. Different perspectives, experiences, and unique ideas increase the likelihood of success. The opportunity for parallel experimentation is a critical aspect of such arrangements. Although shared creativity can reduce the risk of failure, the potential for creative synergism may be far more of a motivating factor for seeking alliances than risk avoidance.

Gaining Competitive Advantage

Some alliances are formed specifically for the purpose of gaining and maintaining competitive advantage. This breed of alliance differs significantly from a simple cooperative agreement. Strategic alliances aimed at gaining competitive advantage become an integral part of a firm's long-term strategic commitment.[11] The goal of an alliance that seeks to leverage critical capabilities, increase innovation, and improve flexibility in response to market and technological changes is typically to institute a quantum change in competitive position.[12]

A NEW MIND-SET

Alliances—particularly strategic or extended enterprise arrangements— are not business as usual. They are formed with the intention of exploiting new business opportunities and taking advantage of synergies associated with collaboration. Alliance firms proactively seek new ways of doing business and willingly accept the idea of working with partners to gain efficiencies that, hopefully, will lead to competitive advantage. For many firms, the notion of "alliancing" requires a new mind-set. It is increasingly becoming a matter of survival, not merely a matter of competitive advantage!

Critical Success Factors

Successful alliances share a number of common elements. Although alliance arrangements vary and exceptions are noted, the following is an itemization of the "critical success factors."[13]

Selective Matching

Alliance participants must work closely together to form an ongoing, dynamic relationship. It is imperative that corporate values and cultures of the proposed partners be compatible. The newly formed business relationship will represent a different approach to doing business. However, the partners' underlying philosophies will provide the foundation for structuring and planning. Separate philosophies must blend together, hopefully with a minimum of disruption. Selective matching requires that firms take care to pick participants that are in the alliance for the long run and that share common beliefs and values. This typically means that time and care must be taken in selecting partners to an alliance.

Information Sharing

Information is the lifeline of a strategic alliance. Successful alliance partners regularly share strategic and technical information. Such openness and willingness to reveal proprietary information contrasts sharply with standard business practices of hoarding and releasing information only on a need-to-know basis. The element of mutual trust residing in a partnership prompts an open exchange of information between partners.[14]

Most alliance partners are electronically linked to permit access to database. Electronic integration has the potential to permeate organizational boundaries. Electronic linkage generally speeds up the pace; thus decisions can be made faster and the overall alliance becomes more responsive to customer needs.

Each alliance is highly individualized and customized to meet the needs of participating organizations. However, information sharing is always crucial for support and to enhance performance. Because of the critical and unique nature of information interchange needed to support alliances, participants frequently find it necessary to develop customized information systems.

Role Specification

Alliance arrangements by their very nature are boundary spanning. The intermingling of resources and blurring of corporate boundaries become common. In many situations, employees of alliance members share facilities and work side by side. It is essential that specific roles of each alliance member be specified. Precise role specification permits focused responsibility and accountability. It is important to define ground rules and gain commitment from personnel from the start. All alliances need "champions" who are committed to making the arrangement a success.

Role specification helps to maintain a balance of power within the cooperative arrangement. "Mutuality" is the operative term. Strategic alliances that are particularly successful express concern with equalizing rather than monopolizing power.[15] Typically one party to an alliance is dominant. However, the dominant partner cannot abuse or exploit the situation if the relationship is to last over the long term.

Ground Rules

When an alliance is formed, clear-cut ground rules and policies are required. Ground rules commonly establish procedures for handling both routine and unexpected events. Ground rules serve to specify both performance expectations and ways to improve inferior or substandard performance.

Dependable service is an especially critical issue in most just-in-time or quick response logistics systems. Such time-based strategies require precise performance and provision for backup or contingency services when and where needed. Ground rules may also define how alliance participants will share rewards and thereby serve as further incentives for improving overall quality.

Ground rules provide guidelines for the day-to-day alliance operations. Ground rules can become critical in avoiding and resolving conflict. Although not all problems can be anticipated, many events are routine and repetitive. Developing empowerment procedures to handle such situations at the time of occurrence frees management to handle planning and development requirements.

Tables 7-1 and 7-2 provide recaps of guidelines used by Kraft General Foods and Schneider National, Inc., respectively, when establishing an alliance. Each serves to illustrate the importance of establishing ground rules up front to guide the establishment and conduct of an alliance.

Exit Provisions

In addition to specifying the formation policies and operating rules for an alliance, it is important to establish procedures to guide potential dissolution of the arrangement. A good time to discuss termination

---

TABLE 7-1: Principles to Guide Channel Alliance

- Share All Relevant Non-Proprietary Information
- Clearly Define Common Interest Boundaries
- Share Forecasts
- Develop Common Performance Measures for Continuous Improvement
- Establish Guidelines to Resolve Issues—Empower Local Resolution Whenever Possible
- Share Risk
- Discourage Adversarial Relationships by Eliminating Short-Term Quid-Pro-Quo Mentality
- Share Benefits

Source: Reproduced with permission of Kraft General Foods, Inc.

TABLE 7-2: Basic Ingredients for a Successful Logistics Alliance

---

- Thorough Assessment of Participant Strengths
- Value Consistency
- Clear Understanding of Objectives
- Agreement on Measurement Standards
- Long-term Focus
- Multiple Level Commitment
- Working Relationship at Interface Level
- Limited Number of Relationships
- Elimination of "Quid-Pro-Quo" Mentality
- Negotiated Prices—Not Bid and Subject to Change

Source: Reproduced with permission of Schneider National, Inc.

guidelines is during the formation period when firms believe everything will go well and therefore are more apt to agree to fair and rational termination procedures. Although most alliance arrangements are voluntary and, in effect, can be dissolved at any point, the formal specification of procedures for voiding responsibility is advisable. The planned duration and termination guidelines are ideally part of the formation agreement.

Exit provisions are especially important when customized equipment or facilities are involved. Buy-sell agreements can be developed that specify who has the right or obligation to purchase or assume lease obligations.

Why Alliances Fail

The typical alliance represents a radical departure from business as usual. Many alliances fail because they were never properly positioned for success. The following events can become major obstacles to alliance success.

Lack of Senior Management Support

To succeed, alliances must have managerial and resource commitment. Equally important is getting mid- and lower-level managers to participate with enthusiasm and make the alliance work. Too often managers consider new ways of doing business a threat to their own careers.

They must be informed of the potential benefits and "converted" to the cause.

In addition to the backing of key managers at all levels, the alliance must be supported with adequate resources. Unless sufficient funds are allocated, the alliance is almost certainly doomed. Funding to provide needed communications support is especially critical. The kinds of activities being developed typically cut across jobs and involve cross-functional or process-related activities. Therefore, an alliance may not have a natural champion in terms of traditional performance centers in an enterprise. The allocation of resources to an alliance may require special appropriations from the top down.

Lack of Trust

Developing internal support for the alliance is closely related to building mutual trust among the participants. It is difficult to promote an atmosphere of trust and willingness to share proprietary information among trading partners. Traditionally, information has been hoarded. The release of information has been considered equivalent to "giving away the store." Unless there can be a free exchange of ideas and a discussion of potential solutions, the alliance foundation will not be strong enough to make the partnership work.

Fuzzy Goals

Planning and discussion of mutual objectives and goals up front are essential. Unless all parties to an alliance share clear-cut goals from the outset, chances for a successful relationship are diminished considerably. Each party must define exactly what is expected to be accomplished, as well as detailing expectations about the responsibilities of other parties. Precise definition of long-term goals can be used to develop strategies, to provide a framework for managing the alliance, and to keep participants focused. Sharing clear-cut goals and related rates also helps to ensure that individual participants remain committed to the overall objectives of the alliance.

Uneven Commitment

In almost every instance, one of the parties to an alliance has more at stake than the others. The party having the most at stake is likely to make the most serious commitment to the long-term welfare of the alliance. Differences in commitment are likely to be directly related to relative power. If the more powerful party tries to leverage its advantage, it is likely to undermine the development of trust and commitment.

Loss of Control

Entering into alliance arrangements means that a certain amount of control is relinquished. Alliance members are likely to be uncomfortable with the idea of relinquishing authority to external partners. In traditional trading arrangements, most decisions were made autonomously. In an alliance, they must be made jointly, which requires open communication and close coordination. Alliance members must feel sufficiently confident in the arrangement to trust that the other members will not take advantage or misuse power.

THE ROLE OF ELECTRONIC DATA INTERCHANGE

Numerous examples of alliances that have been motivated by a desire to reduce costs, to avoid risk, and to stimulate creativity exist. Less frequently reported are alliances aimed at achieving competitive advantage. Such strategic alliances are a relatively recent phenomenon which has been facilitated by advanced electronic data interchange (EDI).

As noted earlier, a fundamental business mandate of an alliance is that participants share information. Exchange of timely, accurate information facilitates coordinated efforts focused on achieving mutual objectives. EDI provides the means for linking independent firms. The following quote from Skagen illustrates how EDI stimulates and facilitates a close working relationship. "EDI fosters customer-supplier partnerships—long-term procurement relationships founded on mutual commitment. A value-added chain connecting retailer to manufacturer to supplier can respond quickly to the marketplace's demands through rapid information exchange. EDI provides the electronic link that makes this possible."[16] Exploiting EDI strategically can position firms to achieve competitive advantage:

> Although technical in execution, the opportunity for successful EDI is not in the technical aspects (most of these issues have been resolved), but in managing a new way of doing business by internal and external relationships, or partnerships . . . the *chief value* of EDI is its ability to position a company to develop long-term, strategic alliances with its supply-chain partners. Further, strategic alliances are the wave of the future in improving

a company's competitive position; EDI is one tool to position companies for this type of relationship.[17]

EDI is the critical component or building block for the establishment of strategic alliances which are aimed at achieving competitive advantage. *EDI is a necessary, but not a sufficient, condition to achieve strategic linkage.* Before developing the ingredients of strategic linkage, the basic constructs of EDI are reviewed.

EDI—The Basics

EDI is defined as intercompany computer-to-computer exchange of business documents in standard formats. Computer-to-computer exchange signifies that information flows directly from the sender's activity, such as purchasing, to a receiver's activity, such as order entry, without human intervention or paper (hard copy). Computer-to-computer communication requires a standard format for message data. Information is formatted following prescribed rules and standards; ultimately, no human involvement is required to complete the transaction.

Information and communication standards are both essential to EDI. For a complete discussion of EDI and EDI standards, readers are referred to the American Management Association publications, *EDI at Work*[18] and *EDI: From Understanding to Implementation*.[19] Space constraints prevent a thorough discussion of detailed EDI standards. In general, communication standards format the language so that two computers can understand each other. Standards for document content govern the format of data content and sequence within a document.

EDI Benefits

EDI has significant potential for facilitating business transactions. In place of manually preparing and mailing business documents, they can be transmitted electronically. Direct benefits are speed, accuracy, and reduced cost. The accuracy issue is critical. Eliminating the need to convert data from hard copy to a different format for computer input dramatically decreases errors.

The most commonly cited direct benefits of EDI are: reductions in labor and material costs associated with printing, mailing, and handling paper-based transactions; reduction of telephone, fax, and telex costs; and reduction in clerical costs. Additional efficiencies are realized in indirect benefits such as: shorter and more dependable order cycles;

decreased labor, freight, and material costs; improved cash flow result-ing from reduced inventory and more timely invoicing and payment; and improvements in overall business efficiency as a result of complete, timely, and accurate information. Exploiting information capabilities also has the potential to improve customer service. Speed is especially important for companies involved in just-in-time (JIT) and quick re-sponse (QR) delivery systems.

The full benefits of EDI are often not realized until the application is developed using proprietary formats.[20] This suggests that basic EDI often needs to be customized for trading partners in order to gain true competitive advantage. Basic or standard applications can achieve cost and time savings, but they will not be unique in an industry. Such applications can be readily duplicated by competitors.

Many industries have developed standards to facilitate the exchange of messages. These industry standards serve to get a large number of firms in a specific industry to exchange basic transaction documents. However, they fail to provide all of the standards required by trading partners who also desire to share operating information such as inven-tory status, forecasts, and production schedules. Operating linkages usually require customizing EDI applications through proprietary con-nections with trading partners and tailoring information linkages to respond to specific requirements.

EDI Risks

EDI usage raises a number of concerns. Managers typically have res-ervations about the complexity involved. EDI systems commonly link a wide range of trading partners at varying levels of computer sophis-tication. Personnel are likely to resist planned changes because of a "fear of technology" and a tendency to view change as an unwelcome dis-ruption in the standard operating procedure. Proposals for developing EDI linkages often are met with a preference to continue to use the telephone or fax. Fear of technology requires training and educational programs to help participants fully understand the associated costs and benefits.

The risk of compromising key information is another typical fear associated with EDI. This is particularly true if outside vendors or third-party services are used. Firms are apprehensive about entrusting vital business information to an outside service. Third-party providers must be especially sensitive to security issues and inform potential users about system controls that limit access and reduce risk.

EDI involvement is sometimes thrust upon a firm. Many suppliers are receiving an "EDI mandate" from key customers, forcing them into involvement. It is not unusual for trading partners to receive notification to become EDI-capable by a specific date or risk losing the business.[21] This forced compliance often raises fear and resistance. Although mandated firms may try to comply with such directives, high levels of resistance are often noted among employees.

Evaluating EDI

Evaluation of EDI applications is typically based on a straightforward cost-benefit analysis. The initial feasibility of adopting EDI typically focuses on the identification and documentation of comparative costs for the paper versus the electronic process. Such direct comparison presents projected savings and estimated payback time. Direct financial evaluations are important but not sufficient to fully evaluate EDI potential. Strategic implications must also be considered. As discussed previously, EDI involvement is frequently required to establish and maintain trading partner relationships. The strategic potential of EDI involvement is difficult to measure and the benefits are not easy to quantify. A wide range of competitive advantages can be generated by strategic linkage. What is at stake is the value of a key customer and a close working relationship. In many situations, there may not be any real cost savings because the new way of doing business is far more comprehensive and requires more involvement. The real value may be satisfied customers.[22] Thus strategic linkage is market driven.

STRATEGIC LINKAGE

Successful strategic ventures share three attributes or characteristics: information access, connectivity, and formalization.[23] Each is discussed and illustrated briefly. Then a model is introduced to illustrate how these three attributes interact.

First, the importance of information access for strategic linkages cannot be overemphasized. Participating firms must formally commit to and develop capabilities for regularly sharing specific key information. Information access focuses on routinely sharing a broad range of database elements without restrictions.

Second, connectivity of strategic linkage refers to the level or capability of the partners' interactivity. Sophisticated communication systems do not guarantee high levels of connectivity. Responsiveness is the critical issue. How quickly can a participant in an alliance make *tailored* information available to the alliance partners? Maximizing responsiveness involves speed and precision—getting the exact information needed and getting it fast. The emphasis is on ease of information transfer between the parties and not on the technical aspects of electronic connection.

Third, as indicated in Chapter Three, formalization is key in a firm's effort to become a leading-edge logistical performer. This same attribute is the key to a firm extending its outreach to work with suppliers and trading partners. Creation of interfirm rules and procedures develops what amounts to an interorganizational culture. The interfirm rules and procedures formalize operating agreements which facilitate the spin-off or absorption of functional responsibilities. Each participant is responsible for defined tasks that permit the realization of benefits associated with specialization.

Achieving Strategic Linkage: An Integrated Model

Examination of the simultaneous interaction of information access, connectivity, and formalization provides the key to distinguishing strategic linkage from other cooperative ventures between trading partners. These three attributes and their simultaneous interaction provide the essential bases for differentiation and gaining competitive advantage. Figure 7-1 presents a three-dimensional model illustrating the interaction of the three key attributes.

All three of the attributes must be present in a strategic linkage arrangement. The synergy resulting from the interaction of the three elements is critical. Firms must commit to establishing levels of excellence and expertise in all three areas. Focusing on one or two of the attributes and ignoring or operating below average on the third will not achieve competitive differentiation.

Individual cooperative ventures can vary significantly. For example, a linkage arrangement may be strong in terms of one of the three attributes and relatively weak with respect to the other two. Or trading partners could have clear-cut agreements in regard to information access while having few formal rules and procedures and a very low level of connectivity. Such a combination of attributes would not constitute strategic linkage.

During the course of examining current business arrangements, few interorganizational arrangements were reviewed which scored high on all three of the attributes. Interviews with firms that are proactively

FIGURE 7-1: Relationship of Key Alliance Attributes

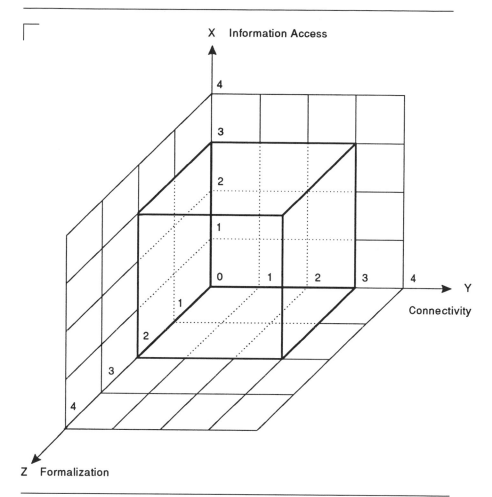

Source: Adapted from Bowersox, et. al., "Logistics Strategy and Structure: Strategic Linkage," a presentation given at the 1990 Council of Logistics Management Annual Conference. Reprinted with permission of the authors.

working to gain competitive advantage through strategic linkages are summarized in Appendix D. Arrangements reviewed that were successful in creating competitive advantage had comparatively high scores on all three of the attributes. It appears that a minimum or threshold level of achievement for each attribute is essential to the realization of a true strategic linkage. However, the minimum requirement for each attribute is relative and specific to each situation. Exactly how much of each attribute is needed to create interorganization synergism cannot be quantified, but a balance of attributes is important. In other words, strategic alliances that excel have a proportionate input of these three attributes. Future research will help to identify how the attributes interact and to determine what the minimum to the ideal combinations are.

Evolution of a Strategic Alliance

As relationships evolve and become strategic, participating parties exhibit a greater commitment to the alliance and its continuation. They actively work to increase interactivity between the organizations. The most advanced state of interaction involves real-time and computer-to-computer connectivity. The strategic partners have directly linked information systems operating in a real-time environment. Predefined information flows freely between partners upon request and in some cases in compliance with planned conditions. The partners have instant access to a wide range of information.

Greater information connectivity is indicative of a strong commitment to supporting and integrating the cooperative venture. The parties involved are proactively involved in reducing barriers to facilitate the free exchange of strategic information.

Generalized patterns illustrate how the attributes of information access, connectivity, and formalization combine into a strategic linkage arrangement and result in competitive advantage. The initial linkage often begins with basic EDI. The cooperative partners may first exchange standard business documents such as purchase orders, invoices, and order status reports as they begin to sort out the strategic potential. The development of information access is often initially prompted by efficiency-related objectives.

As the linkage arrangement matures, information access typically increases in response to a partner's needs. The exchange of basic business documents is soon insufficient. A supplier may desire to routinely access and examine inventory data and automatically create replenishment orders. The benefits of connectivity become part of an arrangement when the supplier provides on-line access to update order status information. Data exchange often includes such information as production status, order picking and loading, or location of materials in transit. Linked partners are able to gain immediate access to such key information. This "as needed" availability is in contrast to requesting the desired information and waiting for answers.

Higher levels of connectivity can facilitate reduced order cycle time and inventory investment. Partners in the arrangement have immediate access to order status and can make desirable changes based upon up-to-date information. Such situations illustrate the relationship between information access and connectivity. As the organizations move toward common formalization, a strategic alliance emerges.

As formalization materializes, planning efforts are coordinated interorganizationally. Order patterns and inventory information become a part of the supplier's forecasting system. Rules and procedures are developed to guide both day-to-day and flexible operating requirements. The traditional buyer-seller relationship is replaced with close interaction and commitment by the partners. The routine way of doing business is electronic. All parties benefit from the reduced administrative costs associated with invoicing, receiving and accounts payable, and from lower inventory levels, shorter order cycles, and the need for fewer adjustments. The resultant strategic linkage forged through interaction and strong commitment creates a competitive advantage.

RISKS ASSOCIATED WITH STRATEGIC ALLIANCES

As previously discussed, a number of benefits accrue to firms entering into alliance arrangements. Alliances have the potential for making a significant contribution to overall corporate success and profitability. The most important benefits include resource sharing and synergy, access to new perspectives and innovative thinking, and the potential for total cost reduction. Unfortunately, there are also risks involved. Following is a brief synopsis of alliance-related disadvantages or risks.

Partners to an alliance may become dependent upon one another. There is always a chance that a partner will not meet performance specifications. An even greater risk exists because of the degree of commitment and information exchanged. Partners "open their books" to each other, and the disclosure of sensitive operating information can be risky.

Problems are likely to ensue when there are differences in the level of commitment made by alliance members. Alliance participants are seldom, if ever, equal in terms of economic and market power and the resource commitment made to support the alliance. Simply put, one alliance partner is likely to dominate the other. For example, when a large organization enters into a partnership or alliance arrangement with a small vendor, the reward potential is much greater for the small firm. The larger firm is likely to be much less concerned with preserving the long-term health and continuation of the alliance.

Alliance arrangements generally increase quality expectations. Typically, commitment to an alliance involves the concentration of business transactions with fewer trading partners—or perhaps with a single trading partner. The guarantee of receiving a larger share of a firm's business is accompanied by an implicit demand for top-notch service. Fewer mistakes and less variance are tolerated.

Alliance participants also confront risks associated with lost opportunities. Committing resources to an alliance precludes taking advantage of other opportunities. Prior to entering into an alliance, the parties must evaluate such tradeoffs and assess the potential benefits. The rewards must be considered as adequately compensating each firm for the loss of its autonomy and the constraints placed on its business operations because of the alliance commitment.

Strategic alliances represent a paradox. The most attractive benefit associated with involvement in a strategic alliance is also its most unappealing feature—being "locked." The positive side of being locked means becoming an active participant in developing a systematic solution that focuses cooperative efforts at achieving mutual gain. The negative component of being locked means that parties involved in strategic alliances are forced to accept the risk associated with the venture and lose a certain amount of control over their own business operations. Fear of losing self-determination works as a barrier to the widespread development of strategic alliances.

SUMMARY

Exploratory research into strategic linkages indicates strong potential for and increasing interest in business arrangements that are more relational than the traditional buyer-seller adversarial practices. Although few true examples of strategic linkages currently exist in North America, greater interest is developing in the creation of alliances aimed at gaining competitive advantage.

Evidence suggests that firms positioning for competitive leadership by developing strategic linkages will rely heavily upon information technology. There are three essential attributes of a strategic alliance: information access, connectivity, and formalization. Strategic linkages represent extended arrangements that transcend an individual firm's legal and economic boundaries. Such arrangements generate their own cultures, roles, rewards, and risks.

Strategic linkages require new approaches to doing business. Developing a new corporate philosophy is not easy. Therefore, strategic linkages must present participants with a clear-cut opportunity to jointly accomplish objectives that could not be achieved operating in isolation or offer the possibility for significant reduction of risks, or both.

Notes

1. Barbara Bund Jackson, *Winning and Keeping Industrial Customers,* (Lexington, Mass.: Lexington Books, 1985); and Robert E. Spekman, "Strategic Supplier Selection: Understanding Long-Term Buyer Relationships," *Business Horizons* 31, 4 (July–August, 1988): 75–81.

2. David L. Anderson and Robert Calabro, "Logistics Productivity Through Strategic Alliances," *Proceedings of the Annual Conference of the Council of Logistics Management* (1987): 61–74; John F. Davisson, "Third-Party Distribution," *Handling and Shipping Management,* 27: 11 (October 1986): 69–71; and Evert Gummeson "The New Marketing—Developing Long-term Interactive Relationships," *Long Range Planning* 20, 4 (August 1987): 10–20.

3. John Gardner and Martha C. Cooper, "Elements of Strategic Partnership," in *Partnerships: A Natural Evolution in Logistics,* Proceedings of the 1988 Logistics Resource Forum (1988): 6.

4. Donald J. Bowersox, "The Strategic Benefits of Logistics Alliances," *Harvard Business Review,* 68, 4 (July–August 1990): 36.

5. Joe Dysart, "Partnerships with Electronic Handshakes," *Transport Topics,* No. 2863, (June 18, 1990): 14.

6. David Cassak, "The Corporate Alliance," *IN VIVO (The Business and Medicine Report)* (September 1989): 14–16.

7. C. K. Prahalad and Gary Hamel, "The Core Competence of the Corporation," *Harvard Business Review* 68, 3 (May–June 1990): 80.

8. Kenichi Ohmae, "The Global Logic of Strategic Alliances," *Harvard Business Review* 67, 2 (March–April 1989): 146.

9. Lane F. Cooper, Alex Linder, David Hold, and Stephanie Whitman, "EDI Part of Service Strategy Management Program at Motorola," *EDI News* 4, 9 (May 7, 1990): 3.

10. Joyce Barrett, "Administration Drafts Bill to Allow Joint Production," *Electronic News* 36, 1804 (April 9, 1990): 9.

11. Godfrey Devlin and Mark Bleackley, "Strategic Alliances—Guidelines for Success," *Long Range Planning* 21, 5 (1988): 18.

12. Stanley J. Modic, "Strategic Alliances," *Industry Week* 237, 7 (October 3, 1988): 46.

13. Donald J. Bowersox, "Logistical Partnerships," *Partnerships: A Natural Evolution in Logistics,* Proceedings of the 1988 Logistics Resource Forum (1988): 1–14.

14. Bernard J. LaLonde and Martha C. Cooper, *Partnerships in Providing Customer Service: A Third-Party Perspective* (Oak Brook, Ill.: Council of Logistics Management, 1989), p. 120.

15. Rosabeth Moss Kanter, "Becoming PALS: Pooling, Allying and Linking Across Companies," *The Academy of Management EXECUTIVE* III, 3, (August 1989): 191.

16. Anne E. Skagen, "Nurturing Relationships, Enhancing Quality with Electronic Data Interchange," *Management Review* 78, 2 (February 1989): 28. Reprinted with permission. © 1989 American Management Association, New York. All rights reserved.

17. Gene R. Tyndall, "Supply-chain Management Innovations Spur Long-term Strategic Retail Alliances," *Marketing News* 22, 26, (December 19, 1988): 10.

18. *EDI at Work* (New York: American Management Association: Membership Publications Division, 1989).

19. Kathleen Hinge, *EDI: From Understanding to Implementation,* (New York: American Management Association: Membership Publications Division, 1988).

20. *EDI News* 4, 11, (June 4, 1990).

21. Skagen, "Nurturing Relationships," *Management Review* 78, 2, (February 1989): 28.

22. Collin Canright, "Seizing the Electronic Information Advantage," *Business Marketing* 73, 1 (January 1988): 84.

23. Donald J., Bowersox, Patricia J. Daugherty, and Maurice P. Lundrigan, "Logistics Strategy and Structure: Strategic Linkage," a presentation given at the 1990 Council of Logistics Management Annual Conference.

The Day After Success

WHEN THE RESULTS started to become apparent, Charlie scheduled a meeting with key personnel to recap how the successful alliance with Super was established. He reported that Super's management was truly impressed with the alliance, and Dan's people were committed to expanding the scope of the arrangement. Charlie emphasized it was critical that their people develop a continued level of commitment. He restated the responsibilities and the potential for sharing of benefits—"we're all in this together."

In order to bring home his point, he spent a great deal of time elaborating on "what's in it for us." He not only mentioned improvements in business efficiency, he also brought it down to the personal level—job security. Logistics capabilities had to be developed, implemented, and continuously improved in order to maintain a competitive edge. The new cooperative venture would allow each of the alliance partners to focus on what they were capable of doing best, thus realizing improvements via reduced costs and improved service. It would also give each of the partners new perspectives, thus introducing the possibility of developing innovative solutions to business problems.

Charlie concluded by saying, "That's history. Our ideas were good enough and the potential for improvement great enough to convince Super to work with us *now*. But what's ahead? How do we ensure that this alliance continues to grow and succeed? And how do we develop other key customer or supplier alliance arrangements?"

People really got involved; ideas were introduced one after another and intense discussion followed. Many of the key ideas focused on remaining *aware.* Too often in the past, things got bogged down because people became too involved in day-to-day "fire fighting" to concentrate on the bigger picture. Although Charlie's team had a pretty good idea of "where the company has been" and "where we are now," they recognized the importance of developing a future orientation. A future orientation involves monitoring the external environment, really establishing a dialogue with customers, investigating new technologies, etc. These things could not be left to chance. It was decided that formal guidelines and the designation of specific responsibilities were necessary to ensure continued development and progression of the firm's logistical excellence.

Just as Charlie and the others were trying to specify and formalize the initiative, Charlie got a call from Randy Good's office. The CEO wanted to see Charlie in fifteen minutes. Leaving the others to develop future-oriented management guidelines, Charlie headed for Randy's office.

Charlie assumed the CEO wanted to hear more about the strategic alliance with Super. However, as he entered Randy's office, he sensed that Super was not the topic at all.

Charlie was soon to learn that the Board had finalized a merger with a major competitor. Charlie was surprised, but he was also pleased. The combined operations would clearly be the industry leader. They've been doing a lot of things right—but not everything. Charlie started to think about how the two firms could be blended together to form one "new and improved" operation. What synergies were possible? Undoubtedly, a merger would require significant rationalization to eliminate duplication. His mind quickly reviewed which areas would offer the best opportunities for "collapsing" and the elimination of personnel, equipment, etc. Charlie could envision an exciting opportunity for significant synergism. As he began to think about what might be, he heard Randy say: "You're the man for the job—you develop the big picture, you find out what has to be done and you get it done."

The winds of change will affect each organization in a unique way and thus its managerial accommodation will naturally be different. Experience dictates that a select few managers will fully grasp the meaning and motivation for change and will be able to isolate unique opportunities. The ability to perceive the opportunity that is embedded in change is the essential difference between a reactor and a leader.

This book has developed a model of what is required for logistical excellence. The overall process of managing change was presented and substantiated as two inherently related initiatives. They are illustrated in Figure 8-1.

The link or bond between internal and external initiatives is the overall vision as well as the formalized rules and procedures that guide routine logistics operations and facilitate day-to-day decision making. One of the lessons learned from research into the practices of leading-edge firms is that the process of establishing these essential attributes

FIGURE 8-1: *Logistical Excellence Establishing Flexibility*

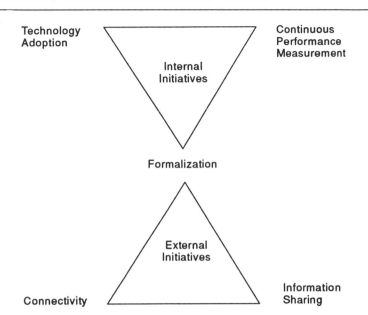

can be managed. Technology adoption and successful implementation do not simply happen. Technology adoption is a process that must be managed. The same is true of continuous performance measurement, information sharing, and connectivity. Although change management requires some unique managerial skills, the process itself and the attributes of leading-edge performance are accessible to all firms who are willing to mount and sustain the initiative.

The primary benefit of logistical excellence is flexibility. The soundly designed logistical system is so well adapted to handling the countless daily details and complexity involved in satisfying customers that it creates an in-place capacity to surge and capture extraordinary opportunities. It is the ready and waiting reserve to do the extraordinary that adds up to using logistical competency to gain competitive advantage.

As noted above, the exact dimension of change that each organization will face and must manage will be different in scope and magnitude. In a general sense, the entire logistical profession will face some *common* forces. In the 1980s, the drivers were unusual political or legal change, the technology explosion, business and economic structural changes, and globalization. At the outset of the 1990s, it appears logistical initiative during the forthcoming decade will focus around the impact of at least three fundamental orientations: speed, quality, and organizational structure change. How individual firms accommodate these forces will define the magnitude and direction of leading-edge practice.

The following eight propositions hypothesize likely change.

PROPOSITION 1: The Basic Demand For Logistical Services Will Expand

World population growth and a commitment to greater equality in the standard of living will be the main drivers of a worldwide demand for logistical services. The demand for basic transportation and storage will be particularly apparent in developing nations. Assuming a decade relatively free from political conflict and military confrontation, this demand will drive a new level of both primary and counter trade worldwide.

Development of major trading blocs of industrialized nations will further fuel the demand for logistical services. Free trading within the blocs will necessitate new logistical arrangements. Growth in trading among the blocs will be dependent upon working out arrangements to facilitate logistical coordination. The impact of the stateless corporation, which seeks a competitive advantage through sourcing on a global basis, will also depend upon logistical proficiency. Thus, logistics will increasingly be viewed as the key process to facilitate potential economic growth.

New demands will be placed on logistical systems. Product proliferation provides an excellent example of such demands. Manufacturers will continue to increase the number of offerings within individual product categories. Ordering patterns will change accordingly. Retailers will increasingly order smaller quantities of a wider assortment of SKUs and will demand more split cases and special packs than in the past. Business operations will become more complex in order to accommodate such requests. Information capability will be key to helping firms develop complex and affordable solutions to providing new customer services.

Within the most advanced industrialized societies, there is every reason to believe that consumers will continue to demand expanded services as part of the total product package they purchase. Logistics systems of the future will need to distribute products in nonconventional configurations. For example, live fish will be delivered direct to retail stores, an increasing quantity of food products will be sold ready to eat, deliveries will increasingly be direct to consumers, and the size of individual orders will decrease. These and other value-added services will serve to increase the pressure on logistics organizations to perform.

Finally, the cost of nonperformance will increase. The cost of losing a customer as a result of poor logistical performance will become greater due to the close operational linkages resulting from strategic alliances. Logistics cost as a percentage of product value will demand exacting performance. Although whole raw chicken may be worth only 25 cents per pound, a pound of fully cooked boned premium chicken breasts may have a value exceeding $4.00 per pound. The raw logistical cost associated with each of them would be nearly identical. Failure to perform and comply with logistical requirements would be far more detrimental in lost earnings for the processor of premium chickens.

All of the above forces and others will combine in the 1990s to stimulate an unprecedented demand for logistics services.

PROPOSITION 2: Environmental and Infrastructure Constraints Will Become Increasingly Restrictive

Logistics considerations related to environmental impact and infrastructure limitations will be pervasive during the 1990s. From the viewpoint of the environment, logistical operations are a major source of potential contamination. Emissions from transportation are significant. In particular, trucks which transport the majority of the logistical ton-miles are significant environmental polluters. The disposal of materials used in unit loading, such as shrink wrap, also offer an environmental challenge. In addition, the safe transport of toxic and hazardous materials requires continuous scrutiny. Hardly a week goes by that one does not witness some type of major material spill that requires environmental cleanup.

Logistical operations are also limited by some major problems within the basic infrastructure. The infrastructure upon which logistics operates requires continuous repair and restoration. The federal freeway system represents the backbone of logistics. While construction started following World War II, the system as originally planned has not to this date been completed. In fact, despite massive repair initiatives, the highway and bridge system is deteriorating at a rate faster than it can be repaired. The nation faces similar concerns related to rail, water, air, and pipeline transportation.

Perhaps the most significant aspects of the environmental and infrastructure impacts upon logistics are the looming limitations of congestion. Gridlock currently exists in many metropolitan areas and at many airports. The reality of the matter is that while national growth occurs, the basic infrastructure remains static. The result is that more movement and tonnage is forced to flow within an infrastructure with a fixed capacity.

Logistics managers face serious limitations in the continuation of traditional work practices. Faced with gridlock, all firms will not be able to get delivery of freight every morning and pickups every night. In fact, several metropolitan areas are considering ordinances that will prevent commercial delivery during selected hours of the day, resulting in the need for pickup and delivery patterns in off-peak hours. Speed limits on trains are being imposed by several local communities, and some are seeking to "fence off" their areas by prohibiting selected types of hazardous materials from moving through commercial and residential districts.

All of the above factors add up to increasing restrictions within which logistical operations will have to be planned and administered. For many firms, new methods of doing business will have to be explored. For some it will mean night-time delivery and a variety of new and different working arrangements. Logistics has always been an around-the-clock business for transportation carriers, and the demand for continuous service seven days a week is bound to expand to all sections of the logistical community during the 1990s. Only by voluntary modification of how the available capacity is used will it be possible to prevent infrastructure rationing.

PROPOSITION 3: Human Resources Will Be A Critical Concern

Most firms have already faced problems attracting and retaining personnel to meet their logistical requirements. Relief is not in sight. In fact, the problem is likely to become even more pronounced in the future because of two important demographic trends: (1) the lower birthrate associated with the baby boom generation; and (2) the general aging of the population. Simply put, there will be fewer people available and interested in performing the physical jobs of logistics.

Entry-level logistical jobs are often less than attractive with their long hours, minimum-wage pay, and less than ideal work conditions, all of which are common. Potential employees must believe there is chance for advancement in order to make the more immediate "sacrifices" seem worthwhile. The shortage of workers will not be of the same intensity in all geographical areas. However, generally severe shortages are anticipated in most industrial areas and more effective methods of using available labor will be required.

Firms will be forced to carefully reassess how jobs are performed and eliminate unnecessary tasks. Innovative thinking and reengineering of the work process will be required. Greater effort must be placed on developing new ways of handling routine business needs. Some firms will be able to adopt automation and thereby reduce the number of employees needed for routinized tasks. The mobile nature of the logistics process places limitations on the potential for automation. However, to the degree possible, automation can free employees from the more mundane, labor-intensive jobs and provide at least a partial solution to the problem.

The aging of the work force will necessitate a reevaluation of work assignments. Many logistical tasks involve manual labor—lifting and moving heavy objects. Older employees are restricted in what they can handle. Another issue related to human resources concerns the concentrated effort to bring more women into the work force to fill jobs traditionally held by men. Many firms have successfully experimented with split shifts and unique working hour arrangements to accommodate the special needs of women who desire both to raise families and to hold formal positions in the work force.

Firms may be able to cross-train employees to perform different jobs as a way to achieve improvements in productivity. By training employees to do multiple jobs, they can be assigned to facilitate adoption of new processes. Having an internal flexible work force may also facilitate the use of outside specialists. A trend of the 1980s was the widespread use of outside service providers. Numerous firms are available that will provide any or all of a firm's logistical needs. Thus, the firm can decide to outsource all or part of its logistical service requirements. In fact, it is becoming commonplace to hire a third party to provide turnkey performance of many logistical requirements. The use of outside logistical service providers will continue to grow as one way for available human resources to be most effectively utilized.

PROPOSITION 4: Logistical Competency Will Increasingly Be Viewed As A Strategic Resource

Logistical competency will be valued as a strategic resource in the future. Firms will increasingly be forced to enter new markets. In order to reach and successfully serve these new markets, logistical competencies will be required. Escalating competition in the 1990s will force firms to seek new ways of gaining and maintaining a competitive edge. Firms will increasingly realize that long-term differentiation through product or service formulation will not always be possible because, in most situations, such efforts can be rapidly duplicated by competitors. Therefore, logistical service dependability and quality will take on even greater importance in future years. If and when a product becomes almost a commodity, the deciding factor between alternative suppliers may become the level of logistical support. An increasing number of firms have come to realize the potential for gaining competitive advantage by providing superior logistical services. As a result, they view their logistical strategies and processes as proprietary assets not to be shared. Such proprietary attitudes will become increasingly common during the 1990s.

In the future, more firms will come to realize the competitive value of creating new solutions to business problems and improved ways of handling routine operations. They will also realize that unique approaches can be used strategically and that the importance of confidentiality cannot be ignored. More firms will place restrictions on the discussion or disclosure of operating strategies and procedures. Revealing too much information could mean risking the loss of competitive advantage.

PROPOSITION 5: Logistics Arrangements Will Become More Relational

Significant growth in the number of partnership arrangements and strategic alliances was a major development in the 1980s. Arrangements in which firms move from a transactional to relational perspective will become even more common in the decade ahead. Attitudes fostering adversarial relations between buyers and sellers have been demonstrated to be shortsighted. More firms will come to realize the advantages associated with building long-term, mutually rewarding working relationships with key customers and suppliers.

The entire business process will continue to change at a pace that will force firms to consider new approaches. In the past, too many managers focused on short-term results. In the future, more executives will realize the importance of working *with* trading partners. Rather than trying to negotiate the absolutely best deal for each individual transaction, a *mutually beneficial* long-term arrangement will become the goal. Such cooperation is especially necessary with respect to obtaining essential logistical support. Both buyers and sellers have much to gain from the development of well-coordinated, long-term relationships.

Through close communication and cooperation, firms can jointly act as architects to tailor or customize logistical services to meet customer needs. Precise specification of fundamental requirements during planning is critical to long-term success. A customer has a greater probability of receiving dependable, high-quality service by explicitly stating up front what is expected. A supplier has a greater likelihood of developing a successful ongoing relationship providing that an appropriate service package can be put together and delivered on a consistent basis.

There is another important reason for working to create closer relationships that will continue to materialize in the future. Selling firms commit a great deal of their resources in the form of time and effort to developing tailored services. It will become increasingly impractical to make such commitments on a short-term or transaction-by-transaction basis. Customers also make a considerable investment when setting up long-term relationships and coordinating planning. Once the relationships are established and operating, business operations can be handled more efficiently by concentrating purchases with the selected trading partner(s) rather than dealing with a number of vendors on a nonroutine basis. This trend will accelerate in the 1990s.

PROPOSITION 6: Technology Will Continue To Reshape Conventional Logistics Processes and Channels

As technology continues to advance at an accelerated rate, new developments will have an important impact on the logistics process. Speed in decision making will be enhanced as information is developed, processed, formatted, and moved at ever-faster rates and at lower cost. Firms are currently able to move information quickly using technologies ranging from simple fax machines to sophisticated satellite systems. New communication technologies will continue to be commercialized. As customers become more committed to technology, supplying firms will need to keep pace or be left out.

Already commonplace among Wall Street trading firms, knowledge-based expert systems will continue to filter into the leading-edge logistics organization. These "smart" systems will enable organizations to go beyond the rudimentary transactional nature of early information systems and assist users in applying information to decisions. Firms that utilize expert systems are able to design capabilities into their information systems that make the user a better and more accurate decision maker.

Neural networks or "fuzzy logic" technology, which mimic the functioning of the human brain, will give logistics personnel the ability to make better decisions when working with incomplete and inadequate information. Fuzzy logic is currently being designed into select consumer products. For example, cameras are being designed with fuzzy logic chips, which gives the camera the ability to make decisions normally reserved for the photographer. This technology will be increasingly applied to logistics systems and manufacturing processes during the 1990s.

Leading-edge logistics organizations of the 1990s will have integrated databases that allow easier access to all relevant operational information. Managers will be able to quickly grab data out of the system, examine those data, and turn them into useful information. The utilization of commercial databases will continue to increase. Third-party information services will provide logistics organizations with a variety of new capabilities. These services will make it easier to perform competitive research, examine supplier or customer finances, benchmark operations, and communicate with external entities who may have input into the organization needs.

Interactive home delivery systems that utilize videotext or high-quality graphics will be commercialized. Logistics organizations will find themselves increasingly dealing with final consumers. The net result of continued technological impact will be to render the logistics channel of the 1990s more direct. Maintaining the economies of direct logistics will become the challenge of the 1990s.

PROPOSITION 7: Management Emphasis Will Focus On Process Accountability

Accounting techniques and practices were originally developed to manage individual business functions. In order to control the total business, measurement and performance standards were imposed separately for each business function. The intent of managerial attention at the functional level was to facilitate efficiency. The experience of the 1980s has highlighted that focusing on functions can ignore the total process, often to the detriment of customer satisfaction. Individual functions may appear to be operating efficiently, but at the same time important interfunctional tradeoffs may be neglected.

In the 1990s, basic changes in business operations and the blurring lines of demarcation between functions will work to make organizations more process based. The supply chain perspective of process management will become commonplace. It will be more difficult and, more importantly, less appropriate to rely on function-based accountability. Management will focus on satisfying customers at reasonable total cost rather than closely examining each step in the process as a separate, unrelated entity. Improved process accountability will result in greater coordination and synergism of business functions. The quality of information used to manage the business will improve as methods of measuring true organizational success or failure are adjusted to focus on the overall process.

PROPOSITION 8: Logistics Organizations Will Become Increasingly Transparent

As the business playing field continues to change, logistics organizations will adapt. Demands for logistical performance will increase to meet constantly changing customer requirements. Emphasis will be placed on making logistics *customer responsive.* Customers will continue to have high expectations regarding the speed and quality of service.

In order to enable quicker and better response, authority will continue to be pushed down the organization. Although strategic direction can be expected to originate at headquarters, operational adaptations will increasingly be made on the front lines. Because of enhanced information system capabilities, organizational strategy will be translated into operational competencies much more fluidly. Front-line managers will be expected to define strategy and apply it directly to operations.

Centralization and decentralization will increasingly become meaningless terms. The availability and accessibility of information will make the *location* of decision makers much less important than in the past. Decisions can be made and disseminated instantaneously. The posture of the organization of the future will seek to capture the best of centralization and decentralization without complete commitment to either concept.

The notion that integrated logistics means "all functions are grouped under a single authority" will be reexamined. Firms will increasingly discover they can reap the benefits of integrated logistics without a restrictive command and control organizational structure. By exploiting information capabilities, crucial system checks and balances can be maintained without bogging down the logistics process with excess personnel and counterproductive controls.

Organizations have become leaner and flatter than they were five years ago. This trend will continue. As information becomes more fluid and more easily accessible, logistics organizations will be better positioned to adapt. Logistics managers cannot survive by simply reading reports and then acting. They will have to be able to manipulate the technology to produce information. Tomorrow's leading-edge managers will be those who not only understand logistics, but also know how to use technology to enhance that process.

POSTSCRIPT

In retrospect, a case can be made that the decade of the 1980s was a logistical renaissance. During the 1980s, logistics practices underwent more change than in all of the years since the industrial revolution. The functional management of logistical activities for some firms was catapulted from near green-eye-shade status to the corporate boardroom. *Logistical Excellence* offers a chronicle of the deep-rooted cultural change required for a firm's management to position logistical performance as a strategic resource.

The dialogue of Charlie Change is a story of change management. Charlie's challenge, while fictional, contains many insights concerning challenges related to exploiting logistical competency. Some lessons learned are:

- To significantly improve performance of a process that is not broken, takes considerable time and will often be resisted by those who have the most to gain.
- The vast majority of business managers simply have neither the training nor the work experience to position them to manage true integration. As a result, the vast majority of available technology capable of facilitating process integration is underutilized.
- Improving quality is illusive in a service such as logistics that is performed across a global playing field, and is difficult to mea-

sure. Therefore, the early advantage favors those who are critical of proposed change. Getting buy-in and ownership when long-standing paradigms are being challenged is most difficult.

■ Finally, the process of improvement must be a continuous effort—the job is never done.

As business faces a new millennium, the 1980/90 paradigms of strategic logistics will be fully tested and retested. The best practices of the 1990s will spawn new and exciting ways to leverage excellence beyond the year 2000. History suggests that today's logistics leaders—those who manage logistics in leading-edge firms—may well become tomorrow's barriers to change. Solutions, no matter how good today, will not remain relevant long in a dynamic environment.

The challenge is significant. A careful examination of the best logistical practice in 1992 suggests that less than 50 percent of North American firms have made significant progress towards achieving logistical excellence. Most of these firms, which include manufacturers, wholesalers, and retailers throughout North America, are struggling to achieve improved logistical integration. Reengineering a value-added process that spans from procurement to final consumption is an awesome task. Approximately 10 percent of North American firms have achieved a level of integration that permits the use of logistical competency in the overall effort to gain and maintain customer loyalty.

The flip side of the coin contains the real challenge for North American business. Approximately 50 percent of all firms have not truly started the journey toward logistical excellence. So for some firms, the challenge is far greater than maintaining momentum.

Logistics-Related Sources

THIS APPENDIX lists logistics-related sources of information and expertise: trade and professional associations, executive management programs, and project management software packages as well as textbooks and selected journals and periodicals. Addresses and phone numbers are provided for the associations and for the software and executive management programs to facilitate making contact.

Additional sources of information can be identified by examining the chapter endnotes throughout this book.

Associations

American Retail Federation (ARF)
Tracy Mullin
President
American Retail Federation
701 Pennsylvania Avenue, N.W., Suite 710
Washington, D.C. 20004
202-783-7971

Association of Retail Marketing Services (ARMS)
George Meredith
Executive Director
Association of Retail Marketing Services
3 Caro Court
Red Bank, NJ 07701
908-842-5070

American Society of Transportation & Logistics, Inc.
Carter M. Harrison, CM
Executive Director
American Society of Transportation & Logistics
P.O. Box 33095
Louisville, KY 40232
502-451-8150

American Warehousemen's Association
Jerry Leatham
President
American Warehousemen's Association
1165 N. Clark Street
Chicago, IL 60610
312-787-3377

Association of Transportation Practitioners
E. Dale Jones
Executive Director
Association of Transportation Practitioners
1725 K Street, NW—Suite #301
Washington, DC 20006-1401
202-466-2080

Canadian Industrial Transportation League
Maria Rehner
President
Canadian Industrial Transportation League
480 University Avenue
Toronto, Ontario M5G 1V2
416-596-7833

Council of Logistics Management
George A. Gecowets
Executive Vice President
Council of Logistics Management
2803 Butterfield Road—Suite #380
Oak Brook, IL 60521
708-574-0985

Delta Nu Alpha
Thomas W. Dardis
Executive Director
Delta Nu Alpha
621 Plainfield Road—Suite #308
Willowbrook, IL 60521
708-850-7100

Eno Foundation for Transportation, Inc.
Roland A. Ouellette
President
Eno Foundation for Transportation, Inc.

270 Saugatuck Avenue
P.O. Box 2055
Westport, CT 06880
203-227-4852

Institute of Logistics & Distribution Management
Raymond C. Horsley
Chief Executive
Institute of Logistics & Distribution Management
4th Floor, Douglas House
Queens Square
Corby, Northants
England, NN17 1PL
(0536) 205500

International Customer Service Association (ICSA)
Madalyn B. Duerr
Executive Director
International Customer Service Association
401 N. Michigan Avenue
Chicago, IL 60611-4267
312-644-6610

International Mass Retailing Association
Richard Hirsch
President
International Mass Retailing Association
570 7th Avenue
New York, NY 10018
212-354-6600

International Material Management Society
Peter Youngs
Executive Director
International Material Management Society

8720 Red Oak Boulevard—Suite
#224
Charlotte, NC 28217
704-525-4667

**The National Association of
Purchasing Management**
Roland J. Baker, CPM
Executive Vice President
National Association of Purchasing
Management
2055 E. Centennial Circle, P.O.
Box 22160
Tempe, AZ 85285-2160
602-752-6276

**National Association of
Wholesaler-Distributors/
Distribution Research and
Education Foundation
(NAW/DREF)**
Ron Schreibman
Executive Director
NAW/DREF
1725 K Street, N.W.—Suite 710
Washington D.C. 20006

**The National Defense
Transportation Association**
Lt. Gen. Edward Honor, USA
(Ret.)
President
National Defense Transportation
Association
50 S. Pickett Street—Suite #220
Alexandria, VA 22304-3008
703-751-5011

**National Food Distributors
Association (NFDA)**
Arthur H. Klawans
Managing Director
National Food Distributors
Association

401 N. Michigan Avenue—24th
Floor
Chicago, IL 60611
312-644-6610

**The National Industrial
Transportation League**
James E. Bartley
National Industrial Transportation
League
1700 North Moore Street—Suite
1900
Arlington, VA 22209-1904
703-524-5011

**National Retail Merchants
Association (NRMA)**
Jack Fraser
Vice President
National Retail Merchants
Association
100 West 31st Street
New York, NY 10001
212-244-8780

**National Wholesale Druggists'
Association**
Charles S. Trefrey
President
National Wholesale Druggists'
Association
P.O. Box 238
Alexandria, VA 22313
703-684-6400

**Society of Logistics Engineers
(SOLE)**
Steven R. Jones
Executive Director
Society of Logistics Engineers
125 W. Park Loop
Huntsville, AL 35806-1745
205-837-1092

Southern Wholesalers Association (SWA)
Frank Rizzo
Executive Vice President
Southern Wholesalers Association
3584 Habersham at Northlake
Tucker, GA 30084
404-939-9882

Transportation Research Forum
William M. Drohan, CAE
Executive Director
Transportation Research Forum
1600 Wilson Boulevard—Suite
  #905
Arlington, VA 22209
703-525-1191

Warehousing Education and Research Council (WERC)
Thomas E. Sharpe
Executive Director
Warehousing Education &
  Research Council
1100 Jorie Blvd.—Suite #170
Oak Brook, IL 60521
708-990-0001

Management Programs

Michigan State University
Logistics Management
  Executive Development
  Seminar
Graduate School of Business
  Administration
Eppley Center
Michigan State University
East Lansing, MI 48824-1121
517-353-6381

Northwestern University—The
  Transportation Center
Logistics/Distribution
  Management
Executive Management Programs
Northwestern University
  Transportation Center
1936 Sheridan Road
Evanston, IL 60208
708-491-3225

Penn State Executive Programs
Program for Logistics
  Executives
Penn State Executive Programs
310 Business Administration
  Building
Pennyslvania State University
University Park, PA 16802
814-865-3435

University of Nevada, Reno
Center for Logistics
  Management Executive
  Programs
Center for Logistics Management
College of Business Administration
University of Nevada, Reno
Reno, NV 89557-0016
702-784-4912

University of South Florida
Managing Inventories in
  Uncertain Times and
  Measuring the Profit Impact
  of Logistics
Professional Development Center
College of Business Administration
University of South Florida
Tampa, FL 33620
813-974-4264

University of Tennessee—
  Management Development
  Center
Executive Development
  Program for Distribution
  Managers; The Logistics
  Institute; and International
  Logistics Program
University of Tennessee
  Management Development
  Center

708 Stokley Management Center
University of Tennessee
Knoxville, TN 37996-0570
615-974-5001

University of Wisconsin—
  Madison
Various programs throughout
  the year
University of Wisconsin—Madison
Management Institute
432 North Lake Street
Madison, WI 53706
608-262-2155

Project Management Software

Harvard Project Manager
Software Publishing Corporation
1901 Landings Drive
Mountain View, CA 94039-7210
415-962-8910

Instaplan 5000
Micro Planning International, Inc.
655 Redwood Highway
Suite 311
Mill Valley, CA 94941
415-389-1414

Microsoft Project for Windows
Microsoft Corporation
1 Microsoft Way
Redmond, WA 98052-6399
206-882-8080

Project Scheduler 5
Scitor Corporation
393 Vintage Park Drive
Suite 140
Foster City, CA 94404
415-570-7700

Superproject Expert
Computer Associates International,
  Inc.
1240 McKay Drive
San Jose, CA 95131
800-531-5236

Time Line
Symantec Corporation
10201 Torre Avenue
Cupertino, CA 95014-2132
408-253-9600

Textbooks

Ronald H. Ballou, *Basic Business Logistics,* 2d ed. (Englewood Cliffs, N.J.: Prentice-Hall, 1987).

Ronald H. Ballou, *Business Logistics Management,* 3d ed. (Englewood Cliffs, N.J.: Prentice-Hall, 1992).

Donald J. Bowersox, David J. Closs, and Omar K. Helferich, *Logistical Management,* 3rd ed. (New York: Macmillan Publishing Co., 1986).

John J. Coyle, Edward J. Bardi, and C. John Langley, Jr., *The Management of Business Logistics,* 4th ed. (St. Paul, Minn.: West Publishing Co., 1988).

James C. Johnson and Donald F. Wood, *Contemporary Logistics,* 4th ed. (New York: Macmillan Publishing Co., 1990).

John F. Magee, William C. Copacino, and Donald B. Rosenfield, *Modern Logistics Management—Integrating Marketing, Manufacturing, and Physical Distribution* (New York: Wiley, 1985).

Philip B. Schary, *Logistics Decisions—Text and Cases.* (New York: Dryden Press, 1984).

Roy D. Shapiro and James L. Heskett, *Logistics Strategy—Cases and Concepts* (St. Paul, Minn.: West Publishing Co., 1985).

James R. Stock and Douglas M. Lambert, *Strategic Logistics Management,* 2d ed. (Homewood, Ill.: Richard D. Irwin, 1987).

Journals and Other Publications

Bibliography on Logistics Management (published annually by the Council of Logistics Management and The Ohio State University)

Council of Logistics Management—Proceedings of the Annual Meeting

Distribution

Handling & Shipping Management

International Journal of Logistics Management

International Journal of Physical Distribution & Logistics Management

Journal of Business Logistics

Journal of Purchasing and Materials Management

The Logistics and Transportation Review

Logistics Information Management

Logistics Spectrum

Logistics World

Purchasing World

Traffic Management

Traffic World

Transportation & Distribution

The Transportation Journal

Transportation Quarterly

Transportation Research Forum, Proceedings

Warehousing Forum

Statistical Tools

WHEN PERFORMING an assessment of logistics processes, it is absolutely necessary to understand relevant data thoroughly. Statistical tools allow the change agent to gain a comprehensive understanding of the data that otherwise would be impossible.

Almost all members of the organization need some training in statistical techniques. Certainly the people responsible for changing an organization need to have a clear understanding of statistical tools and techniques. Statistical techniques allow organization change agents to examine logistics processes and focus on problems rather than continuously putting out fires.

Often, instead of controlling the process, many firms simply hire more expediters or else let their current managers work longer hours to get the product out the door. Statistical analysis increases the organization's ability to bring manufacturing and logistical processes under control. It also increases the likelihood that organizational change will be successful. The careful examination of data through an ordered process can do much to improve operational management.

The statistical tools discussed in this appendix are simple, straightforward, and useful. They are not intended to represent a complete list. There are many books and articles that describe in detail analytical tools and how they are used. Some of these references are listed at the end of this appendix.

Statistical Tools

The statistical tools discussed briefly in this section are as follows:

1. Shewhart cycle
2. Cause-and-Effect diagrams (fishbone)
3. Flow charts
4. Pareto charts

5. Trend charts
6. Histograms
7. Control charts
8. Scatter diagrams

Shewhart Cycle

As mentioned in Chapter Four, the Shrewhart cycle is a methodical way to test specific variables (see Table B-1). It has sometimes been referred to as the "PDCA Cycle," which stands for Plan, Do, Check, Act. It is a simple method used to structure the methodical solving of problems. The first step in this cycle is to study a process and decide what changes might be desirable. The second step is testing, or making a change. This testing is usually made on a small scale. The third step is observing the effects of the test and step four is studying the results and determining what was learned. The cycle is a closed loop so that following step four, step one is repeated with new knowledge from the previous iteration of the cycle.

Cause-and-Effect Diagrams (Fishbone)

Cause-and-effect diagrams are good tools for graphically depicting the relationship between the occurrence of an event and the likely causes of that event. These diagrams are sometimes referred to as Ishikawa diagrams after the University of Tokyo professor who invented these charts. These cause-and-effect diagrams are also sometimes called "fishbone" diagrams because of their skeletonlike appearance.

Fishbone diagrams are used to graphically depict the causes of a specific problem. They are often constructed during brainstorming sessions in which key personnel work together to determine causes of a selected

---

TABLE B-1: Shewhart Cycle

Step 1: What could be the most important accomplishment of this team? What changes might be desirable? What data are available? Are new observations needed? If yes, plan a change or test.
Step 2: Carry out the tests, or change, on a small scale.
Step 3: Observe effects of the change or test.
Step 4: Study the results. Determine what was learned.
Step 5: Return to Step 1 with new knowledge accumulated.

Source: Mary Walton, *The Deming Management Method* (New York: Perigee Books, 1986). Reprinted by permission of The Putnam Publishing Group from *The Deming Management Method* by Mary Walton. Copyright © 1986 by Mary Walton.

problem. The fishbone diagram consists of a "head" where the problem is briefly described. The "head" is connected to a long branch which has minor branches extending from the major branch. Additional smaller branches, or "twigs," are attached to the minor branches during the session determining the cause of the problem. Each minor branch is labeled. Four categories that are commonly used to label minor branches are materials, methods, manpower, and machines. These categories are sometimes referred to as the four "Ms." The underlying concept behind the four "Ms" is that the causes of most problems can be found somewhere within these four categories.

The benefits resulting from intelligent utilization of cause-and-effect diagrams are many. Development of a good cause-and-effect diagram can be enlightening. The capturing of causes on paper is an excellent formal way to detail information. People learn from each other as the diagram is put together. Learning might not take place without the structured discussion during development of a fishbone diagram. Logistics managers are likely to glean information that otherwise would be missed. A fishbone diagram captures reasons for problems and categorizes those reasons.

An example of a preliminary fishbone diagram that focuses on the causes of slow delivery time is depicted below in Figure B-1. Figure B-2 identifies a few of the causes for the slow delivery times.

Flow Charts

Flow charting is another technique for data collection. Flow charts allow the user to understand a process flow. It is impossible to assess and improve a process unless the process is clearly understood in detail. Management's view of the process flow can be much different from the actual logistics process flow. The difference between the actual process and the perception of the process leads to bad decisions. Thus, documenting actual logistics processes can be informative.

Pareto Charts

Pareto charts are bar graphs that show the relative magnitudes of problem causes. Pareto charts are named for Vilfredo Pareto, the originator of the "80-20 rule." They are used to collect data relating to the causes of problems and to determine priorities. They can be used in conjunction with cause-and-effect diagrams. After a cause-and-effect diagram has been completed to determine the probable reasons for a problem, Pareto charts can be used to display the relative size of problem causes.

Problems are often comprised of several smaller problems. Pareto charts prioritize the smaller problems that make up the larger problem. Pareto diagrams are useful because they clearly display the main associated

FIGURE B-1: Initial Fishbone Diagram

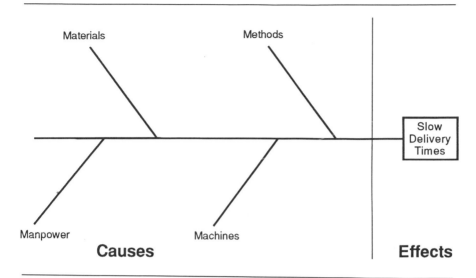

FIGURE B-2: Modified Fishbone Diagram

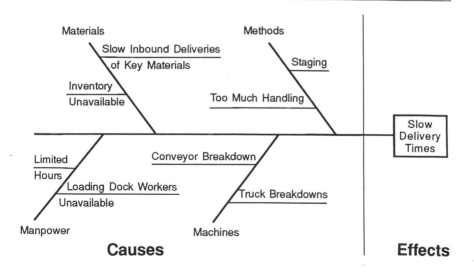

problems with a specific process. They enable logistics personnel to focus on the greatest problems. With limited resources, most organizations can work only on a small number of problems. These limitations force organizations to prioritize. The taller bars on the Pareto chart show the largest problems. Over time, Pareto charts show whether attempts at process improvement have been successful. As a problem cause is determined and the incidence of that cause decreased, the size of the bar representing that cause is reduced. As the incidence of problems is reduced, they move from the left of the Pareto chart to the right as depicted in Figure B-3.

After continually working on the causes of the major problems, inventory unavailability and limited hours to accomplish the logistics mission, these problems are shown to be reduced. The Pareto chart for slow delivery in Figure B-4 reveals the following results.

Trend Charts

Trend charts represent a very simple tool. They are used to track trends over time. Time is always charted on the X-axis while the variable that is to be tracked is on the Y-axis.

Histograms

Histograms are used to determine how often a specific event occurs. For example, charting sales of an item on a histogram can assist logistics

---

FIGURE B-3: Slow Delivery Pareto Chart 1

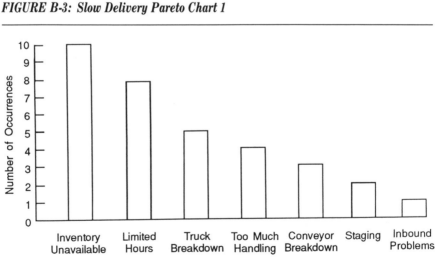

SLOW DELIVERY CAUSES

FIGURE B-4: Slow Delivery Pareto Chart 2

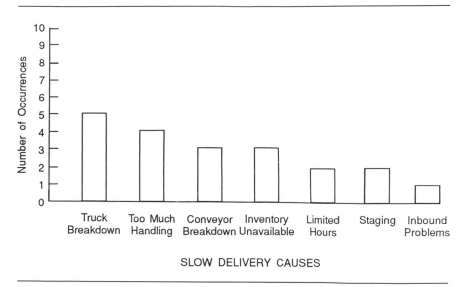

personnel in visualizing where safety stock levels should be set. Figure B-5 shows an example of a historgram of weekly pallet sales for a selected item. This histogram displays a clearly visible sales pattern.

Control Charts

Control charts are structured similar to trend charts with time depicted on the X-axis. Control charts have an important extra ingredient however. Upper or lower control lines, or both, are superimposed on the graph. The control limits are used to determine whether the pattern or process is out of control. Control charts are a good method to graphically display unacceptable process variation. Upper and lower control limits are often calculated based on standard deviations from the mean.

In the packing errors control chart in Figure B-6, cumulative numbers of packing errors for 10 weeks were charted. An upper control limit was set at approximately 23 errors per week. After working to bring this process under control to where there are never more than 23 packing errors per week, the upper control limit can be lowered. This method of bringing the process under control, tightening the control limits, and then repeating the process results in less variation in key logistics operations.

FIGURE B-5: Histogram of Weekly Sales (in pallets)

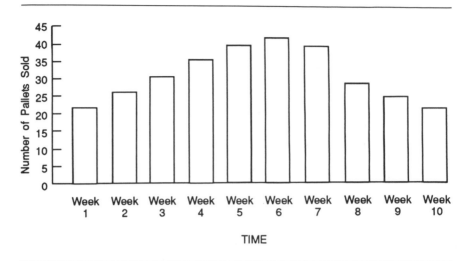

FIGURE B-6: Packing Errors Control Chart

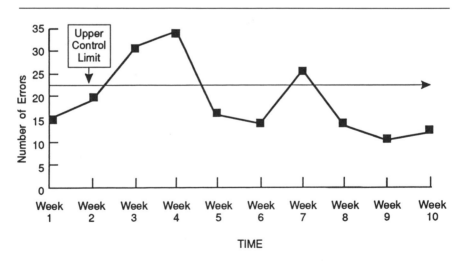

Scatter Diagrams

Scatter diagrams are simple *X-Y* graphs where the relationship between two variables is examined. These charts assist logistics personnel to clearly see correlations between variables. In the example of a scatter diagram in Figure B-7, inventory errors are compared to shipping problems for a selected period. This comparison shows that there may be some correlation between inventory errors and shipping problems. It helps to establish a relationship between two separate problems.

References

The following references can be helpful in studying in greater detail the use of these statistical tools.

Kaoru Ishikawa, *Guide to Quality Control* (Tokyo: Asian Productivity Organization, 1976).

Soichiro Nagashima, *100 Management Charts* (Tokyo: Asian Productivity Organization, 1987).

Mary Walton, *The Deming Management Method* (New York: Perigee Books, 1986).

Western Electric, *Statistical Quality Control Handbook* (Indianapolis: Western Electric, Inc. 1956).

FIGURE B-7: *Scatter Diagram (Comparison of Inventory Errors to Shipping Problems)*

Statistical Analysis

APPENDIX C describes the method used in the analysis presented in Chapter Six and is organized in the following manner. First, the sampling design is described. This is followed by a description of the sample itself. Next, the scales used are discussed and the statistical tests employed are presented. Lastly, the tables are listed and then the tables themselves are presented.

DESCRIPTION OF THE SAMPLING PROCESS

A series of self-administered questionnaires were designed by a panel of academicians and industry executives. These questionnaires were extensively pretested prior to mailing.

Two separate sampling frames were obtained: one for manufacturers and the other for wholesale and retail merchandisers. The manufacturer sampling frame was provided by A.T. Kearney, Inc., in conjunction with the Council of Logistics Management. A total of 680 questionnaires were mailed and 380 (55.9%) usable forms were returned. A second questionnaire containing the technology and performance measurement scales was designed by the advisory panel and mailed to the 380 respondents of the first questionnaire. A total of 187 (49.2%) of these forms were returned.

The merchandiser questionnaire was also designed by the advisory panel and pretested before final mailing. A sampling frame consisting of the name and address of the CEO of 6,678 U.S. and Canadian wholesalers and retailers was purchased from Dun and Bradstreet. A total of 369 (5.5%) of the questionnaires were returned. In order to correctly identify the type of firm, respondents were asked to select as many types as were applicable from the categories of manufacturer, wholesaler, and retailer. Several firms selected the manufacturer response only. The names of these organizations were carefully screened by the authors and it was decided that 92 of the 369 organizations that responded to the merchandiser study were primarily manufacturers. This difficulty can be attributed to two factors. First, the sampling frame itself may have been flawed. Second, manufacturing organizations with merchandise subsidiaries may have responded. The screening of the firms by name was conducted to ensure that every organization was properly categorized as either a manufacturer or a merchandiser. Several firms also selected the manufacturer response as well as one or both of wholesaler or retailer. These firms were also screened individually to determine if they were predominantly manufacturers or merchandisers.

A total of 556 organizations are included in the analysis. Of these, a total of 279 are manufacturers (187 plus 92) and the remaining 277 are merchandisers.

DESCRIPTION OF THE SAMPLE

The 556 organizations in the sample vary considerably in terms of size and primary class of trade. Mean annual dollar sales of all the firms is $1.5 billion with a standard deviation of $6.49 billion. The mean annual sales of the manufacturers is $1.7 (with a standard deviation of $8.01 billion) and mean annual sales of the merchandisers is $1.29 billion (with a standard deviation of $4.43 billion). In the manufacturer study, 2-digit Standard Industrial codes were collected to determine the class of trade industry. In the merchandiser study, respondents were asked to select the most appropriate class of trade from a list provided in the questionnaire. The classifications used in the two surveys are not entirely alike. Table C-1 presents the class of trade distribution for the firms in the analysis.

DESCRIPTION OF THE SCALES

A wide variety of scales were used during the analysis, although for the most part an attempt was made to avoid perceptual scales (e.g., Likert scales or semantic differential scales). Many of the scales used were the sum of a series of yes/no items. In the subsections that follow, the scales used to measure formalization, performance measurement, technology (and information quality), and flexibility are described.

Formalization

The formalization variables were broken down into variables that describe formal mission and strategy, empowerment of logistics, and organization.

TABLE C-1: Class of Trade Distributions

Class of trade	Manu-facturer study	Class of trade	Merchandiser Study Manu-facturers	Merchan-disers
Mining, metals, petroleum	21	Building materials	13	49
		General merchandise	3	35
Food, tobacco, beverage	45	Food	36	54
Textiles, apparel, leather	12	Automotive	3	27
Furniture, forest related	24	Apparel	2	26
Electronic/scientific equipment	26	Furniture	22	26
		Eat/drink	—	4
Transportation equipment	16	Drugs	2	16
		Fuel	4	20
Pharmaceuticals	35	Paper/office supplies	6	11
Missing	8	Other	1	3
		Missing	0	1

Unless otherwise mentioned, identical scaling methods were employed in the merchandiser and manufacturer questionnaires.

Formal mission and strategy:

Formal mission logistics statement: measured on a single yes/no scale. Formal logistics strategic plan: measured on a single yes/no scale.

Empowerment of logistics:

Title level of the senior logistics executive: measured in two different but equivalent ways in the merchandiser and manufacturer questionnaires. In the merchandiser questionnaire, respondents were asked to select from among president, executive vice president, senior vice president, vice president, director, or manager. The president response was coded as a 7, the executive vice president response was coded as a 6, and so on. In the manufacturer questionnaire, a free response scale was used. These were coded by hand into equivalent response categories as those in the merchandiser questionnaire.

Participation by the senior logistics executive in business unit strategic planning was measured on a 3-point scale. Respondents were asked to rate the extent of participation using the following response categories: (1) no, provides no input; (2) no, but provides input through other executives; and (3) yes.

Organization:

Number of times logistics has been reorganized during the past five years was measured on a free response scale.

Length of time logistics formally organized was measured on a free response scale.

Total number of activities controlled by or reporting to logistics was measured by a series of summed yes/no scales. A list of activities was provided and respondents were asked whether logistics has line and/or staff responsibility over each. The sum was then taken. For manufacturers, the list included the following 15 activities: (1) sales forecasting; (2) production planning; (3) sourcing/purchasing; (4) inbound transportation; (5) outbound transportation; (6) intra-company transportation; (7) finished goods field warehousing; (8) raw/WIP inventory control; (9) finished goods inventory control; (10) order processing; (11) customer service; (12) logistics systems planning; (13) logistics engineering; (14) logistics administration; and (15) international logistics. For merchandisers, the list included the following 16 activities: (1) sales forecasting; (2) purchasing; (3) inbound transportation; (4) outbound transportation; (5) intra-company transportation; (6) warehousing; (7) inventory control; (8) order processing; (9) customer service; (10) logistics systems planning; (11) facilities design; (12) logistics administration; (13) international logistics; (14) materials handling; (15) capital equipment procurement; and (16) data processing for distribution applications.

Performance Measurement

Several measures of the extent to which the firm engaged in performance measurement were utilized. These were divided into two broad categories: (1) internal performance measurement; and (2) benchmarking performance measurement or the comparison of the firm to competition.

Internal Performance Measurement:

Respondents were asked if they used each of 38 measures to monitor operations or identify problems. These 38 measures were then classified as belonging to one of seven types.

Total cost performance measurement: sum of 6 yes/no measures: (1) total logistics cost analysis; (2) logistics cost per unit; (3) logistics cost as a percentage of sales; (4) comparison of actual to budgeted costs; (5) cost trend analysis; and (6) direct product profitability.

Logistics cost components: sum of 6 yes/no measures: (1) inbound freight costs; (2) outbound freight costs; (3) warehouse costs; (4) administration costs; (5) order-processing costs; and (6) direct labor costs.

Asset management: sum of 6 yes/no measures: (1) inventory turns; (2) inventory-carrying costs; (3) inventory levels (number of days supply); (4) obsolete inventory; (5) return on net assets; and (6) return on investment.

Service: sum of 6 yes/no measures: (1) fill rate; (2) stockouts; (3) shipping errors; (4) on-time delivery; (5) back orders; and (6) cycle time.

Feedback: sum of 3 yes/no measures: (1) sales force feedback; (2) customer feedback; and (3) customer surveys.

Productivity: sum of 6 yes/no measures: (1) units shipped per employee; (2) units per labor dollar; (3) orders per sales representative; (4) comparison to historical standards; (5) goal programs; and (6) productivity index.

Quality of service: sum of 5 yes/no measures: (1) frequency of damage; (2) dollar amount of damage; (3) number of customer returns; (4) number of credit claims; and (5) cost of returned goods.

Benchmarking Measurement:

Benchmarking was defined in the questionnaire as: "a management process used to monitor and measure performance against competitors." Respondents were asked whether they benchmarked in each of ten areas. The ten areas were classified as belonging to one of two groups.

Components: sum of 5 yes/no benchmarking areas related to major logistical components: (1) logistics costs; (2) asset management; (3) customer service; (4) productivity; and (5) quality of service.

Operations/strategy: sum of 5 yes/no benchmarking areas related to operations and strategy: (1) logistics strategy; (2) technology deployment; (3) transportation operations; (4) warehouse operations; and (5) order-processing operations.

Technology

Three major types of technology were measured: (1) computer software; (2) electronic data interchange (EDI); and (3) hardware technology. In addition, the quality of information was also measured.

Computer Software:

A total of 23 computer applications were examined. Respondents were asked whether or not each installation (or application) was currently computerized. The 23 applications were categorized as belonging to one of two major types.

> Basic installations: sum of 4 yes/no applications that are primarily transactional in nature: (1) purchasing; (2) inventory control; (3) order processing; and (4) order entry.

> Other installations: sum of 19 other computer applications: (1) freight/audit and payment; (2) sales forecasting; (3) warehouse order selection; (4) warehouse on-line receiving; (5) warehouse merchandise locator; (6) warehouse workload balancing; (7) warehouse short interval scheduling; (8) vehicle routing and scheduling; (9) inbound freight consolidation; (10) outbound freight consolidation; (11) supporting financials; (12) performance measurement; (13) distribution modeling; (14) direct product profitability; (15) direct store delivery; (16) shelf management; (17) electronic order transmission; (18) computer aided warehouse design; (19) artificial intelligence.

Electronic Data Interchange:

Respondents were asked whether they are currently linked with each of eight organizational entities. These were classified as being related to one of two types.

> EDI with channel members: sum of links out of four trading partner entities: (1) manufacturers; (2) wholesalers; (3) retailers; and (4) customers.
> EDI with third parties: sum of links out of four service providers: (1) public warehouses; (2) carriers; (3) financial institutions; and (4) copackers/contractors.

Hardware Technology:

Respondents were asked whether or not each of 17 hardware technologies were used in logistics. These were categorized as being one of two types.

> Operational hardware: sum of 7 yes/no items: (1) bar codes; (2) optical-scanning devices; (3) robotics; (4) automated storage and retrieval systems; (5) automated material handling equipment; (6) computers on-board delivery vehicles; and (7) computers on-board lift trucks.

> Computer hardware: sum of 10 yes/no items: (1) local area networks; (2) hand-held data-entry devices; (3) voice data capture; (4) IBM PC or PC XT compatible; (5) 80286 microcomputers (IBM AT or compatible); (6) 80386 microcomputers; (7) CD-ROM; (8) WORM (write once, read many) discs; (9) 68020-based microcomputers (Macintosh 2 or Sun); and (10) fiber optics.

Quality of Information:

Respondents were asked to rate on five scales the quality of information used to manage logistics: (1) timeliness of information; (2) accuracy of information; (3) readily available information; (4) information formatted on an exception basis; and (5) information appropriately formatted to facilitate use. For each information characteristic, a 5-point scale was used: (1) never; (2) rarely; (3) sometimes; (4) often; and (5) always. A "not applicable" response category was also available, and these were coded as "missing" values.

Short-Run Logistical Flexibility

The flexibility of the organization was measured on eight dimensions. Respondents were asked to rate the ability of the firm to accommodate each of the following specific events: (1) special customer service requests; (2) sales and marketing incentive programs; (3) product introduction; (4) product phaseout; (5) disruption in supply; (6) product recall; (7) customization of service levels to specific markets or customers; and (8) product modification or customization while in the logistics system (e.g., pricing, packaging, or mixing). In the merchandiser questionnaire, each of the events were measured on a 5-point scale: (1) cannot accommodate; (2) accommodates with difficulty; (3) accommodates with few problems; (4) accommodates easily; and (5) accommodates very easily. In addition, a "not applicable" response category was available, and these were treated as "missing" values.

DESCRIPTION OF STATISTICAL METHODOLOGY AND SUMMARY OF MAJOR RESULTS

The analysis occurred in two stages. In the first stage, relationships between pairs of variables were examined one pair at a time. Simple linear correlations were estimated whenever possible in Tables C-2 through C-19. Only in the case of the two binary variables (the existence of a formal mission statement and the existence of a formal logistics strategic plan) were *t*-tests used. All remaining variables were treated as interval-scaled. Lettered superscripts in Tables C-2 through C-19 indicate significance at the 1% level (a), 5 % level (b), or 10% level (c). When no correlation or *t*-statistic appears as indicated by a blank space, then the relationship between the pair of variables was not significant at the 10% level.

The second stage of the analysis involved testing whether the relationships between variables were consistent across the manufacturer and merchandiser groups. Two different approaches were taken. The first approach involved testing whether the manufacturer versus merchandiser variable was a significant covariate. In this case, a separate ANCOVA model was estimated for each relationship. The results are reported in Tables C-20 through C-25. In these tables, a "Me" entry indicates that the relationship was stronger in the merchandiser group, a "Ma" entry indicates that the relationship was stronger in the manufacturer group (the significance level is also provided), and no entry (indicated by a dot) means that the manufacturer/merchandiser covariate was not significant.

Tables C-20 through C-25 therefore report the results of a total of 455 ANCOVA models. Of these, the manufacturer/merchandiser covariate was significant a total of 43 times (or 9.45%). The proportion of times that the manufacturer/merchandiser covariate was significant is less than 10 percent, which is less than the proportion one would expect on the basis of chance alone. The conclusion drawn from this analysis is that the relationships underlying organizational design do not differ markedly between manufacturers and merchandisers.

The second approach to determining whether the relationships differed across manufacturers and merchandisers involved the use of rank order correlations (Tables C-26 through C-29). The 25 predictor variables (the 5 formalization variables, 9 performance measurement variables, and 11 technology and quality of information variables) were rank ordered in terms of the strength of their relationship with each flexibility variable. It should be pointed out that the formal logistics mission statement and formal logistics strategic plan variables could not be included in such an analysis because of their binary nature. Nonsignificant relationships were given a rank of zero, the most significant relationship was given a rank of 25. The average rank order (over the 8 flexibility measures) was then estimated for each of the 25 predictor variables. This process, conducted for all 556 firms together, yielded a rank order of the 25 predictor variables in terms of how related they were, on average, with the 8 measures of logistical flexibility. The process was then repeated for each of the manufacturer and merchandiser subgroups. The rank order of the two subgroups was then compared.

Take, for example, the case of basic computer installations. Table C-26 reports that it received a rank of 20 (24 being the most strongly related, zero being the least related) in terms of how highly it was related to flexibility at accommodating customer service requests (column 1). Looking across this row, it can be seen that basic installations received a rank order of 24 for the following 5 measures of flexibility and a rank order of 16 for the last two measures. Its mean score across all measures of short-run logistical flexibility (across all firms) was 21.50, the highest rank order among all 25 predictor variables (see Table C-29). Among manufacturers, the mean ranking for basic installations was 23.50 (Table C-27) while among merchandisers, the mean ranking was 8.38. These were ranked 1st and 15th, respectively.

The complete rank order of the 25 predictor variables is shown in Table C-29 for all firms and for the manufacturer and merchandiser subgroups separately. A rank order correlation was then estimated to determine whether the rank order of the 25 predictor variables between manufacturers and merchandisers differed. The rank order correlation was 0.497, which was significant at the .01 level. Based on this finding, the conclusion was drawn that the manner in which formalization, performance measurement, and technology (and quality of information) relate to flexibility does not differ significantly between manufacturers and merchandisers.

LIST OF TABLES

Table C-1, as already mentioned, contains the class of trade industry distributions for the organizations participating in the study. The remaining tables are organized into various sets. The first set of tables presents the results of the relationships among formalization, performance measurement, technology, and short-run logistical flexibility for all firms ($n=556$).

Table C-5: Formalization and Flexibility
Table C-6: Performance Measurement and Flexibility
Table C-7: Technology and Flexibility

The second and third sets of tables are similar to the first set, except that they present results for the manufacturer subgroup ($n=279$) and the merchandiser subgroup ($n = 277$), respectively.

Set 2 Table C-8: Formalization and Performance Measurement (Manufacturers Only)

Table C-9: Formalization and Technology (Manufacturers Only)

Table C-10: Performance Measurement and Technology (Manufacturers Only)

Table C-11: Formalization and Flexibility (Manufacturers Only)

Table C-12: Performance Measurement and Flexibility (Manufacturers Only)

Table C-13: Technology and Flexibility (Manufacturers Only)

Set 3 Table C-14: Formalization and Performance Measurement (Merchandisers Only)

Table C-15: Formalization and Technology (Merchandisers Only)

Table C-16: Performance Measurement and Technology (Merchandisers Only)

Table C-17: Formalization and Flexibility (Merchandisers Only)

Table C-18: Performance Measurement and Flexibility (Merchandisers Only)

Table C-19: Technology and Flexibility (Merchandisers Only)

It is important to recall that for Tables C-2 through C-19, the values reported are correlations except for mission statement and strategic plan where t-values from two-tailed t-tests are reported.

The fourth set of tables presents the results of the first analysis concerning whether the relationships between pairs of variables differ across manufacturers versus merchandisers.

Set 4 Table C-20: Formalization and Performance Measurement (Differences Based on ANCOVA Models)

Table C-21: Formalization and Technology (Differences Based on ANCOVA Models)

It is important to recall that for Tables C-2 through C-25, superscript "a" (^{a}) means that the relationship is significant at alpha equal to 0.01, superscript "b" (^{b}) means that it is significant at 0.05, and superscript "c" (^{c}) indicates significance at 0.10.

The fifth and last set of tables presents results of the second analysis concerning whether relationships differ between manufacturers and merchandisers.

ABLE C-2: Formalization and Performance Measurement (All Firms: Max n = 556)

	(1)	(2)	(3)	(4)	(5)	(6)	(7)
Performance Measurement							
Internal							
Total cost	5.601[a]	6.302[a]		.172[a]	.096[b]		.252[a]
Cost components	5.667[a]	5.332[a]		.129[a]			.275[a]
Asset management	4.068[a]	3.747[a]		.114[a]			.157[a]
Service	6.392[a]	5.835[a]		.126[a]			.258[a]
Feedback	4.841[a]	3.657[a]					.157[a]
Productivity	4.591[a]	4.985[a]		.196[a]			.231[a]
Quality	5.613[a]	5.605[a]	−.106[b]	.131[a]	.096[b]		.196[a]
Benchmarking							
Components	4.152[a]	4.028[a]	−.080[c]		.107[b]		.132[a]
Operations/strategy	5.902[a]	5.824[a]		.125[a]	.159[a]		.156[a]

1 = Mission statement   4 = Participation   6 = Number of reorganizations
2 = Strategic plan   5 = Years organized   7 = Total activities
3 = Title level

TABLE C-3: Formalization and Technology (All Firms: Max n = 556)

	(1)	(2)	(3)	(4)	(5)	(6)	(7)
Technology							
Software							
Basic installations	5.889[a]	5.288[a]	−.156[a]		.106[b]		.196[a]
Other installations	7.496[a]	7.263[a]		.231[a]	.127[a]		.218[a]
EDI							
Members	2.890[a]	3.841[a]	.108[b]	.101[b]	.127[a]		.102[b]
Third parties	3.637[a]	3.271[a]		.136[a]	.101[b]		.139[a]
Hardware							
Operational technology	5.412[a]	6.672[a]	.094[b]	.150[a]	.104[b]		.176[a]
Hardware technology	4.948[a]	5.987[a]	.120[a]	.183[a]		.078[c]	.236[a]
Information Characteristics							
Timely	2.992[a]	2.479[a]			.148[a]	−.146[a]	.145[a]
Accurate	3.355[a]	2.830[a]			.133[a]		.195[a]
Readily available	3.764[a]	3.141[a]		.103[b]	.198[a]	−.103[b]	.148[a]
Exception formatted	3.567[a]	3.821[a]					.208[a]
Appropriately formatted	3.414[a]	2.935[a]		.135[a]	.139[a]		.236[a]

1 = Mission statement   4 = Participation   6 = Number of reorganizations
2 = Strategic plan   5 = Years organized   7 = Total activities
3 = Title level

TABLE C-4: Performance Measurement and Technology

	(1)	(2)	(3)	(4)	(5)	(6)	(7)	(8)	(9)
Technology									
Software									
Basic installations	.277[a]	.302[a]	.197[a]	.385[a]	.264[a]	.220[a]	.330[a]	.280[a]	.254[a]
Other installations	.345[a]	.420[a]	.293[a]	.471[a]	.259[a]	.460[a]	.382[a]	.197[a]	.293[a]
EDI									
Members	.095[b]	.085[b]	.079[c]	.169[a]	.107[b]	.086[b]			.080[b]
Third parties	.169[a]	.169[a]		.072[c]			.147[a]	.096[b]	.173[a]
Hardware									
Operational technology	.171[a]	.247[a]	.138[a]	.254[a]	.094[b]	.261[a]	.210[a]	.120[a]	.211[a]
Hardware technology	.183[a]	.214[a]	.156[a]	.265[a]	.163[a]	.236[a]	.232[a]	.166[a]	.217[a]
Information Characteristics									
Timely	.226[a]	.183[a]	.091[b]	.146[a]	.094[b]	.162[a]	.153[a]	.160[a]	.143[a]
Accurate	.241[a]	.223[a]	.104[b]	.150[a]	.118[a]	.125[a]	.187[a]	.135[a]	.147[a]
Readily available	.248[a]	.208[a]	.140[a]	.166[a]	.113[a]	.097[b]	.154[a]	.170[a]	.128[a]
Exception formatted	.253[a]	.246[a]	.167[a]	.311[a]	.217[a]	.214[a]	.262[a]	.189[a]	.206[a]
Appropriately formatted	.251[a]	.219[a]	.174[a]	.208[a]	.192[a]	.174[a]	.205[a]	.233[a]	.200[a]

ernal
1 = Total cost   4 = Service   6 = Productivity
2 = Cost components   5 = Feedback   7 = Quality
3 = Asset management

nchmarking
8 = Components   9 = Operations/strategy

TABLE C-5: Formalization and Flexibility (All Firms: Max n = 556)

	(1)	(2)	(3)	(4)	(5)	(6)	(7)	(8)
Formalization								
Formal Mission/Plan								
Mission statement		2.353^b	3.929^a	3.204^a	3.455^a	4.089^a	1.895^c	2.942^a
Strategic plan	2.402^b	1.753^c	3.224^a	2.098^b	3.243^a	4.412^a	2.260^b	3.529^a
Empowerment								
Title level				$-.085^c$	$-.087^b$	$-.113^b$		$-.099^b$
Participation								
Organization								
Years organized		$.093^c$	$.109^b$		$.103^b$	$.094^b$		
No. of reorganizations							$-.082^c$	
Total activities	$.090^b$		$.218^a$	$.201^a$	$.186^a$	$.218^a$		$.200^a$

1 = Customer service requirements   4 = Product phaseout   7 = Customized service
2 = Sales/marketing incentives   5 = Disruption in supply   8 = Modification in system
3 = Product introduction   6 = Product recall

TABLE C-6: Performance Measurement and Flexibility

	(1)	(2)	(3)	(4)	(5)	(6)	(7)	(8)
Performance Measurement								
Internal								
Total cost	$.154^a$	$.158^a$	$.218^a$	$.204^a$	$.196^a$	$.189^a$	$.145^a$	$.169^a$
Cost components		$.075^c$	$.163^a$	$.147^a$	$.092^b$	$.158^a$	$.073^c$	$.173^a$
Asset management	$.119^a$	$.168^a$	$.180^a$	$.172^a$	$.075^c$	$.112^b$	$.133^a$	$.171^a$
Service	$.141^a$	$.087^b$	$.241^a$	$.235^a$	$.200^a$	$.318^a$		$.120^a$
Feedback	$.160^a$	$.220^a$	$.204^a$	$.180^a$	$.160^a$	$.113^a$	$.139^a$	$.139^a$
Productivity	$.090^b$	$.116^a$	$.222^a$	$.223^a$		$.219^a$	$.083^c$	$.086^b$
Quality	$.194^a$	$.179^a$	$.257^a$	$.275^a$	$.211^a$	$.316^a$	$.176^a$	$.197^a$
Benchmarking								
Components	$.191^a$	$.249^a$	$.174^a$	$.202^a$	$.178^a$	$.191^a$	$.162^a$	$.146^a$
Operations/strategy	$.135^a$	$.199^a$	$.240^a$	$.174^a$	$.164^a$	$.165^a$	$.128^a$	$.188^a$

1 = Customer service requirements   4 = Product phaseout   7 = Customized service
2 = Sales/marketing incentives   5 = Disruption in supply   8 = Modification in system
3 = Product introduction   6 = Product recall

TABLE C-7: Technology and Flexibility

	(1)	(2)	(3)	(4)	(5)	(6)	(7)	(8)
Technology								
Software								
Basic installations	.164[a]	.259[a]	.283[a]	.317[a]	.317[a]	.338[a]	.130[a]	.175[a]
Other installations		.098[b]	.246[a]	.242[a]	.141[a]	.244[a]		.103[b]
EDI								
Members			.107[b]		.108[b]			
Third parties			.120[a]	.095[b]	.141[a]	.091[b]		.092[b]
Hardware								
Operational technology			.134[a]	.153[a]	.087[b]	.189[a]		
Hardware technology	.099[b]	.091[b]	.216[a]	.161[a]	.096[b]	.198[a]	.072[c]	.108[b]
Information Characteristics								
Timely	.187[a]	.191[a]	.234[a]	.177[a]	.247[a]	.207[a]	.183[a]	.182[a]
Accurate	.216[a]	.195[a]	.249[a]	.215[a]	.249[a]	.215[a]	.172[a]	.190[a]
Readily available	.162[a]	.195[a]	.201[a]	.159[a]	.244[a]	.192[a]	.199[a]	.189[a]
Exception formatted	.117[a]	.190[a]	.226[a]	.156[a]	.206[a]	.238[a]	.104[b]	.194[a]
Appropriately formatted		.257[a]	.244[a]	.193[a]	.240[a]	.199[a]	.080[c]	.187[a]

1 = Customer service requirements   4 = Product phaseout   7 = Customized service
2 = Sales/marketing incentives   5 = Disruption in supply   8 = Modification in system
3 = Product introduction   6 = Product recall

TABLE C-8: *Formalization and Performance Measurement*
(Manufacturers Only: Max n = 279)

	(1)	(2)	(3)	(4)	(5)	(6)	(7)
Performance Measurement							
Internal							
Total cost	1.953[c]	4.469[a]		.233[a]			.195[a]
Cost components	3.673[a]	5.094[a]		.132[b]			.254[a]
Asset management	2.523[b]	3.736[a]					.144[b]
Service	3.419[a]	4.179[a]		.104[c]			.193[a]
Feedback	4.229[a]	3.646[a]					.152[b]
Productivity	2.109[c]	3.185[a]		.265[a]			.199[a]
Quality	3.014[a]	4.015[a]		.166[a]			.111[c]
Benchmarking							
Components	2.400[b]	2.743[a]		.104[c]	.219[a]		
Operations/strategy	3.174[a]	4.025[a]		.158[a]			.115[c]

1 = Mission statement 4 = Participation   6 = Number of reorganizations
2 = Strategic plan   5 = Years organized   7 = Total activities
3 = Title level

ABLE C-9: Formalization and Technology (Manufacturers Only: Max n = 279)

	(1)	(2)	(3)	(4)	(5)	(6)	(7)
echnology							
oftware							
asic installations	4.398[a]	3.852[a]		.117[c]	.152[b]		.177[a]
ther installations	4.633[a]	4.326[a]	.105[c]	.260[a]			.182[a]
DI							
embers	2.061[b]	3.176[a]	.182[a]	.150[b]	.135[b]		.125[b]
hird parties				.149[b]			.125[b]
ardware							
perational technology	3.142[a]	2.564[b]	.163[a]	.191[a]			.173[a]
ardware technology	3.579[a]	5.401[a]	.176[a]	.188[a]		.161[b]	.194[a]
formation Characteristics							
mely	2.124[b]				.159[b]	−.168[a]	.106[c]
ccurate	1.920[c]				.107[c]		.138[b]
adily available	2.573[b]				.225[a]		.102[c]
ception formatted	2.571[b]	3.431[a]					.180[a]
ppropriately formatted	2.379[b]	2.168[b]			.117[c]	.117[c]	.203[a]

= Mission statement	4 = Participation	6 = Number of reorganizations
= Strategic plan	5 = Years organized	7 = Total activities
= Title level		

TABLE C-10: Performance Measurement and Technology (Manufacturers Only: Max n = 279

	(1)	(2)	(3)	(4)	(5)	(6)	(7)	(8)	(9)
Technology									
Software									
Basic installations	.255[a]	.309[a]	.159[a]	.366[a]	.252[a]	.147[b]	.271[a]	.331[a]	.327[a]
Other installations	.398[a]	.426[a]	.257[a]	.426[a]	.293[a]	.433[a]	.379[a]	.274[a]	.325[a]
EDI									
Members	.118[b]	.136[b]		.206[a]	.110[c]				.110[c]
Third parties	.144[b]	.182[a]					.124[b]		.120[b]
Hardware									
Operational technology	.139[b]	.207[a]	.136[b]	.262[a]		.175[a]	.166[a]	.184[a]	.187[a]
Hardware technology	.168[a]	.157[a]		.295[a]	.137[b]	.225[a]	.196[a]	.203[a]	.246[a]
Information Characteristics									
Timely	.197[a]	.165[a]			.105[c]	.157[a]		.122[b]	.106[c]
Accurate	.202[a]	.237[a]			.146[b]				.107[c]
Readily available	.141[b]	.161[a]		.130[b]	.122[b]			.166[a]	.160[a]
Exception formatted	.300[a]	.326[a]	.233[a]	.264[a]	.175[a]	.166[a]	.262[a]	.147[b]	.151[b]
Appropriately formatted	.171[a]	.232[a]		.111[c]			.167[a]	.136[b]	.120[b]

Internal
1 = Total cost   4 = Service   6 = Productivity
2 = Cost components   5 = Feedback   7 = Quality
3 = Asset management

Benchmarking
8 = Components   9 = Operations/strategy

BLE C-11: Formalization and Flexibility (Manufacturers Only: Max n = 279)

	(1)	(2)	(3)	(4)	(5)	(6)	(7)	(8)
rmalization								
rmal Mission/Plan								
ission statement		3.108[a]	3.098[a]	2.342[b]	2.980[a]	3.436[a]		1.717[c]
ategic plan	2.834[a]	3.409[a]	4.107[a]	2.617[a]	3.688[a]	3.660[a]	2.144[b]	3.502[a]
powerment								
le level								
rticipation			.126[b]					.129[b]
ganization								
ars organized		.142[b]			.143[b]	.187[a]		
. of reorganizations								
tal activities		.138[b]	.261[a]	.202[a]	.193[a]	.207[a]		.117[c]

Customer service requirements	4 = Product phaseout	7 = Customized service
Sales/marketing incentives	5 = Disruption in supply	8 = Modification in system
Product introduction	6 = Product recall	

BLE C-12: Performance Measurement and Flexibility (Manufacturers Only: Max n = 279)

	(1)	(2)	(3)	(4)	(5)	(6)	(7)	(8)
formance Measurement								
nal								
l cost	.152[b]	.271[a]	.224[a]	.221[a]	.111[c]	.180[a]	.112[c]	.133[b]
t components	.141[b]	.265[a]	.231[a]	.285[a]	.169[a]	.223[a]	.126[b]	.169[a]
t management	.117[c]	.171[a]	.158[b]	.109[c]		.164[a]	.158[a]	.213[a]
ice			.141[b]		.123[b]	.226[a]		
back	.155[b]		.128[b]		.149[b]		.104[c]	
uctivity	.133[b]	.156[b]	.224[a]	.225[a]		.181[a]		
lity	.150[b]	.150[b]	.110[c]	.153[b]	.142[b]	.272[a]	.147[b]	.143[b]
hmarking								
ponents	.119[b]	.201[a]	.175[a]	.199[a]	.177[a]	.215[a]	.141[b]	
rations/strategy	.189[a]	.227[a]	.242[a]	.215[a]	.229[a]	.235[a]	.187[a]	.140[b]

Customer service requirements	4 = Product phaseout	7 = Customized service
ales/marketing incentives	5 = Disruption in supply	8 = Modification in system
roduct introduction	6 = Product recall	

TABLE C-13: Technology and Flexibility (Manufacturers Only: Max n = 279)

	(1)	(2)	(3)	(4)	(5)	(6)	(7)	(8)
Technology								
Software								
Basic installations	.270[a]	.366[a]	.338[a]	.331[a]	.369[a]	.399[a]	.188[a]	.187[a]
Other installations		.118[c]	.238[a]	.209[a]	.139[b]	.238[a]		
EDI								
Members								
Third parties					.130[b]			
Hardware								
Operational technology			.185[a]	.179[a]	.161[a]	.210[a]		
Hardware technology			.247[a]	.161[a]	.107[c]	.228[a]		
Information Characteristics								
Timely	.135[b]	.127[b]	.187[a]	.124[b]	.208[a]	.170[a]	.207[a]	.172[a]
Accurate	.224[a]	.168[a]	.226[a]	.204[a]	.218[a]	.224[a]	.196[a]	.226[a]
Readily available	.122[b]	.163[a]	.193[a]	.127[b]	.225[a]	.215[a]	.173[a]	.180[a]
Exception formatted	.253[a]		.174[a]	.121[c]	.123[b]	.275[a]		.128[b]
Appropriately formatted	.118[c]	.195[a]	.190[a]	.131[b]	.254[a]	.214[a]	.146[b]	.145[b]

1 = Customer service requirements   4 = Product phaseout   7 = Customized service
2 = Sales/marketing incentives   5 = Disruption in supply 8 = Modification in system
3 = Product introduction   6 = Product recall

ABLE C-14: *Formalization and Performance Measurement*
(Merchandisers Only: Max n = 277)

	(1)	(2)	(3)	(4)	(5)	(6)	(7)
erformance Measurement							
ternal							
otal cost	6.020[a]	4.503[a]	.136[b]	.184[a]	.140[b]		.281[a]
ost components	4.436[a]	2.478[b]		.129[b]			.294[a]
sset management	3.107[a]			.160[a]	.119[c]		.165[a]
rvice	5.477[a]	4.077[a]		.181[a]	.119[c]		.306[a]
edback	2.166[b]						.146[b]
oductivity	4.571[a]	3.877[a]		.127[b]			.261[a]
ıality	4.728[a]	4.032[a]		.153[b]	.141[b]		.247[a]
nchmarking							
›mponents	3.077[a]	3.073[a]		.104[c]			.143[b]
›erations/strategy	4.748[a]	4.181[a]		.120[b]	.240[a]		.182[a]

Mission statement   4 = Participation   6 = Number of reorganizations
Strategic plan   5 = Years organized   7 = Total activities
Title level

TABLE C-15: Formalization and Technology (Merchandisers Only: Max n = 277)

	(1)	(2)	(3)	(4)	(5)	(6)	(7)
Technology							
Software							
Basic installations	3.581[a]	3.967[a]			.142[b]		.189[a]
Other installations	6.294[a]	6.025[a]		.186[a]	.233[a]		.261[a]
EDI							
Members	2.099[b]	2.338[b]			.114[c]		
Third parties	3.593[a]	3.802[a]		.158[a]	.154[b]		.146[b]
Hardware							
Operational technology	4.715[a]	4.184[a]		.101[c]	.121[c]		.185[a]
Hardware technology	3.460[a]	2.906[a]		.187[c]			.280[a]
Information Characteristics							
Timely	2.125[b]	2.179[b]			.141[b]	−.128[b]	.167[a]
Accurate	2.733[a]	2.322[b]			.148[b]		.225[a]
Readily available	2.580[b]	2.757[a]		.193[a]	.186[a]	−.120[c]	.172[a]
Exception formatted	2.304[b]	1.191[b]		.126[b]			.215[a]
Appropriately formatted	2.311[b]	1.964[c]		.189[a]	.160[b]		.245[a]

1 = Mission statement   4 = Participation   6 = Number of reorganizations
2 = Strategic plan   5 = Years organized   7 = Total activities
3 = Title level

**TABLE C-16: Performance Measurement and Technology
(Merchandisers Only: Max n = 277)**

	(1)	(2)	(3)	(4)	(5)	(6)	(7)	(8)	(9)
Technology									
Software									
Basic installations	.208[a]	.340[a]	.238[a]	.399[a]	.206[a]	.326[a]	.315[a]		.143[b]
Other installations	.337[a]	.417[a]	.334[a]	.537[a]	.257[a]	.491[a]	.425[a]	.193[a]	.278[a]
ROI									
Members	.110[c]		.158[a]	.149[b]	.134[b]	.155[a]		.150[b]	
Third parties	.172[a]	.158[a]				.137[b]	.148[b]		.227[a]
Hardware									
Operational technology	.217[a]	.289[a]	.143[b]	.251[a]	.101[c]	.358[a]	.269[a]		.243[a]
Hardware technology	.200[a]	.277[a]	.222[a]	.230[a]	.191[a]	.249[a]	.274[a]	.135[b]	.183[a]
Information Characteristics									
Timely	.250[a]	.199[a]	.120[b]	.223[a]		.169[a]	.197[a]	.193[a]	.175[a]
Accurate	.270[a]	.218[a]	.109[c]	.198[a]		.152[b]	.249[a]	.176[a]	.177[a]
Readily available	.321[a]	.245[a]	.169[a]	.194[a]	.102[c]	.133[b]	.210[a]	.170[a]	.102[c]
Exception formatted	.201[a]	.194[a]	.117[c]	.343[a]	.232[a]	.257[a]	.245[a]	.186[a]	.240[a]
Appropriately formatted	.283[a]	.218[a]	.224[a]	.272[a]	.249[a]	.249[a]	.209[a]	.263[a]	.249[a]

Internal
   Total cost   4 = Service   6 = Productivity
   Cost components   5 = Feedback   7 = Quality
   Asset management

Benchmarking
   Components   9 = Operations/strategy

TABLE C-17: Formalization and Flexibility (Merchandisers Only: Max n = 277)

	(1)	(2)	(3)	(4)	(5)	(6)	(7)	(8)
Formalization								
Formal Mission/Plan								
Mission statement			2.342[b]	1.683[c]		2.118[b]		2.118[b]
Strategic plan						2.682[a]		1.863[c]
Empowerment								
Title level			.114[c]					
Participation						.117[c]		
Organization								
Years organized		.110[c]	.157[b]		.117[c]			
No. of reorganizations								
Total activities			.183[a]	.179[a]	.159[a]	2.05[a]		2.31[a]

1 = Customer service requirements　　4 = Product phaseout　　7 = Customized service
2 = Sales/marketing incentives　　5 = Disruption in supply　　8 = Modification in system
3 = Product introduction　　6 = Product recall

TABLE C-18: Performance Measurement and Flexibility
(Merchandisers Only: Max n = 277)

	(1)	(2)	(3)	(4)	(5)	(6)	(7)	(8)
Performance Measurement								
Internal								
Total cost	.119[b]		.190[a]	.144[b]	.202[a]	.134[b]	.126[b]	.146[b]
Cost components			.124[b]			.112[c]		.185[a]
Asset management	.114[c]	.162[a]	.192[a]	.209[a]			.108[c]	.138[b]
Service	.166[a]	.106[c]	.302[a]	.313[a]	.243[a]	.362[a]		.167[a]
Feedback	.133[b]	.258[a]	.235[a]	.225[a]	.120[b]		.131[b]	.155[a]
Productivity			.227[a]	.227[a]	.109[c]	.243[a]		.129[b]
Quality	.195[a]	.145[b]	.331[a]	.314[a]	.210[a]	.296[a]	.159[a]	.187[a]
Benchmarking								
Components	.187[a]	.199[a]	.132[b]	.122[b]			.110[c]	.106[c]
Operations/strategy		.155[a]	.230[a]	.119[b]				.205[a]

1 = Customer service requirements　　4 = Product phaseout　　7 = Customized service
2 = Sales/marketing incentives　　5 = Disruption in supply　　8 = Modification in system
3 = Product introduction　　6 = Product recall

ABLE C-19: Technology and Flexibility (Merchandisers Only: Max n = 277)

	(1)	(2)	(3)	(4)	(5)	(6)	(7)	(8)
echnology								
ftware								
asic installations			.214[a]	.229[a]	.172[a]	.204[a]		
ther installations	.110[c]	.112[c]	.271[a]	.294[a]	.183[a]	.273[a]		.136[b]
DI								
embers		.197[a]	.174[a]	.163[a]	.165[a]	.106[c]		
hird parties			.137[a]		.119[b]			.154[b]
ardware								
perational technology	−.126[b]		.107[c]	.145[b]		.188[a]		
ardware technology	.106[c]	.110[c]	.199[a]	.159[a]		.166[a]		.122[b]
formation Characteristics								
mely	.219[a]	.231[a]	.259[a]	.208[a]	.275[a]	.230[a]	.169[a]	.189[a]
ccurate	.211[a]	.209[a]	.258[a]	.221[a]	.268[a]	.206[a]	.157[a]	.172[a]
adily available	.181[a]	.212[a]	.204[a]	.174[a]	.256[a]	.174[a]	.212[a]	.192[a]
cception formatted		.219[a]	.239[a]	.149[b]	.228[a]	.191[a]		.207[a]
propriately formatted		.263[a]	.256[a]	.198[a]	.205[a]	.166[a]		.186[a]

= Customer service requirements	4 = Product phaseout	7 = Customized service
= Sales/marketing incentives	5 = Disruption in supply	8 = Modification in system
= Product introduction	6 = Product recall	

**TABLE C-20: *Formalization and Performance Measurement
(Differences based on ANCOVA Models)***

	(1)	(2)	(3)	(4)	(5)	(6)	(7)
Performance Measurement							
Internal							
Total Cost						Ma[b]	
Cost components							
Asset management							
Service							
Feedback							
Productivity							
Quality							
Benchmarking							
Components		Ma[b]					
Operations/strategy							

---

1 = Title level	4 = Participation	6 = Mission statement
2 = Years organized	5 = Total activities	7 = Strategic plan
3 = No. of reorganizations		

Ma = significant interaction: relationship greater in manufacturer group.
Me = significant interaction: relationship greater in merchandiser group.

TABLE C-21: *Formalization and Technology (Differences Based on ANCOVA Models)*

	(1)	(2)	(3)	(4)	(5)	(6)	(7)
Technology							
Software							
Basic installations							
Other installations		Me[b]					
IDI							
Members	Ma[b]					Me[c]	
Third parties							
Hardware							
Operational technology	Ma[c]						
Hardware technology			Ma[b]			Ma[b]	
Information Characteristics							
Timely							
Accurate							
Readily available			Me[a]				
Exception formatted							
Appropriately formatted							

1 = Title level   4 = Participation   6 = Mission statement
2 = Years organized   5 = Total activities   7 = Strategic plan
3 = No. of reorganizations

a = significant interaction: relationship greater in manufacturer group.
e = significant interaction: relationship greater in merchandiser group.

TABLE C-22: *Performance Measurement and Technology (Differences Based on ANCOVA Models)*

	(1)	(2)	(3)	(4)	(5)	(6)	(7)	(8)	(9)
Technology									
Software									
Basic installations						Me[b]		Ma[a]	Ma[b]
Other installations									
EDI									
Members			Me[c]						
Third parties						Me[b]			
Hardware									
Operational technology						Me[b]			
Hardware technology		Me[c]	Me[c]						
Information Characteristics									
Timely									
Accurate									
Readily available									
Exception formatted	Ma[c]	Ma[c]	Ma[c]						
Appropriately formatted									

Internal
1 = Total cost 4 = Service 6 = Productivity
2 = Cost components 5 = Feedback 7 = Quality
3 = Asset management

Benchmarking
8 = Components 9 = Operations/strategy

Ma = significant interaction: relationship greater in manufacturer group.
Me = significant interaction: relationship greater in merchandiser group.

ABLE C-23: Formalization and Flexibility (Differences Based on ANCOVA Models)

	(1)	(2)	(3)	(4)	(5)	(6)	(7)	(8)
ormalization								
ormal Mission/Plan								
lission statement								
rategic plan		Ma[b]						
npowerment								
itle level								
articipation								
rganization								
ears organized								
o. of reorganizations								
otal activities								

= Customer service requirements   4 = Product phaseout   7 = Customized service
= Sales/marketing incentives   5 = Disruption in supply   8 = Modification in system
= Product introduction   6 = Product recall

a = significant interaction: relationship greater in manufacturer group.
e = significant interaction: relationship greater in merchandiser group.

BLE C-24: Performance Measurement and Flexibility (Differences Based on ANCOVA Models)

	(1)	(2)	(3)	(4)	(5)	(6)	(7)	(8)
erformance Measurement								
ernal								
tal cost	Ma[b]							
st components	Ma[a]		Ma[b]					
set management								
rvice			Me[a]	Me[a]	Me[b]	Me[b]		Me[b]
edback	Me[b]	Me[b]	Me[b]					
oductivity								
ality			Me[c]	Me[b]				
achmarking								
mponents								
erations/strategy								

Customer service requirements   4 = Product phaseout   7 = Customized service
Sales/marketing incentives   5 = Disruption in supply   8 = Modification in system
Product introduction   6 = Product recall

= significant interaction: relationship greater in manufacturer group.
= significant interaction: relationship greater in merchandiser group.

TABLE C-25: Technology and Flexibility (Differences Based on ANCOVA Models)

	(1)	(2)	(3)	(4)	(5)	(6)	(7)	(8)
Technology								
Software								
Basic installations	Ma[a]	Ma[a]					Ma[b]	
Other installations				Me[c]				
EDI								
Members		Me[a]	Me[b]	Me[b]				
Third parties								Me[b]
Hardware								
Operational technology	Ma[b]							
Hardware technology								
Information Characteristics								
Timely								
Accurate								
Readily available								
Exception formatted	Ma[a]							
Appropriately formatted								

1 = Customer service requirements   4 = Product phaseout   7 = Customized service
2 = Sales/marketing incentives   5 = Disruption in supply   8 = Modification in system
3 = Product introduction   6 = Product recall

Ma = significant interaction: relationship greater in manufacturer group.
Me = significant interaction: relationship greater in merchandiser group.

ABLE C-26: Rankings of Flexibility Predictor Variables (All Firms)

	(1)	(2)	(3)	(4)	(5)	(6)	(7)	(8)	Ranking
ormalization									
tle level	0	0	0	0	0	0	0	0	0
articipation	0	0	0	0	0	0	0	0	0
ears organized	0	10	4	0	8	5	0	0	3.38
o. of reorganizations	0	0	0	0	0	0	0	0	0
otal activities	11.5	0	13.5	16	15	18	0	24	12.25
erformance Measurement									
ternal									
otal cost	17	13	13.5	18	16	10.5	19	13	15.00
ost components	0	7	7	6	6	8	11	15	7.50
set management	14	14	9	11	4	6	17	14	11.13
rvice	16	18	19	21	17	23	0	10	14.25
edback	18	21	11	14	12	7	18	11	14.00
oductivity	11.5	12	15	20	0	19	13	6	12.06
uality	23	15	23	23	19	22	23	25	21.25
achmarking									
mponents	22	22	8	17	14	12	20	12	15.88
erations/strategy	15	20	18	12	13	9	15	19	15.13
chnology									
iware									
ic installations	20	24	24	24	24	24	16	16	21.50
her installations	0	11	21	22	10.5	21	0	8	11.69
I									
mbers	0	0	3	0	9	0	0	0	1.50
rd parties	0	0	7	5	10.5	4	0	7	4.19
dware									
erational technology	0	0	8	7	5	10.5	0	0	3.81
dware technology	13	9	12	10	7	14	10	9	10.50
rmation Characteristics									
ely	21	17	17	13	22	16	23	17	18.25
urate	24	18.5	22	19	23	17	21	23	20.69
dily available	19	18.5	10	9	21	13	24	20	16.81
eption formatted	14	16	16	8	18	20	14	22	16.00
ropriately formatted	0	23	20	15	20	15	12	18	15.38

ies represent rank order of column-wise relative strength of correlation. Greatest correlation
ned a rank of 24, next greatest a value of 23 and so on. Nonsignificant correlations assigned a
: of zero. The last column, labeled Ranking, represents the mean across the eight flexibility
bles.

Customer service requirements	4 = Product phaseout	7 = Customized service
Sales/marketing incentives	5 = Disruption in supply	8 = Modification in system
Product introduction	6 = Product recall	

TABLE C-27: Rankings of Flexibility Predictor Variables (Manufacturers)

	(1)	(2)	(3)	(4)	(5)	(6)	(7)	(8)	Ranking
Formalization									
Title level	0	0	0	0	0	0	0	0	0
Participation	0	0	6	0	0	0	0	14	2.50
Years organized	0	13	0	0	13	12	0	0	4.50
No. of reorganizations	0	0	0	0	0	0	0	0	0
Total activities	0	12	23	17	18	11	0	12	11.63
Performance Measurement									
Internal									
Total cost	19	23	16.5	21	7	8	14	15	15.44
Cost components	17	22	19	23	16	16	15	19	18.38
Asset management	11	18	9	8	0	6	19	23	11.75
Service	0	0	8	0	8.5	18	0	0	4.31
Feedback	20	0	7	0	14	0	13	0	6.75
Productivity	15	15	16.5	22	0	9	0	0	9.69
Quality	18	14	5	13	12	22	18	17	14.88
Benchmarking									
Components	13	20	11	16	17	14.5	16	0	13.44
Operations/strategy	21	21	21	20	22	20	21	16	20.25
Technology									
Software									
Basic installations	24	24	24	24	24	24	22	22	23.50
Other installations	0	10	20	19	11	21	0	0	10.13
EDI									
Members	0	0	0	0	0	0	0	0	0
Third parties	0	0	0	0	10	0	0	0	1.25
Hardware									
Operational technology	0	0	12	15	15	12	0	0	6.75
Hardware technology	0	0	22	14	6	19	0	0	7.63
Information Characteristics									
Timely	16	11	13	10	19	7	24	20	15.00
Accurate	22	17	18	18	20	17	23	24	19.88
Readily available	14	16	15	11	21	14.5	20	21	16.56
Exception formatted	23	0	10	9	8.5	23	0	13	10.81
Appropriately formatted	12	19	14	12	23	13	17	18	16.00

Entries represent rank order of column-wise relative strength of correlation. Greatest correlation assigned a rank of 24, next greatest a value of 23 and so on. Nonsignificant correlations assigned a value of zero. The last column, labeled Ranking, represents the mean across the eight flexibility variables.

1 = Customer service requirements 4 = Product phaseout 7 = Customized service
2 = Sales/marketing incentives 5 = Disruption in supply 8 = Modification in system
3 = Product introduction 6 = Product recall

ABLE C-28: Rankings of Flexibility Predictor Variables (Merchandisers)

	(1)	(2)	(3)	(4)	(5)	(6)	(7)	(8)	Ranking
ormalization									
itle level	0	0	3	0	0	0	0	0	0.38
articipation	0	0	0	0	0	10	0	0	1.25
ears organized	0	11.5	7	0	10	12	0	0	3.56
o. of reorganizations	0	0	0	0	0	0	0	0	0
otal activities	0	0	9	14	13	18	0	24	9.75
erformance Measurement									
ternal									
otal cost	17	0	10	8	17	11	19	12	11.75
ost components	0	0	4	0	0	9	0	17	3.75
set management	16	16	11	17	0	0	17	11	11.00
rvice	19	10	23	23	21	24	0	15	16.88
edback	18	23	17	19	12	0	20	14	15.38
oductivity	0	0	15	20	9	21	0	9	6.75
uality	22	14	24	24	19	23	22	19	20.88
nchmarking									
omponents	21	18	5	7	0	0	18	7	9.50
erations/strategy	0	15	16	6	0	0	0	22	7.38
chnology									
ftware									
sic installations	0	0	14	21	15	17	0	0	8.38
her installations	15	13	22	22	16	22	0	10	15.00
I									
mbers	0	17	8	12	14	8	0	0	7.38
rd parties	0	0	6	0	11	0	0	13	3.75
dware									
erational technology	0	0	2	9	0	15	0	0	3.25
rdware technology	14	11.5	12	11	0	12.5	0	8	8.63
rmation Characteristics									
nely	24	22	21	16	24	20	23	20	21.25
urate	23	19	20	18	23	19	21	16	19.88
dily available	20	20	13	13	22	14	24	21	18.38
eption formatted	0	21	18	10	20	16	0	23	13.50
ropriately formatted	0	24	19	15	18	12.5	0	18	13.31

es represent rank order of column-wise relative strength of correlation. Greatest correlation
ned a rank of 24, next greatest a value of 23 and so on. Nonsignificant correlations assigned a
of zero. The last column, labeled Ranking, represents the mean across the eight flexibility
bles.

Customer service requirements	4 = Product phaseout	7 = Customized service
Sales/marketing incentives	5 = Disruption in supply	8 = Modification in system
Product introduction	6 = Product recall	

TABLE C-29: Summary of Ranking Analysis

	All Firms		Manufacturers		Merchandisers		
	Mean	Ranking	Mean	Ranking	Mean	Ranking	$Diff^2$
Formalization							
Title level	0	24	0	24	0.38	24	0.00
Participation	0	24	2.50	21	1.25	23	4.00
Years organized	3.38	21	4.50	19	3.56	21	4.00
No. of reorganizations	0	24	0	25	0	25	0.00
Total activities	12.25	13	11.63	12	9.75	12	0.00
Performance Measurement							
Total cost	15.00	10	15.44	7	11.75	10	9.00
Cost components	7.50	18	18.38	4	3.75	19.5	240.25
Asset management	11.13	16	11.75	11	11.00	11	0.00
Service	14.25	11	4.31	20	16.88	5	225.00
Feedback	14.00	12	6.75	17.5	15.38	6	132.25
Productivity	12.06	14	9.69	15	6.75	18	9.00
Quality	21.25	2	14.88	9	20.88	2	49.00
Components	15.88	8	13.44	10	9.50	13	9.00
Operations/strategy	15.13	9	20.25	2	7.38	16.5	210.25
Technology							
Basic installations	21.50	1	23.50	1	8.38	15	196.00
Other installations	11.69	15	10.13	14	15.00	7	49.00
Members	1.50	22	0	24	7.38	16.5	56.25
Third parties	4.19	19	1.25	22	3.75	19.5	6.25
Operational technology	3.81	20	6.75	17.5	3.25	22	20.25
Hardware technology	10.50	17	7.63	16	8.63	14	4.00
Timely	18.25	4	15.00	8	21.25	1	49.00
Accurate	20.69	3	19.88	3	19.88	3	0.00
Readily available	16.81	5	16.56	5	18.38	4	1.00
Exception formatted	16.00	6	10.81	13	13.50	8	25.00
Appropriately formatted	15.38	7	16.00	6	13.31	9	9.00
Sum							1307.50

Rank order correlation = .497   z-score = .587/.204 = 2.435   One-tailed p-value = .0073
$Diff^2$ = ((merchandiser rank order) − (manufacturer rank order))^2.
Correlation is significantly greater than zero at the .01 level.

Examples of Strategic Linkage

TO GAIN a better understanding of what it takes to implement strategic linkage, eighteen interviews were completed. The firms interviewed were involved in advanced EDI applications and were seeking to gain competitive advantage from their participation. In other words, these firms were actively trying to work out interorganizational arrangements with customers and suppliers that would provide them a unique position in their industry. Because many of these firms are plowing new ground, they have a strong proprietary sense about some of their more creative applications. Although several of them consented to allowing at least a partial writeup of their applications, others did not. All of them provided key information that was used to develop the general model presented in Chapter Seven. Table D-1 provides a list of the firms interviewed. Selected testimonies are reported in this section.

Nabisco Foods Company

EDI involvement often begins with internal linkages to facilitate intracompany processing and exchange of information. Nabisco Foods' involvement in EDI followed this pattern. They initially used EDI to pass information between headquarters and regional distribution centers. Later they expanded EDI applications to the transportation area of their Distribution Operations Control System (DOCS).

The DOCS program became the basis for true partnership arrangements between Nabisco Foods and its key carriers. The EDI application provided information to measure delivery performance and to transmit planned loads to carriers so that they could plan equipment requirements. These load plans become a carrier's freight invoice support data and bills are paid electronically. The overall linkage has resulted in faster deliveries, fewer errors, and improvements in the efficiency of operations for both

TABLE D-1: List of Firms Interviewed

- American President Companies
- Baxter Healthcare Corp.—Value Link Group
- Bergen Brunswig Corporation
- Digital Equipment Corporation
- Drug Transport
- Federal Express
- The Gillette Company
- Johnson & Johnson Hospital Supply—COACT
- Kuppenheimer Men's Clothiers
- Levi Strauss & Company
- Lithonia Lighting
- Nabisco Foods Company
- Owens-Corning Fiberglas Corporation
- JC Penney Company
- Schneider National, Inc.
- J.R. Simplot
- United Parcel Service
- Zellerbach—A Mead Company

Nabisco and the carriers. The system permits tight control over distribution operations critical to achieving those efficiencies. As an example, at one point prior to the system installation, the outstanding transportation claims balance exceeded $2 million. In the first year under DOCS, the claims balance was reduced to less than $500,000. Current claims balance is less than $250,000 and still declining. The ability to avoid claims is a major benefit of the linkage.

The technical side of EDI involvement was not a serious problem at Nabisco. The greatest obstacle to achieving success rested with people. Strong commitment or the "shoulder of management pushing to make it happen" was needed to overcome resistance to change.

Nabisco is an example of linking service suppliers to a firm in a way that favorably impacts each participant's cost structure. The shared information served to reduce uncertainty and facilitated planning. In the final analysis, EDI applications can result in a competitive differential advantage only if the new arrangement lowers operating costs *and* improves customer service.[1]

JC Penney Company

The traditional perspective of successful retailing boils down to three factors: location, location, and location. No one can dispute the importance of location, but the strategic use of information systems is rapidly becoming a prime concern. The JC Penney Company is a leader in exploiting information technology to redefine the rules of retailing. They are effectively using information technology in merchandising, inventory control, and decision support to gain a competitive edge.

Penney has a long history of EDI involvement. They have used EDI for over 15 years. In their initial applications, they used internally developed proprietary standards. Transactions with trading partners were restricted to the exchange of purchase orders and invoices. In the mid–1980s Penney became interested in expanding their EDI commitment. Aware that proprietary standards would severely limit exchange capabilities, they investigated the establishment of industry standards. The creation of a new position, Corporate EDI Coordinator, was necessary to focus on the role EDI was expected to play in future operations.

Penney first focused on the area of transportation. They chose freight bills as the initial area because they accounted for the largest portion of paperwork and could be controlled. EDI applications in the transportation area resulted in speed and accuracy. They also generated another, even more important, benefit: "free data." Upon receipt of freight bills, Penney's system strips out accounting data needed for payment and then structures key information related to the transaction into a database. This database has proven to be extremely valuable for operational analysis. For example, Penney executives use information from the database about past carrier performance, volume of material shipped, and distribution patterns when negotiating new contracts with their carriers.

Penney's next EDI application was freight bill remittance statements. Standard procedure is for buyers to pay a group of freight bills with a single check. The check is accompanied by a remittance statement specifying bills being paid. Carriers were given the option of electronically receiving remittance statements. This form of electronic exchange facilitated accounting because the EDI remittance statements could be entered directly into carrier systems. Penney was very interested in creating electronic linkages with carriers. However, they knew that there "had to be something in it" for the carriers. Handling freight bills by EDI simplified Penney's operations. The remittance statement service was added to make linkage arrangements attractive to the carriers.

From these initial applications, EDI has moved in many directions. Penney has an elaborate point-of-sale (POS) system established in 1981 which tracks all inventory movement. Authorized suppliers can "dial in" the EDI system and pick up daily sales data. Sharing such data facilitates vendor planning.

Penney plans to expand EDI applications in such areas as processing returns to catalogue centers, handling store claims, and expanding quick response inventory programs. The Penney executives interviewed stressed that *internal coordination* is the key to success. Although success came slowly, significant expansion is planned for the future. The Penney strategy is to create expanded linkages with key trading partners.[2]

Kuppenheimer Clothiers

Kuppenheimer, a leading manufacturer and retailer of menswear, is seeking to gain competitive advantage in the way they go to market. Their strategy is to provide outstanding customer service as a means of differentiating Kuppenheimer from the competition. Information system competency is a key toward achieving that goal.

Kuppenheimer recently consolidated logistical operations from a four-warehouse system to one centralized facility near Atlanta. The centralized Georgia facility handles three times the volume previously handled at the four separate locations. The new facility requires approximately half of the previous staff to handle the increased volume.

Merchandise manufactured in the five Kuppenheimer plants as well as merchandise from outside vendors now moves through the distribution center. Coordinated movement through the distribution center permits maximum control of all shipments.

The distribution revamping and changeover required "cultural changes to make it happen." Kuppenheimer's manufacturing plants were not fully automated and did not have state-of-the-art information systems. Plans for updating met with resistance. Employees were generally intimidated by computer systems. Kuppenheimer overcame the obstacles through extensive training programs as preparation for systems installations.

Because Kuppenheimer is a manufacturer and a retailer with few purchases made from external vendors, their EDI system was primarily designed for handling internal communications. They deal with only a limited number of external trading partners and, thus far, have not believed that the expense for external EDI linkages is warranted. The new internal system represents a radical change for Kuppenheimer. Five years ago they operated in a 100-percent paper environment. Paper documents were used to control retail receipts, manufacturing orders, and allocation and transfer of orders. The new EDI-based transaction system and information-processing capacity dramatically improved their ability to provide increased customer service, timely recording of inventory movement, and generated key management control of information.

The Kuppenheimer philosophy is to focus on efficiency improvements throughout the logistical process wherever they can be generated. Typically this means new ways of doing things must be considered. Many of their successes are directly related to EDI and new technology applications. For example, the quick response replenishment system is the result of combining EDI and bar coding.[3]

Lithonia Lighting

Lithonia Lighting, a Georgia-based manufacturer of commercial lighting fixtures, has been extremely successful in using information management and technology to achieve strategic goals. As the lighting industry matured and became more sophisticated in the mid-1970s, Lithonia competitors were "gaining on" them. Lithonia realized they had to think long-term and develop ways to build customer linkages. The lighting industry has traditionally employed an agent system to handle product sales. The industry was undergoing a number of changes. Technology was changing rapidly, products were increasing in complexity, thus making the agent's selling effort more complicated, and the general volume of sales was increasing. Agents were being asked to handle more work-related details and they looked to manufacturers for assistance.

Lithonia decided that the best opportunity to differentiate their products from competitors was to provide exceptional information to support the agents. The company determined that order entry and handling was at the heart of what made the business run. As a result, Lithonia focused its initial efforts on developing an electronic order entry system at a time when such applications were new and revolutionary. Much of Lithonia's initial success was attributed to two factors: (1) it was willing to commit sufficient resources to develop a long-term dynamic solution with the agents; and (2) it understood that Lithonia acting in isolation from the agents could not sustain a competitive advantage.

Since Lithonia was handling a commodity type of product which was easily duplicated, their strategic focus became service. A recent article in *Information Week* summarized their philosophy.

> In a market in which products vary little, if at all, in price and availability, Lithonia seeks to deliver the best service . . . Lithonia, which sells a vast array of lighting and related products, has an integrated group of systems called "Light*Link," which are tied together over a network of dial-up lines. These lines intertwine the diverse players of the lighting industry: the company's 84 agents' offices, customers, electrical distributors, electrical engineers and specifiers, and Lithonia's 35 warehouses across the U.S.

> . . . customers can plug into Lithonia's wires to enter the order, check stock, and get delivery information. To those who do most of their business by phone, those electronic links mean more time to sell.

> . . . Lithonia has an amalgamation of systems, each tailored to a segment of the industry . . . Virtually everyone doing business with Lithonia ties into one of the systems.[4]

Over the years, Lithonia has upgraded and expanded its information exchange. The company has expanded data systems to improve the efficiency of its relationship with the agents. For example, Lithonia developed a wide range of data to permit agents to more efficiently service customers. Lithonia has achieved leadership status in the industry and competitors simply cannot match its information systems support. Information capabilities played a key role in Lithonia's success: "Information systems have made us capable of living up to what we call the Lithonia Way: to provide the best value in lighting and to be easy to do business with."[5]

Bergen Brunswig Corporation

Bergen Brunswig, a leading drug wholesaler, was another EDI pioneer. They were involved as early as the mid-1960s when they experimented with using EDI to handle purchase orders with Eli Lilly. In these early stages, EDI took not only a pioneering spirit, but also a relatively large amount of capital to implement. At first, electronic order entry was a "hard sell" because customers did not feel comfortable switching to a new way of doing business.

From this early start, EDI has become a major technological weapon. Bergen Brunswig is currently linked with approximately 200 vendors representing over 94.5 percent of their drug division sales. Even with such extensive involvement in EDI linkages, it is important to be selective when developing such relationships. Fully integrated alliances must be supported with significant time and resources. Bergen has been careful to "target only a select number" of trading partners for close interactive relationships.

In 1989, Bergen Brunswig introduced the "Electronic Partnership Program" which directly linked its operations with select suppliers. The Electronic Partnership Program covers four broad areas: purchase orders, suppliers' invoices, payments, and the entire chargeback process. Both Bergen and its involved suppliers have enjoyed significant reductions in operating expenses and increases in productivity as a result of the program. The partnership arrangements have been influenced by extensive use of market research and customer advisory groups. Customer reactions to proposed new services, solutions to problems, and recommendations for new services have guided the development of the relationships.

Bergen Brunswig has also been very active in building electronic linkages with their customers. These linkages have revolutionized the retail drug industry. Examples include sophisticated bar coding structures, computer terminals for pharmacy counters, new point-of-sale bar coding readers integrated with the pharmacy computers, plan-o-graming, immediate price change capabilities, and management reports showing such things as profitability information and frequency of movement. Whereas the Bergen

Brunswig EDI solution is standard with suppliers, it is highly proprietary with retail customers. This arrangement provides the balance that achieves maximum competitive advantage. EDI is expected to play an even greater role in health and personal care distribution in the future.

Conclusion: Testimonials

These few examples illustrate the kinds of breakthroughs that can result from advanced EDI applications. Executives among all the firms interviewed anticipate greater involvement in EDI for both internal and external communications. They are still seeking ways to strategically exploit such electronic linkages. It is safe to conclude that basic EDI can result in cost and service improvements. However, these firms realize that there is potential for achieving competitive advantage through strategic alliances and they are among a small group of firms pushing the frontier.

Notes

1. For a supplemental discussion see Francis J. Quinn, "Profile of a Partnership," *Traffic Management* 28,2 (1989): 36.

2. For a supplemental discussion see Alan Alper and James Daly, "Penney Cashes in on Leading Edge," *Computerworld* XXII,25 (1988): 1.

3. For a supplemental discussion see Lane F. Cooper, Alex Linder, and Stephanie Whitman, "Revamped Distribution Center Highlights Quick Response at Kuppenheimer," *EDI News,* 4,7, (April 9, 1990): 5.

4. Michael A. Fillon, "IS Lights the Way at Lithonia," *Information WEEK,* (April 11, 1988): 30.

5. For a supplemental discussion see Michael Fillon and Charles von Simson, "Award-Winning Partners" *Information WEEK* (October 17, 1988): 43.

Index

Abbott Laboratories, 143, 145
Accounting, 100–101
Activity-based costs, 100
Adversarial negotiation, 141
Aging, of work force, 169
Airborne Express, 142
Alco Health Services, 143
Alliances. *See* Strategic alliances
AMC, 37
American Management Association, 153
ANCOVA models, 199
Andersen, Arthur, 55
Antitrust laws, alliances and, 146
Arm and Hammer, 26
Armstrong, 25
Artificial intelligence, 27
Asia, 24
Assessment, 65–89
  benchmarking and, 83–86
  benefits of, 66
  in change management model, 62–63
  cost-benefit analysis and, 87–88
  of customer impact, 75–77
  decision to assess, 67–69
  defined, 66
  deliverable results, 71–72

feedback loop, 89
of flexibility, 82–83
implementation plan and, 88–89
managerial recommendations and, 88
of mission statement, 73–74
objectives of, 67
of organizational structure, 74–75
of performance measurement, 77–80
planning, 69–72
of planning, 74
process of, 67–89
situational analysis, 72–86
statistical methods for, 78–80
supporting logic for, 86–87
task specification and prioritization for, 71
team, 70–71
technology and, 69, 80–82
time and resources for, 71
Asset management, 52
Associations, trade and professional, 177–180
AT&T, 29
Austria, 22
Automation, 107

Index